I0819160

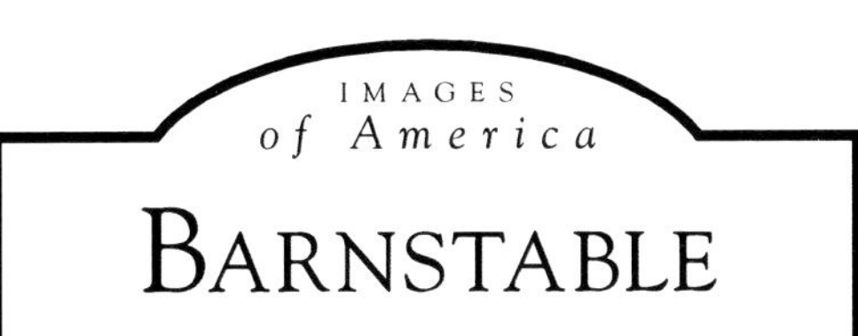
IMAGES
of America
BARNSTABLE

On the Cover: This photograph shows the grandstand on the grounds of the Barnstable County Fair. The fair, established in 1844 by the Barnstable County Agricultural Society, was first held in front of the courthouse in Barnstable Village. By the late 1800s, mainstays of the fair were livestock judging, grange displays, horseracing, and the biggest sports event of the time—baseball.

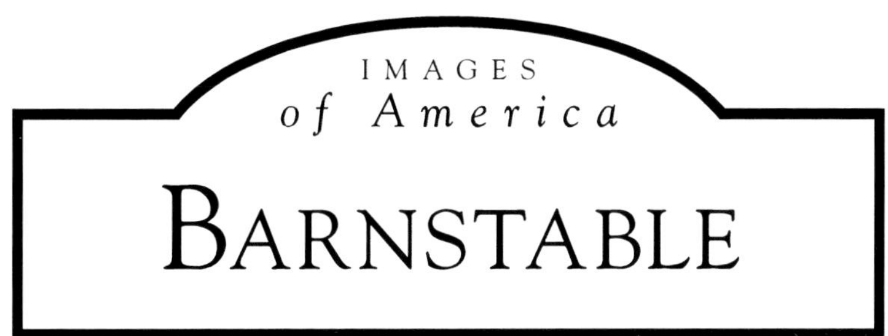

Stephen Robert Lovell Farrar
and the Barnstable Historical Society

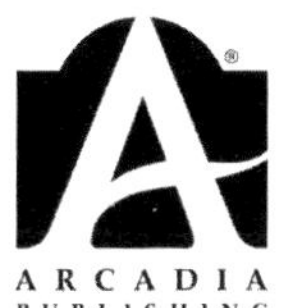

ISBN 978-0-7385-9836-9

Published by Arcadia Publishing
Charleston, South Carolina

Printed in the United States of America

Library of Congress Control Number: 2012947735

For all general information, please contact Arcadia Publishing:
Telephone 843-853-2070
Fax 843-853-0044
E-mail sales@arcadiapublishing.com
For customer service and orders:
Toll-Free 1-888-313-2665

Visit us on the Internet at www.arcadiapublishing.com

This book is dedicated to Robert Stewart, director of the Barnstable Historical Society.

Contents

ACKNOWLEDGMENTS

Several members of the Barnstable Historical Society helped with research, provided input, and donated photographs from their own collections. I would like to thank Lisa Blair, Robert and Prudence Stewart, and Wendy Lapine. I would also like to thank Jim Ellis of Barnstable Village who spent several hours sharing his knowledge of his family and local blacksmiths. Thanks also to Thomas Shanahan, past president of the Barnstable Historical Society; it was his vision that moved this project forward. I would be remiss if I did not thank the myriad of docents and volunteers for their hard work, support, and solidarity, including Pat Coffey, Ski Morton, Dorothy O'Connell, Dorothy Carver, Ruth Anne Allen, Joan Ellis, and of course Irving Stewart. They readily shared their local knowledge and challenged me on a daily basis. I would also like to thank the Sturgis Library. Under the leadership of Lucy Loomis, the Sturgis Library is responsible for digitizing 100 years of the *Barnstable Patriot* newspaper. The digitization of newspapers opens up a new and fascinating avenue of research to historians and genealogists. Although too many to name, I would like to thank our volunteers from the Palaemon House in Barnstable Village. They taught us that everyone can learn and benefit from the preservation of history.

All photographs are courtesy of the Barnstable Historical Society and its members unless otherwise noted.

Introduction

Barnstable occupies a place in American history unlike any other region in the United States. Its gentle dunes and sandy beaches have brought people from all over the world for warm weather recreation. For those who come to Barnstable and are captivated by its wonders, the "sand in their shoes" compels them to return again and again.

As much as it is favored for its summertime pursuits, the region has been blessed with a fascinating history. As we know from our history books, the region was explored by Europeans in the early 1600s, and the Puritans came to live in what is now Plymouth by 1620. By 1639, a scant 19 years from the founding of the Plymouth Colony, the town of Barnstable was the third town founded on Cape Cod, also known as Barnstable County.

The first settlement in Barnstable was founded on the north side and was named Barnstable Village. The area's extensive salt marshes promised instant fodder for animals brought along by early farmers.

Although many Europeans came to the colonies relatively unskilled, they quickly learned how to take advantage of the region's natural resources. Essentially, the colonists who came to Barnstable learned how to tame the wilderness, educated themselves, prospered locally, built ships, created industries, and founded a merchant class that then went off to economically conquer the world. Then, having created vast merchant empires in transportation, commerce, and other industries, they rested from those labors and more often than not came back "home," bringing their riches with them.

By the 1800s, the population of the town of Barnstable had increased, and those who wanted to be part of the burgeoning merchant class needed to go off Cape for increased opportunities. So many moved during this period of economic diaspora that Cape Cod clubs were formed in many cities and towns to continue the connection they had with home. These organizations played a prominent role when a centennial celebration was planned for Barnstable in 1839.

The planning started with a call for citizens to meet on April 23, 1839, at the courthouse in Barnstable Village for "the purpose of taking into consideration such measures as may be thought expedient, preparatory to the celebration in June next, of the second centennial year of the settlement of Barnstable." On April 23, a committee was chosen to report back on ideas and plans for a centennial celebration to be held the following September. A committee was chosen during the April meeting that consisted of David Crocker, Henry Crocker (chairman), Nathaniel Hinckley, Rev. George Woodward, Josiah Hinkley, Zenas Bassett, and Zeno Scudder. In researching town history and while firming up their plan, the committee could not find any absolute evidence of a previous centennial taking pace in 1739. However, modern-day historian Donald Trayser stated in *Three Centuries of a Cape Cod Town* that according to tradition the town did have a centennial celebration in West Barnstable on the end of Hinckley Lane at the home of the Otis and Hinckley families.

On September 3, 1839, Barnstable celebrated its second centennial. John Gorham Palfrey was the principle orator and spoke for two hours in the Unitarian meetinghouse. Many distinguished guests attended, and 1,458 persons sat down to a dinner in a pavilion that was erected west of the courthouse. Gov. Edward Everett, Chief Justice Lemuel Shaw, Robert Winthrop, William Sturgis, and Daniel C. Bacon were among the guests. William Sturgis, a native of Barnstable, who was on the Committee to Procure Collation, insisted that women be allowed to sit down at the banquet table, which was a departure from the social custom of the day. His wishes prevailed, and more than 400 women joined the festivities.

Determined to leave a record for their ancestors (the proceedings of which were published in 1840), the 1839 celebrants toasted their descendents and directed them to have a similar celebration in 1939: "Our descendants in 1939—may they then as we do now—come from North and South, East and West, and celebrate our natal day with an honest pride and pleasure worthy of their ancestors."

A century later, Barnstable honored that request by forming a committee in 1935 "To instruct the Moderator to appoint a Committee of ten towns-people to consider plans and methods for a proper observance of the Towns Tercentenary anniversary in the year 1939 and to report its recommendations at the next annual town meeting."

Donald Trayser, Reginald Bowles, James F. Mclaughlin (chair), Alfred Crocker, Thomas Otis, Genevieve Leonard, Evelyn Crosby, Ora A. Hinkley, Gladys Swift, and Elizabeth Jenkins were appointed to the committee, which came up with a plan involving special church services, an outdoor pageant, memorial tablets, Village Weeks, and the revival of the Barnstable County Fair, which had closed in 1931. The fairgrounds would host the final days of the celebration and provide a place for the tercentenary banquet.

When Arcadia Publishing first approached the Barnstable Historical Society, we decided that our photographic collection would best support a history book covering the years 1839 to 1939. This, we felt, was a time of great change for Barnstable.

Going through a period of prosperity after the War of 1812, the local economy would dip following the Civil War. Steamships replaced sailing vessels, and during the Industrial Revolution, goods were produced in distant factories rather than in village homes and businesses. But rather than fade away because of economic pressure, Barnstable would reinvent itself as a tourist destination in the 1870s and continue to find a way to thrive. This book seeks to document that change based on photographs from our collection.

One

Barnstable Village

Barnstable, the village, and Barnstable, the town, came into existence in 1639; the third Barnstable, the county, did not come along until nearly a half-century later. In 1685, Plymouth Colony, then "being much enlarged," was divided for convenience of administration into the counties of Barnstable, Plymouth, and Bristol. People sometimes confuse the three Barnstables, and this is not surprising, although now and ever in the past, the village, town, and county have been quite separate and distinct entities. In old English terms, Barnstable Village is a shire town, where the county has its seat. It would take a volume to set down the story of Barnstable County since it was created in 1685. From the very first, Barnstable County affairs and those of Barnstable the town have always been interwoven, and men of Barnstable have taken the leadership in county affairs. In turn, being a shire town has greatly influenced Barnstable. The following chapter examines the town as the village and its place as the first village of the town.

In 1634, John Lothrop came to Plymouth Colony and joined members of his congregation in Scituate. In 1639, after spending a number of years in Scituate, he and his flock relocated to the northern part of Barnstable, first called Mattacheese. This area was chosen as a settlement site because of its abundant marshes. The salt hay in these marshes would literally provide instant fodder for farm animals, which was very important for these early settlers and the success of their settlement. Lothrop's house, built in 1646, doubled as a site of worship. A church would later be built in Barnstable village in 1717. Many years later, Capt. William Sturgis purchased Lothrop's house and donated $15,000 to make it a library for the benefit of all.

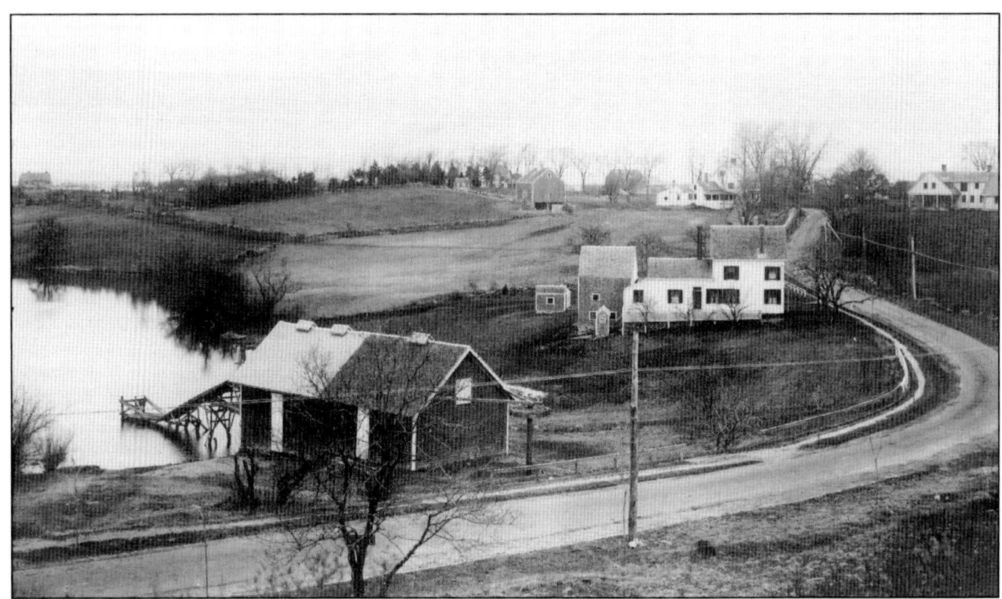

Icehouse, Coggins Pond. An icehouse was built in 1865 on the Coggins (also known as Hinckley) Pond, an area of Barnstable Village known as Pond Village. The icehouse was in operation until 1930. Ice was cut on the pond and then slid over to the conveyor belt, which hoisted it up into the icehouse proper, where it would be covered in sawdust. The conveyer belt was powered by animals, walking to turn a large gear.

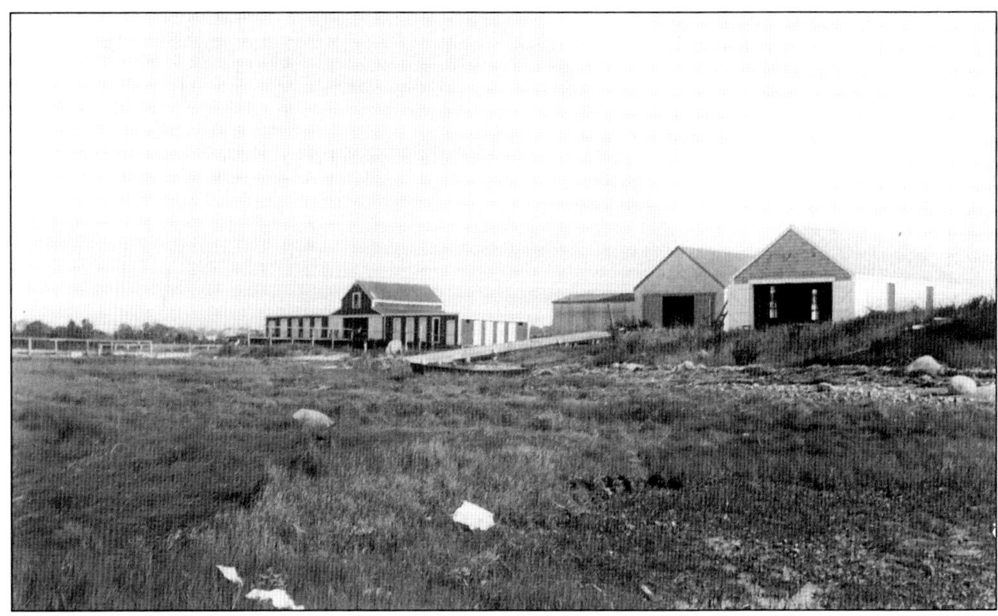

Barnstable Yacht Club. Yacht clubs and yachting in the town of Barnstable become a popular activity prior to the 1900s. By 1905 in Barnstable Village, a group of residents got together and formed the Barnstable Pier Association at Beales Wharf. This association was created to encourage yachting, sports, and social activity. In 1914, Arthur M. Beale gave the wharf to the association. By 1930, the association changed its name to the Barnstable Yacht Club.

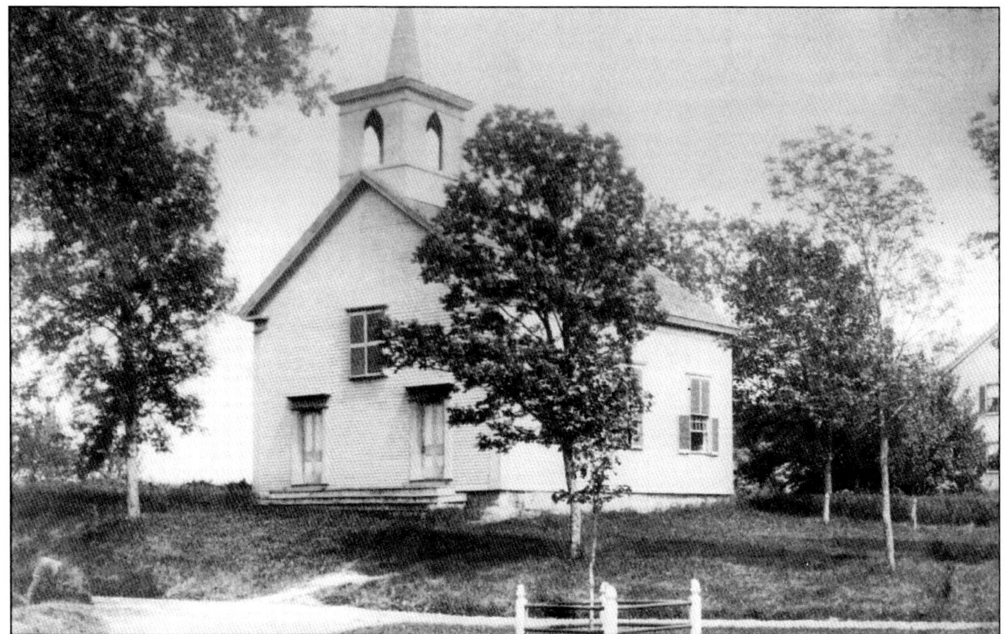

Second Colonial Courthouse. This is a courthouse that was turned into a church. Built in 1772, it served as a court of the English crown until 1774, when it saw a huge crowd gathered outside in Revolutionary protest. It became an official Massachusetts court after the Revolution until 1838, after which it was sold to the Third Baptist Church for a meetinghouse. The Baptists actually turned the building to face Rendezvous Lane and modified it for religious worship.

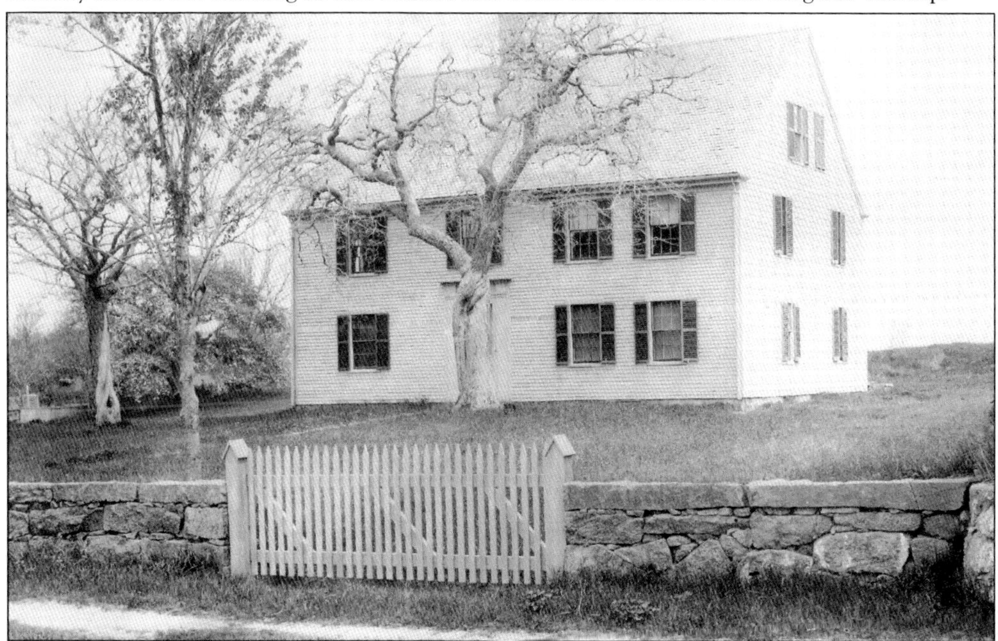

Sturgis Library. In 1863, Capt. William Sturgis died at the age of 81 years. Before his death, he had purchased his childhood home, which had originally been built for John Lothrop in 1644. His will left the house along with a bequest of $15,000 so that it could be turned into a library. The first librarian was Rev. Thomas Weston, who lived on the premises.

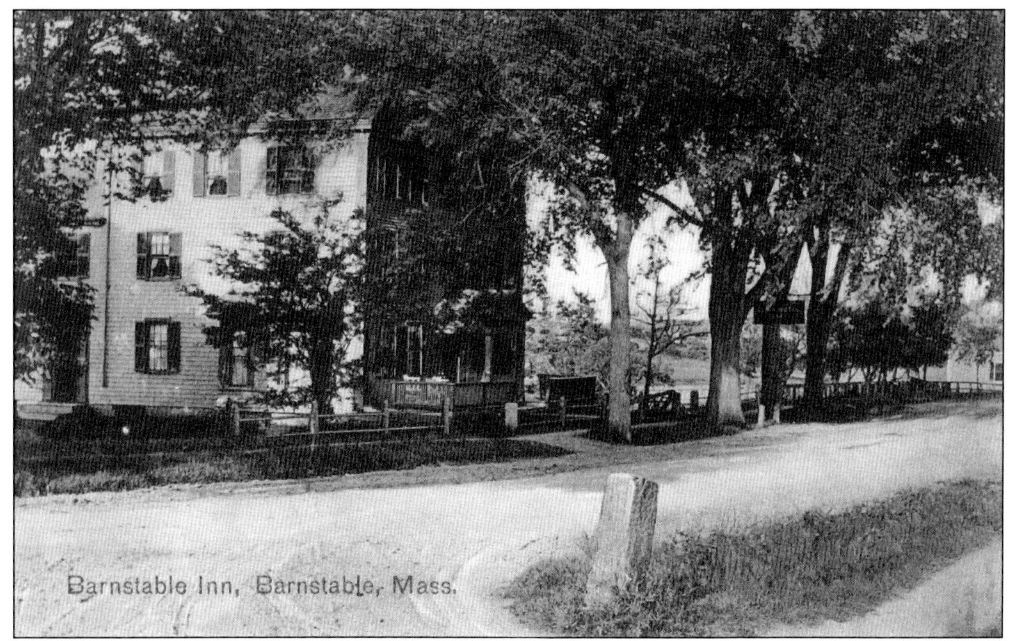

Globe Hotel and Barnstable Inn. The hotel stood on the site of John Lothrop's first house, built when he came to Barnstable. In 1827, the house was turned into a hotel by Eben and Waterman Eldridge. The hotel soon became a popular spot for the thousands of people who stayed there over the years. In 1897, the name "Globe Hotel" was changed to "Barnstable Inn" and by 1924 it was sold to Joseph C. Turpin.

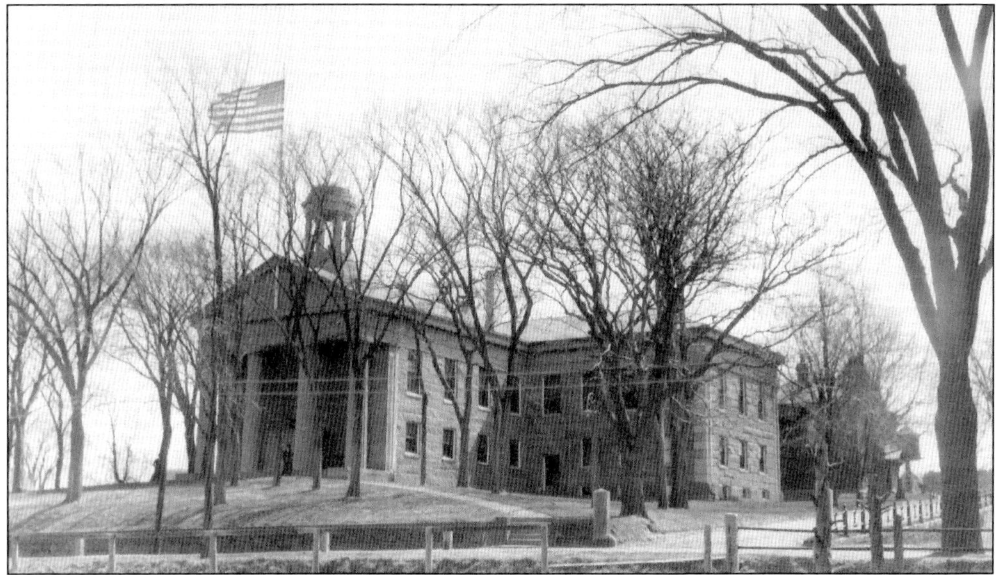

Barnstable Courthouse. In 1827, the county house burned to the ground, taking with it most of the deeds that were stored there. Through the valiant efforts of Josiah Hinckley and several others who were nearby at the Crocker Tavern, many probate records were saved. As a result, the county constructed a new fireproof courthouse with enough room to store documents in 1832. This imposing granite structure was enlarged three times over its first century of operation and new buildings were added to the complex.

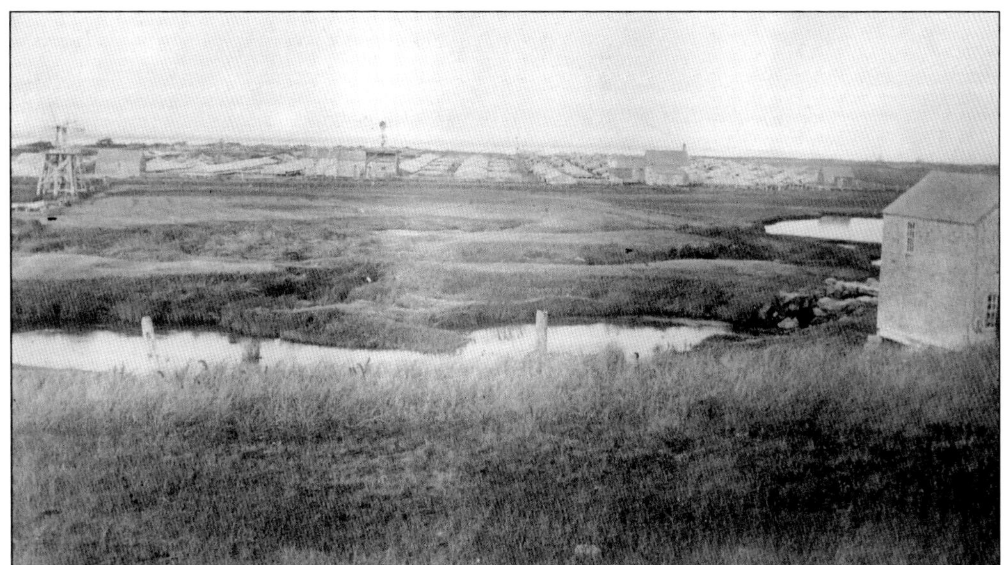

COMMON FIELDS SALT WORKS. Salt works were once a very common site on the shores of Barnstable. Needed to preserve fish, salt was either imported or boiled down in huge iron vats of seawater. The latter method proved very expensive, as the process required two cords of firewood to produce one bushel of salt. During the War of 1812, British frigates threatened the salt works in common fields. The cannon used in their defense are on the grounds of the courthouse in Barnstable.

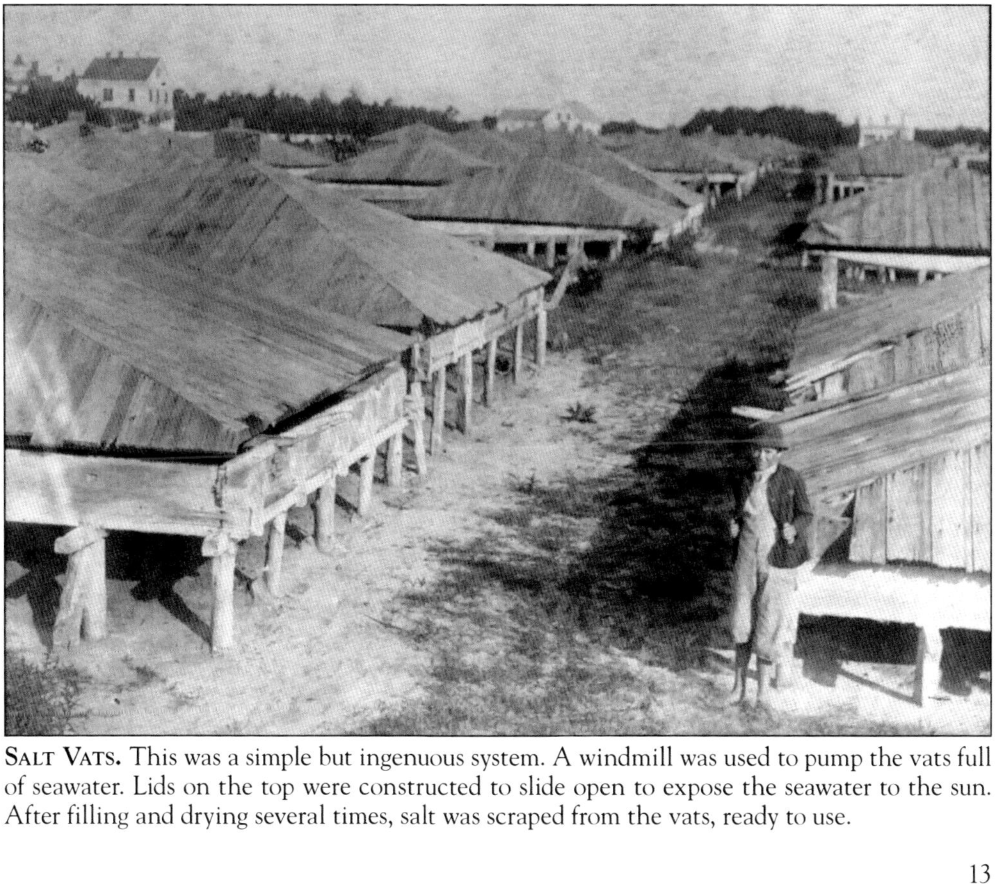

SALT VATS. This was a simple but ingenuous system. A windmill was used to pump the vats full of seawater. Lids on the top were constructed to slide open to expose the seawater to the sun. After filling and drying several times, salt was scraped from the vats, ready to use.

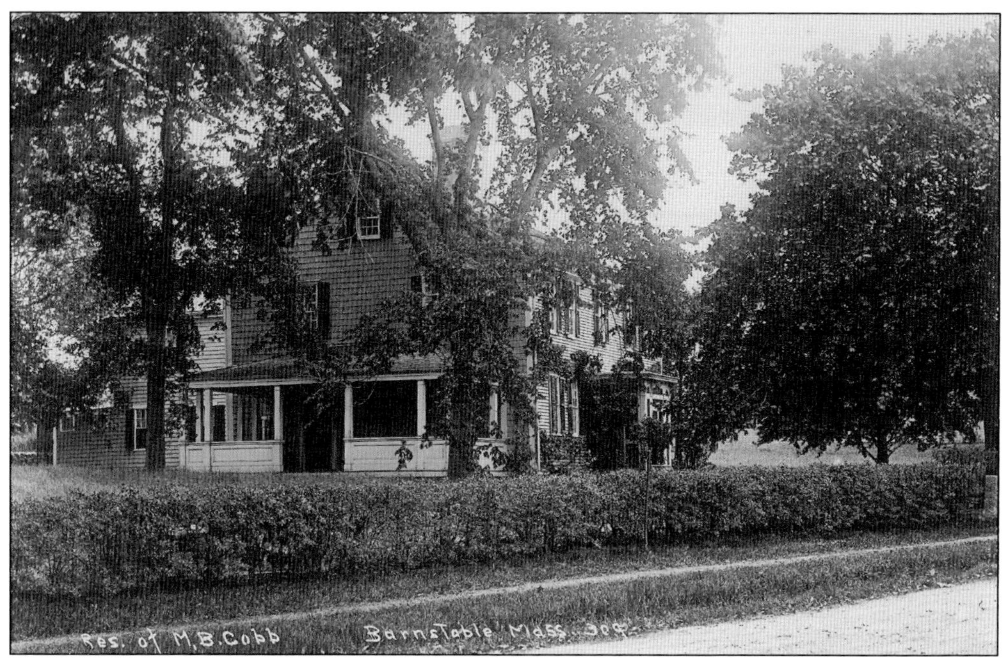

Daniel Davis House. The c. 1739 Daniel Davis House is located next to the Sturgis Library in Barnstable. Daniel Davis was considered a patriot of the Revolution and also served as a judge in the Barnstable court system. Mary Kearny Cobb, a great granddaughter of Davis (several times removed), gave the land across the street from the Davis house for St. Mary's Episcopal Church in 1890.

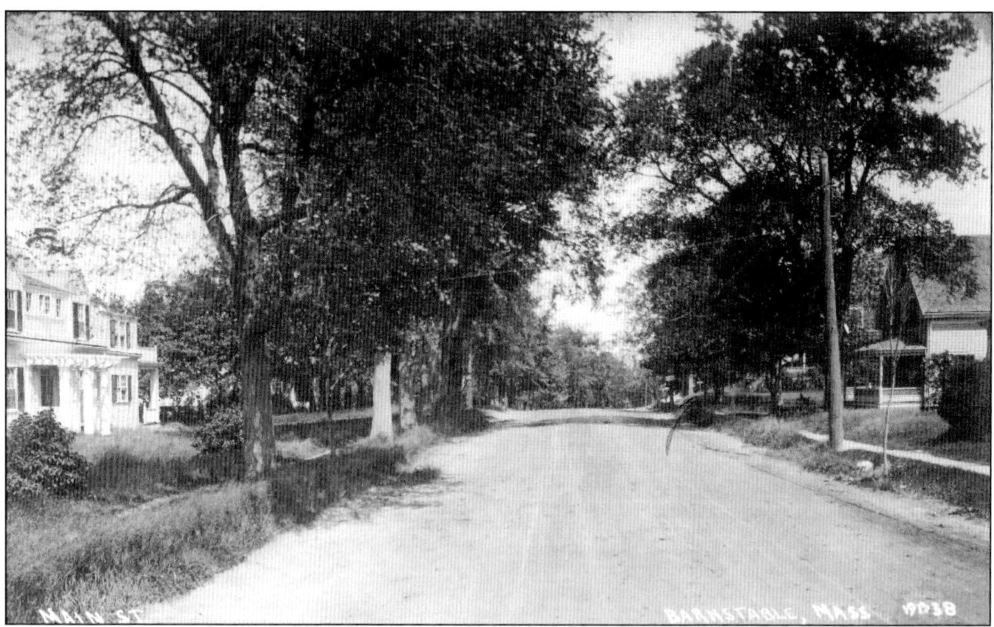

Main Street, Looking East. This pastoral view of Kings Highway (6A) in Barnstable looks east toward the village center. The entrance to the Barnstable Yacht Club is on the left next to the white house, which was once occupied by Arthur Beale, the resident who donated Beale Wharf to the Barnstable Yacht Club.

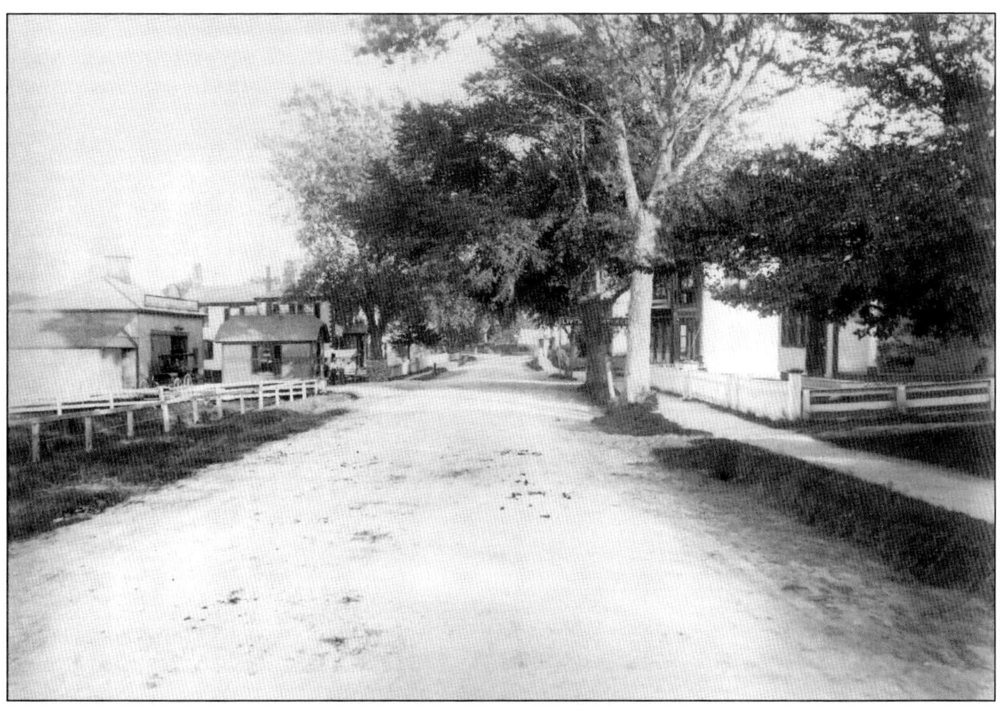

MAIN STREET TOWARDS HYANNIS ROAD. Looking east toward Hyannis Road about 1870, F.S. Kent's garage and blacksmith shop and E.S. Phinney's general store are visible.

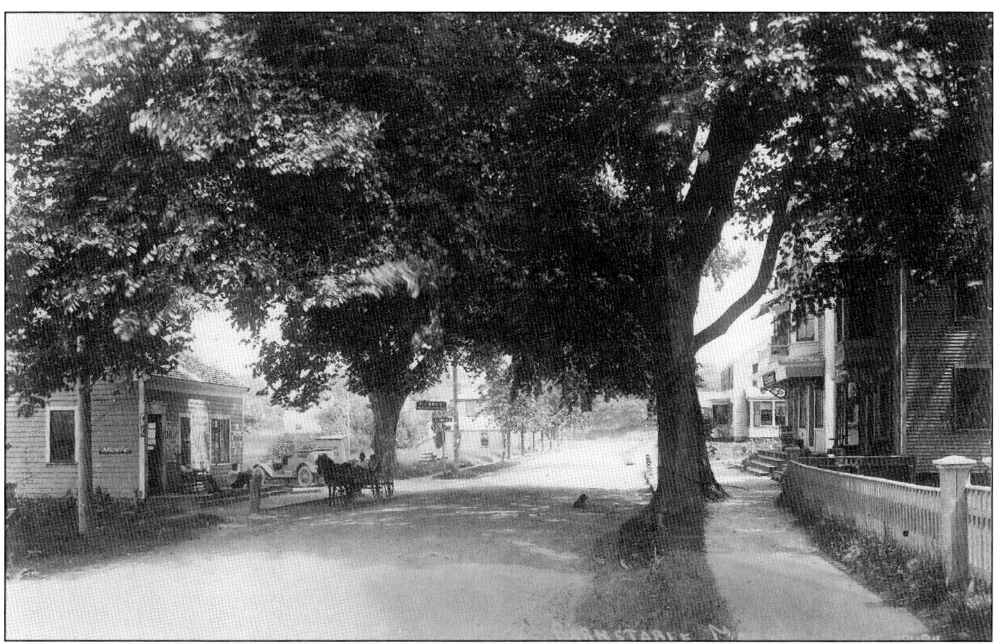

KENT'S GARAGE. This is a closer view of Kent's on Main Street in the early 1900s, showing an automobile next to a gas pump. The sign out front still offers blacksmith services along with mechanic services. During this time, the marsh in the village was much closer to Main Street.

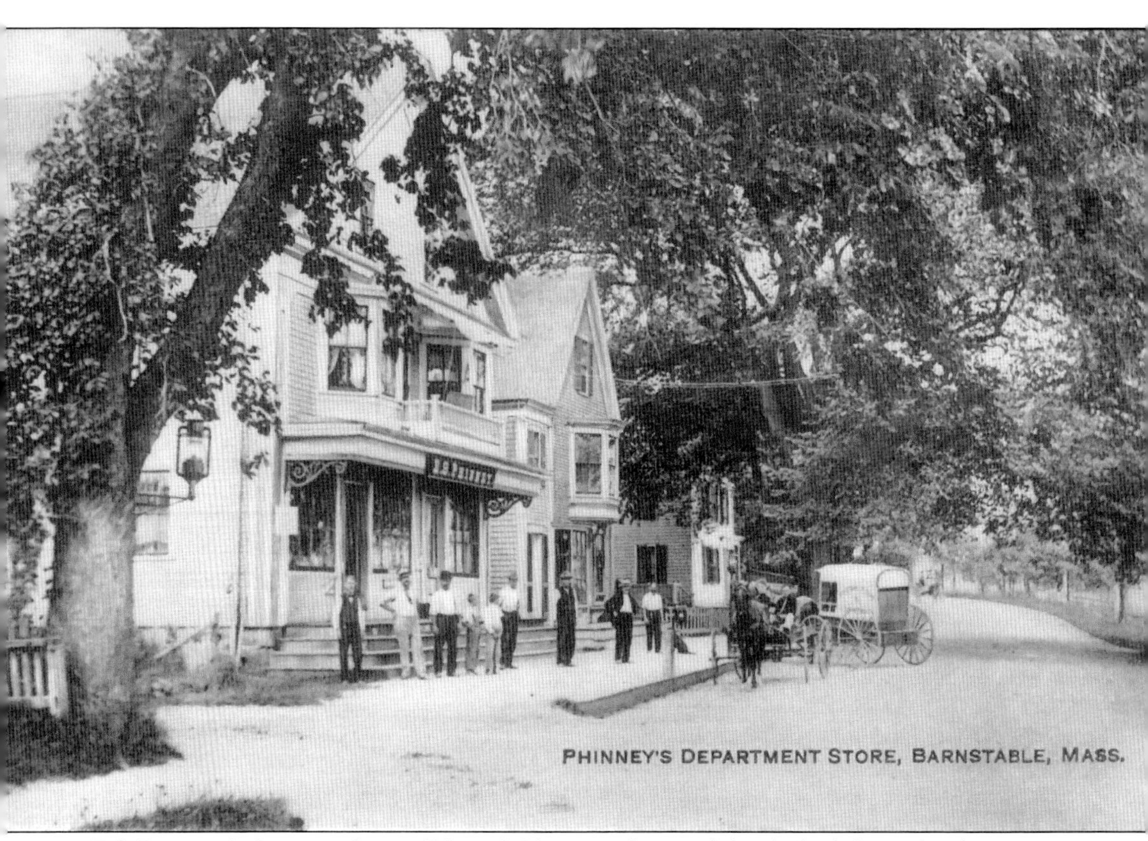

E.S. PHINNEY'S GENERAL STORE. Edwin S. Phinney advertised that he had choice family groceries, dry goods, boots and shoes, crockery, and carpeting, as well as a livery and boarding stable behind the store. Upstairs, he rented rooms to travelers who would find spacious accommodations and a "good table." He rented wagons with either a single hitch or double hitch, and they could come with a driver if needed. Up until 1883, he operated the store in partnership with a variety of co-owners. After that, he operated it himself until about 1923, when he sold the store to A.B. Yaffe of Brockton who renovated it and turned it into the Union Furniture Company. A fire burned down the store the same year it was purchased from Phinney. The same conflagration also burned down two buildings on either side of the old Phinney store. To the west, the D.M. Seabury and Son hardware store was a total loss. To the east, the Crocker residence was also a total loss. Phinney passed away a month before his former store burned down.

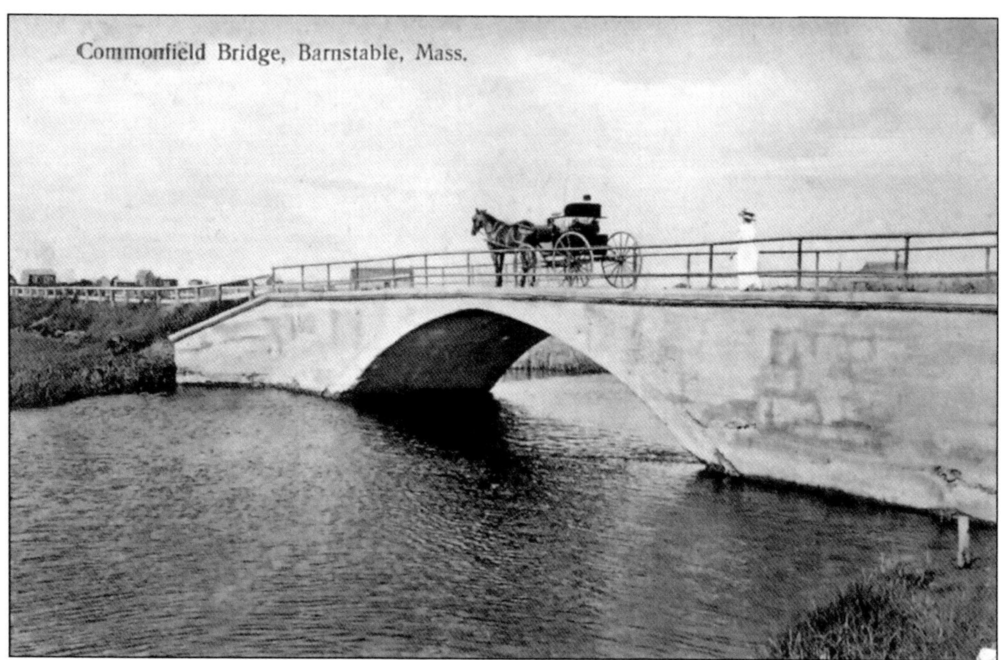

COMMONFIELDS BRIDGE. At town meeting in 1909, an article was considered for the replacement of the Commonfields Bridge, which had been damaged by a large gale. A new stone and concrete bridge was erected in place of the old wooden one. Unfortunately, due to poor construction, the new bridge was often closed for repairs. By 1914, the Commonfields Bridge Committee was again taking bids for bridge replacement. The work to be performed was very specific. This time, solid fill was to be placed under and adjacent to the bridge along with a new culvert pipe. This pipe, 72 feet long and 36 inches in diameter, was to be installed and rest on a properly prepared foundation. Concrete cutoff walls were built at each end of the culvert and a tide gate was built at the downstream end.

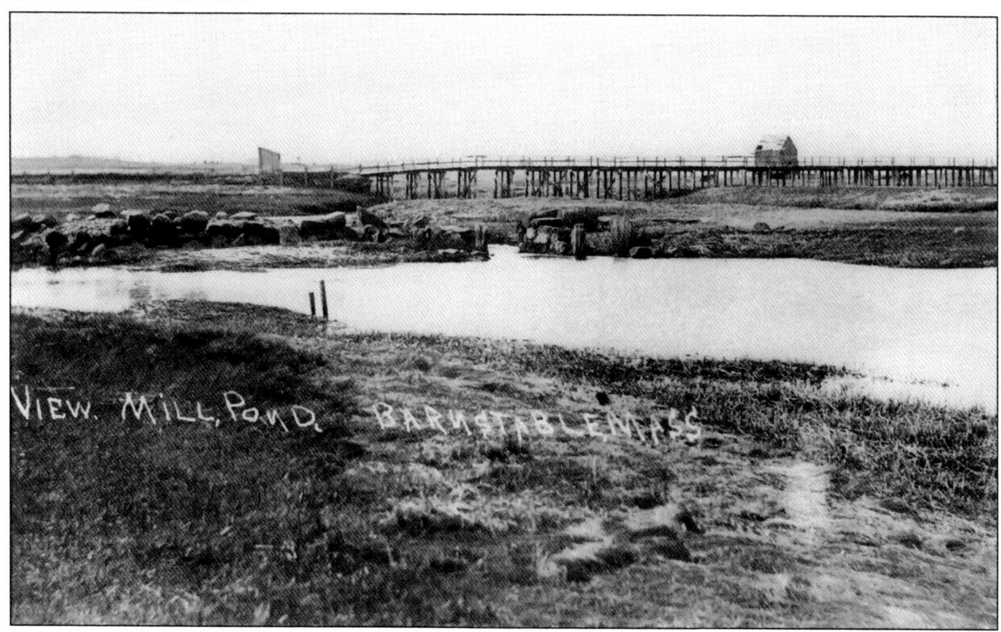

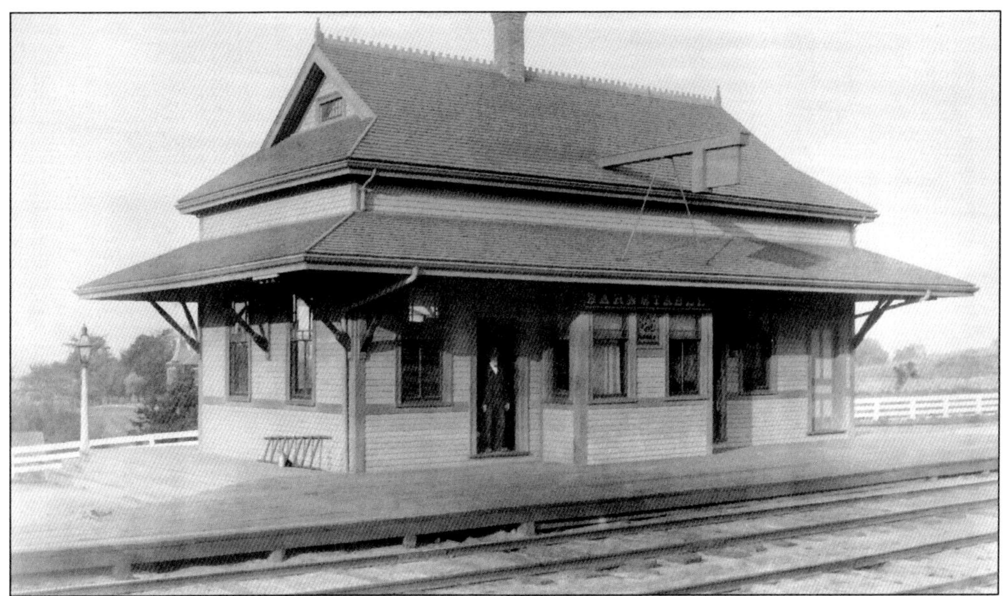

TRAIN STATION, BARNSTABLE VILLAGE. The first train into the new Barnstable station rolled in on May 8, 1854, and the *Barnstable Patriot* stated that most of the village turned out for the event. The train arrived to a crowd of hundreds at the depot and on surrounding hills cheering and ringing bells. As the train came into the station, a cannon was fired in salute.

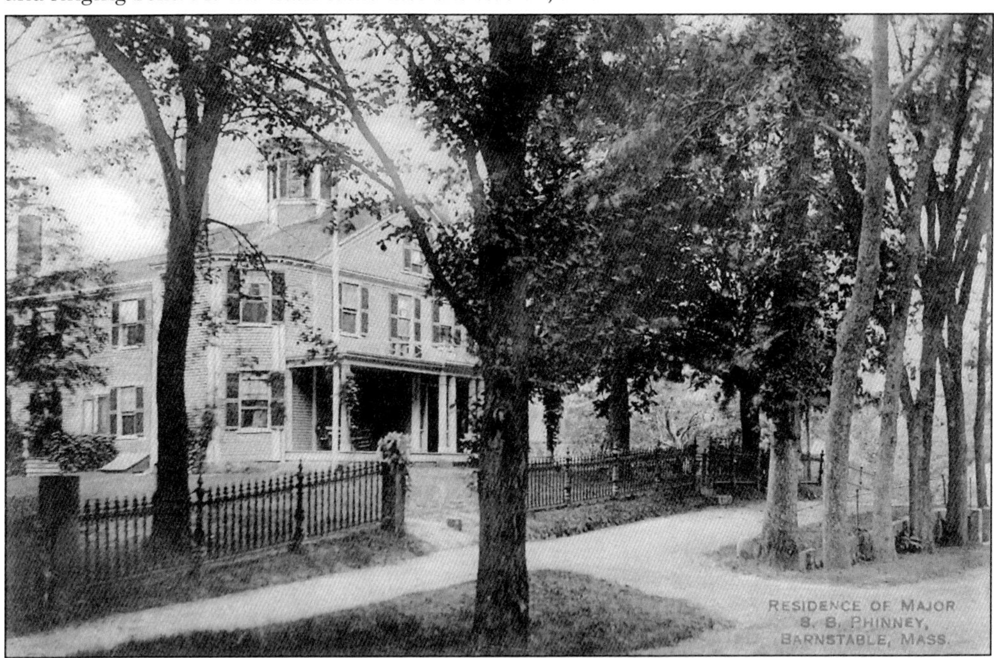

SYLVANUS B. PHINNEY HOUSE. Sylvanus B. Phinney, militia major, publisher of the *Barnstable Patriot*, collector of customs, and witness to the Civil War naval battle between the ironclads *Merrimack* and *Monitor*, lived his entire life in Barnstable Village. The first issue of the *Barnstable Patriot* appeared June 26, 1830. He was an unrepentant Democrat and filled his columns with criticisms of the Whigs and later, the Republican Party. He especially liked his print battles with *Yarmouth Register* publisher Charles Swift.

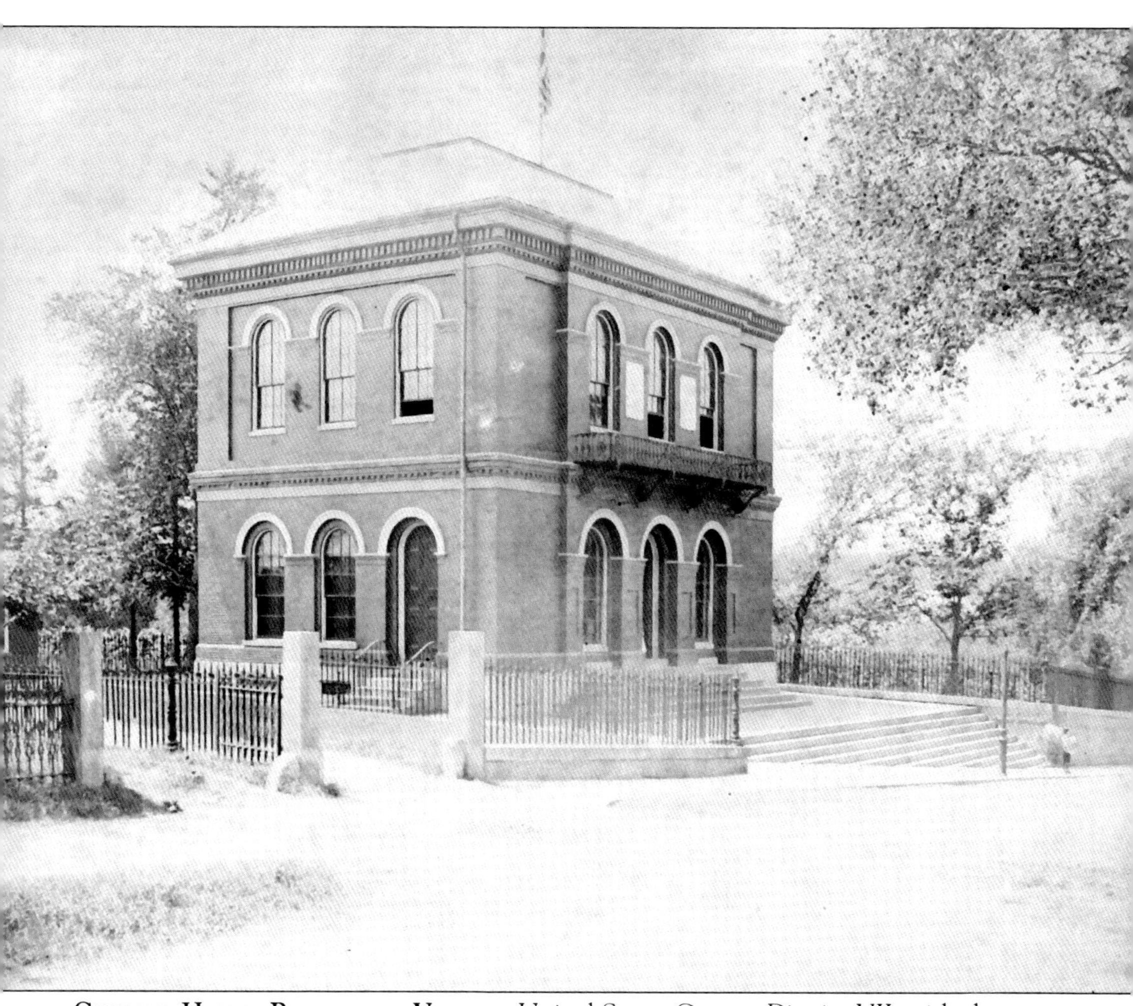

Customs House, Barnstable Village. United States Custom District VII, with the port of Barnstable as headquarters, was established by act of Congress in 1789. Comprising all of Barnstable County, the district was nearly 70 miles in length, had an average width of six miles, and included eight ports of entry: Barnstable, Provincetown, Wellfleet, Sandwich, Falmouth, Hyannis, Chatham, and Dennis. The customs building was designed by Ammi Burnham Young and was built in 1855. Sylvanus B. Phinney was responsible for securing the funding from Congress. Due to falling revenue, District VII was consolidated with New Bedford Custom District IV in 1913 with Barnstable becoming a sub-port under a deputy collector. In 1919, the Customs House was turned over to the postal department. All records were sent to the New Bedford Port and were published as part of a Works Progress Administration (WPA) project.

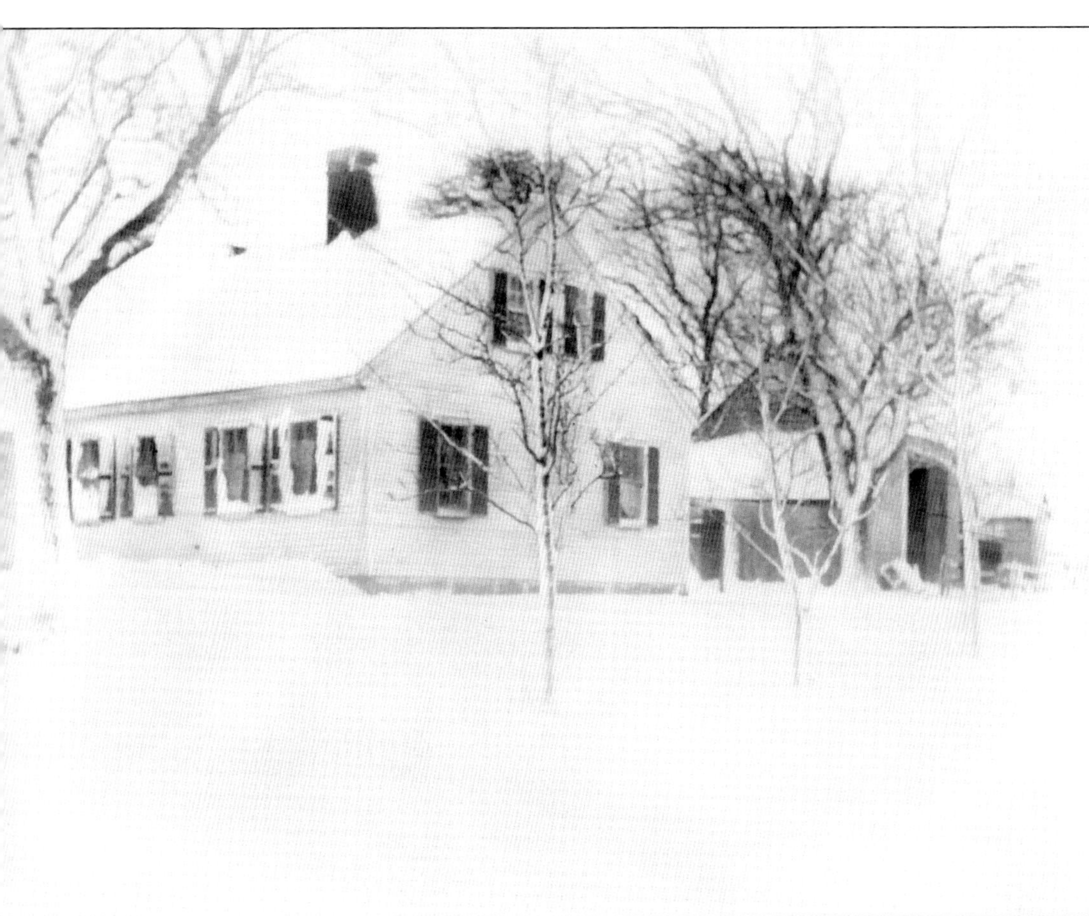

THE THAYER FAMILY. John and Catherine Thayer were married in 1852 in Barnstable. John Thayer was a clerk at the Barnstable Bank and both were members of the Unitarian Church. In 1855, they traveled to Sheboygan, Wisconsin, for economic opportunity. Moving west, John found employment with the local railroad. Within a year, he was elected secretary and treasurer of the Fon Du Lac Railway Company, founded his own private bank and an insurance company, and was elected mayor of Sheboygan in 1864. During this time, the couple retained ownership of their house in Barnstable. Son Frederick would come back to Barnstable and use the family home to start a poultry business. Fredrick's daughter would marry Bruce Jerauld, who would be clerk of courts for 30 years.

Unitarian Church. The first meetinghouse was built on Lothrop Hill in 1646. By 1681, a larger house of worship was built near Coggins Pond close to the house of Thomas Hinckley. No description of these churches has been found. The second church served until Barnstable was divided into two precincts in 1717. The new church for Barnstable was built on Cobb's Hill in the same year.

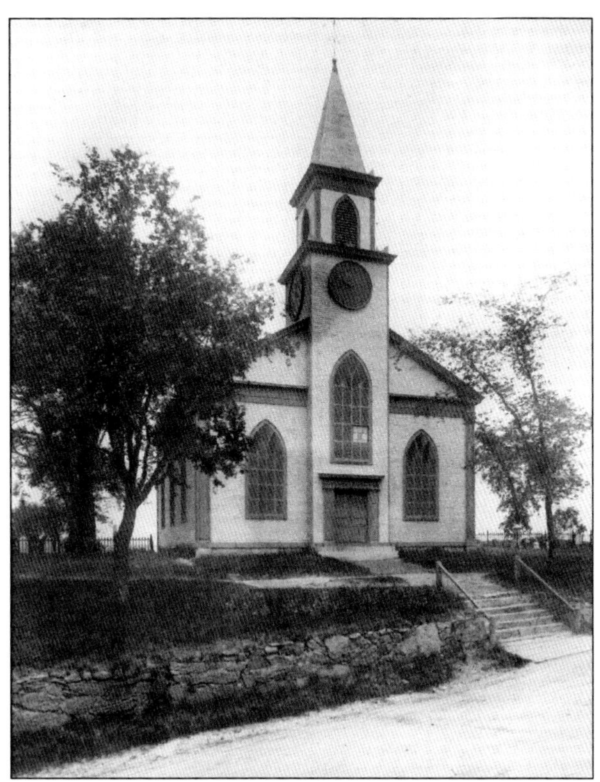

Unitarian Church Interior. This photograph shows the interior of the old Unitarian church as it looked in 1896. Early meetinghouses were often plain, rectangular buildings devoid of ornamentation and generally without a spire. This church, built in 1717, was simple inside but sported a bell tower on the outside. The church was replaced by another structure in 1836.

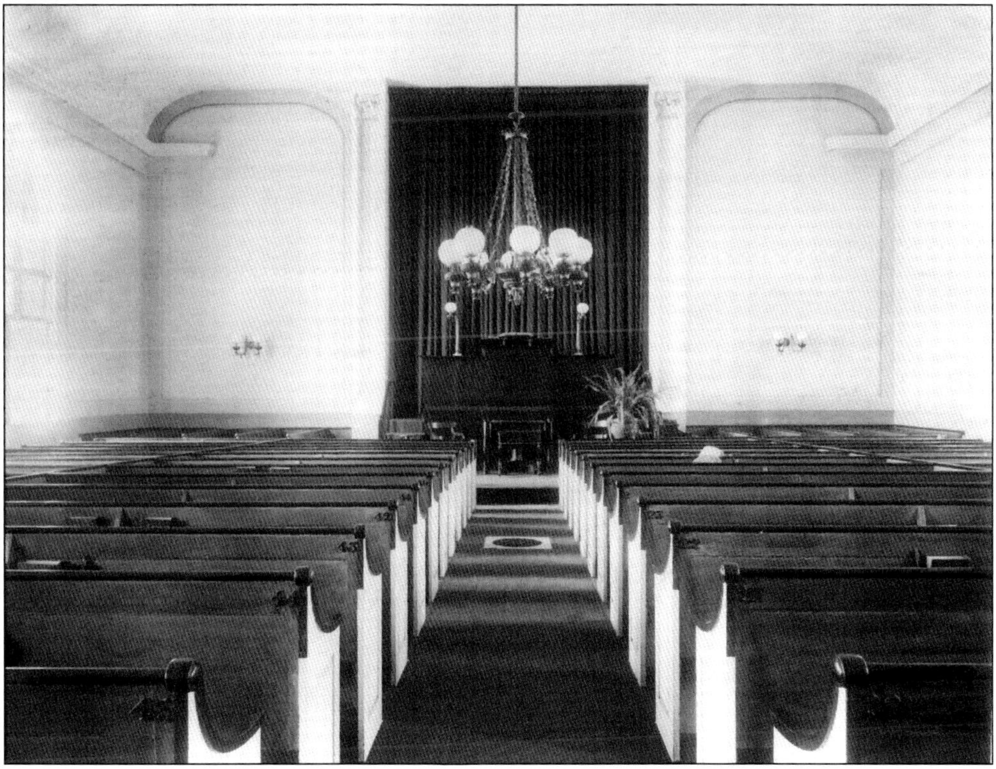

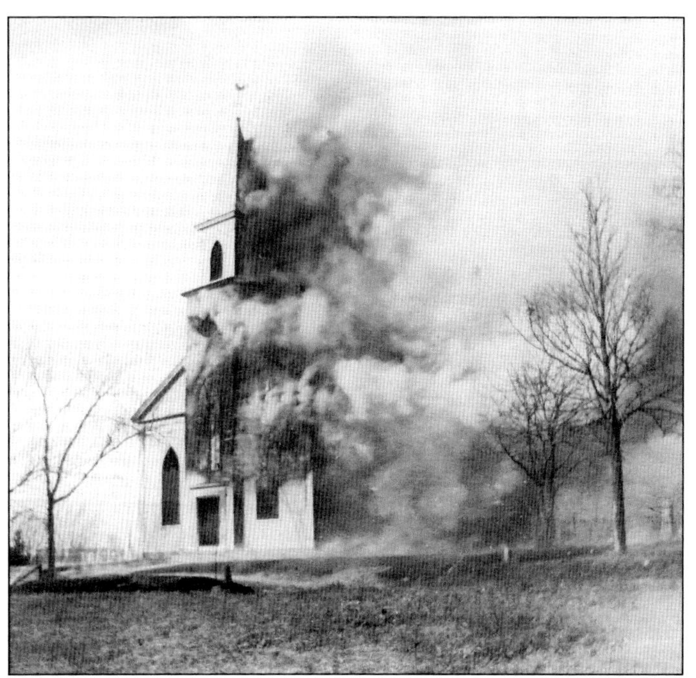

UNITARIAN CHURCH FIRE. On Sunday afternoon January 15, 1905, just after the close of Sunday school, residents discovered the Unitarian church was on fire. A stiff breeze from the Southwest was blowing at the time, and although hand extinguishers were used, the inevitable could not be prevented. The front door and a rug were the only things saved from fire. Officials believed the fire to have started in the furnace.

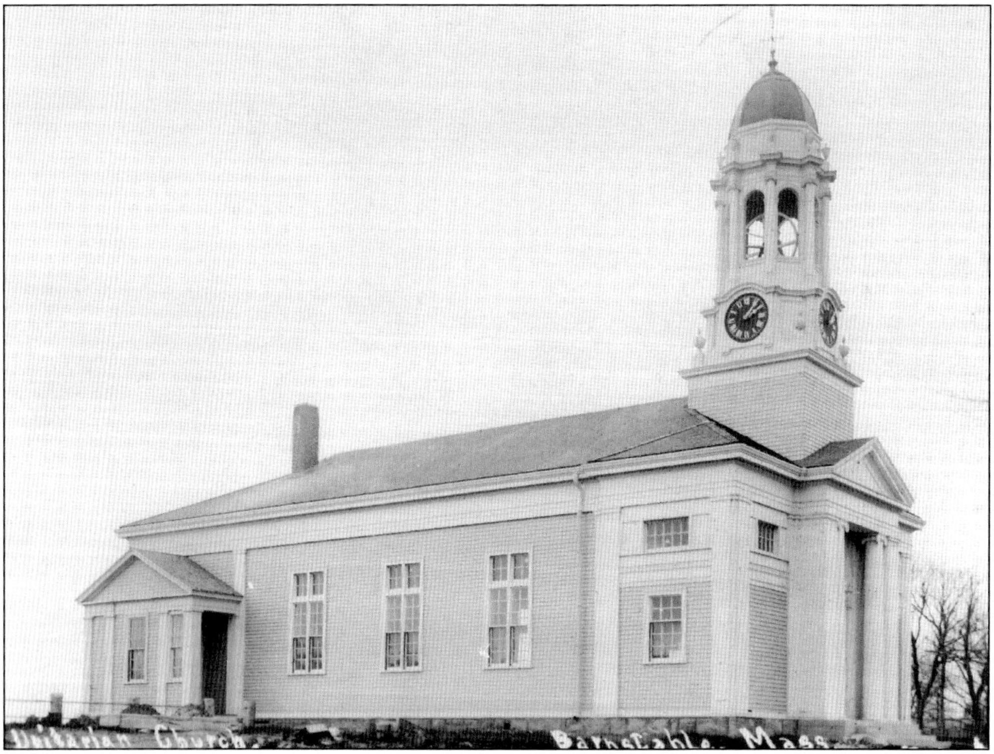

THE NEW CHURCH. Almost before the ashes of the church were cold, money was pledged for a new church. Architect Guy Lowell, who also designed the Boston Museum of Fine Arts, designed the new church. Descendants of John Lothrop donated the bell, and a fragment of the rock used as the first pulpit in Barnstable was added to the foundation. The new church was dedicated in 1907.

Two

Hyannis, the South Sea

The name Hyannis comes from a Native American sachem, Iyanough, who aided the Pilgrims in 1621 when they paused at Barnstable Harbor looking for a lost boy. Iyanough was sachem of the Cummaquids, whose domain lay along the north side of Barnstable and on the site of present-day Hyannis, known then as the South Sea area. It was also known that he summered in the Hyannisport area. In 1623, after the death of Iyanough, people in Barnstable began buying land from a sachem named Yanno who was considered a son of Iyanough. In 1664, this sachem conveyed lands—now known as Hyannis, Hyannisport, Craigville, and Centerville—to Barnstable.

There were only a handful of dwellings in Hyannis in the early 1800s. Amos Otis, Barnstable's renowned 19th-century genealogist, wrote that a Rachel Cathcart, who was born in Hyannis in 1771 and died in 1862, could remember when there were only three houses in the village. Otis conjectured that she meant only the small settlement at the head of Lewis Bay. The actual population of Barnstable was approximately 3,000. At that time, 1,000 people lived alongshore from Hyannis to Cotuit.

Early in the 19th century, Hyannis experienced growth spurred on by the creation of a breakwater in Hyannis Port, stretching 1,170 feet. This barrier to the sea was completed by 1887 at a total cost of $300,000, making Hyannis a safe harbor. With these improvements, the new harbor would be one of the busiest in Barnstable County. At times, 100 ships could be counted waiting out a storm in the harbor. The coming of the railroad train to Hyannis in 1854 and the subsequent building of the railroad wharf in the harbor brought even more prosperity to Hyannis. The post–Civil War era saw a gradual slowdown in maritime business but an increase in tourism by the 1870s. The first Hyannis land boom was aided by the creation of the Hyannis Land Company (1872), which bought 1,000 acres between Hyannis and Craigville. Between 1870 and 1890, life changed in Hyannis as people adapted to the new economy, and Hyannis grew to be the biggest village in the town of Barnstable.

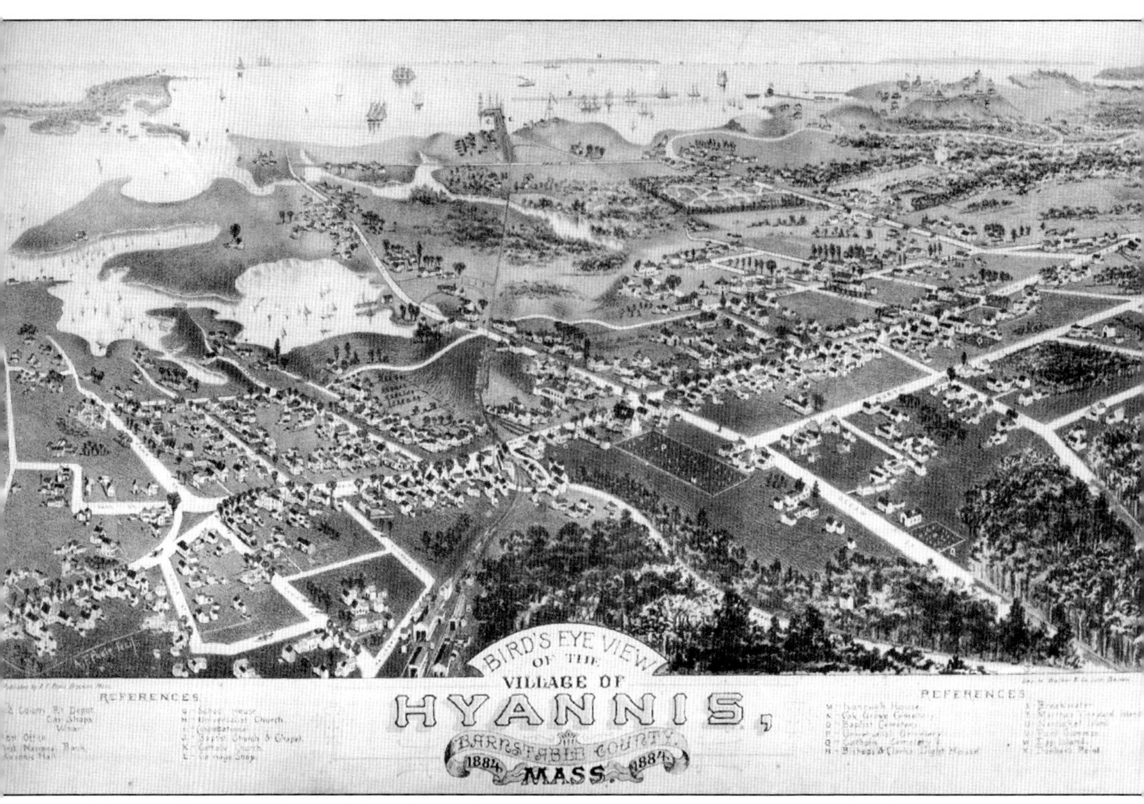

MAP OF HYANNIS, 1884. Maps like this help to preserve an image of what localities like Hyannis once looked like. This map, and others like it, faithfully record the names of families living in the houses that were drawn on the map in addition to street names. These 19th century maps would also often show points of interest such as hotels, churches, businesses, cemeteries, and lighthouses. This map also identifies the railroad station and the train wharf. In general, comparing maps from various years (such as the Hale map of 1835, the Walling map of 1856, and this map) makes it easier to see how the town and its villages grew, or in some cases, didn't grow. In the case of Hyannis, over the years, businesses crept down Main Street, gradually displacing residential housing and a popular baseball field used for the welcome home celebration of 1919.

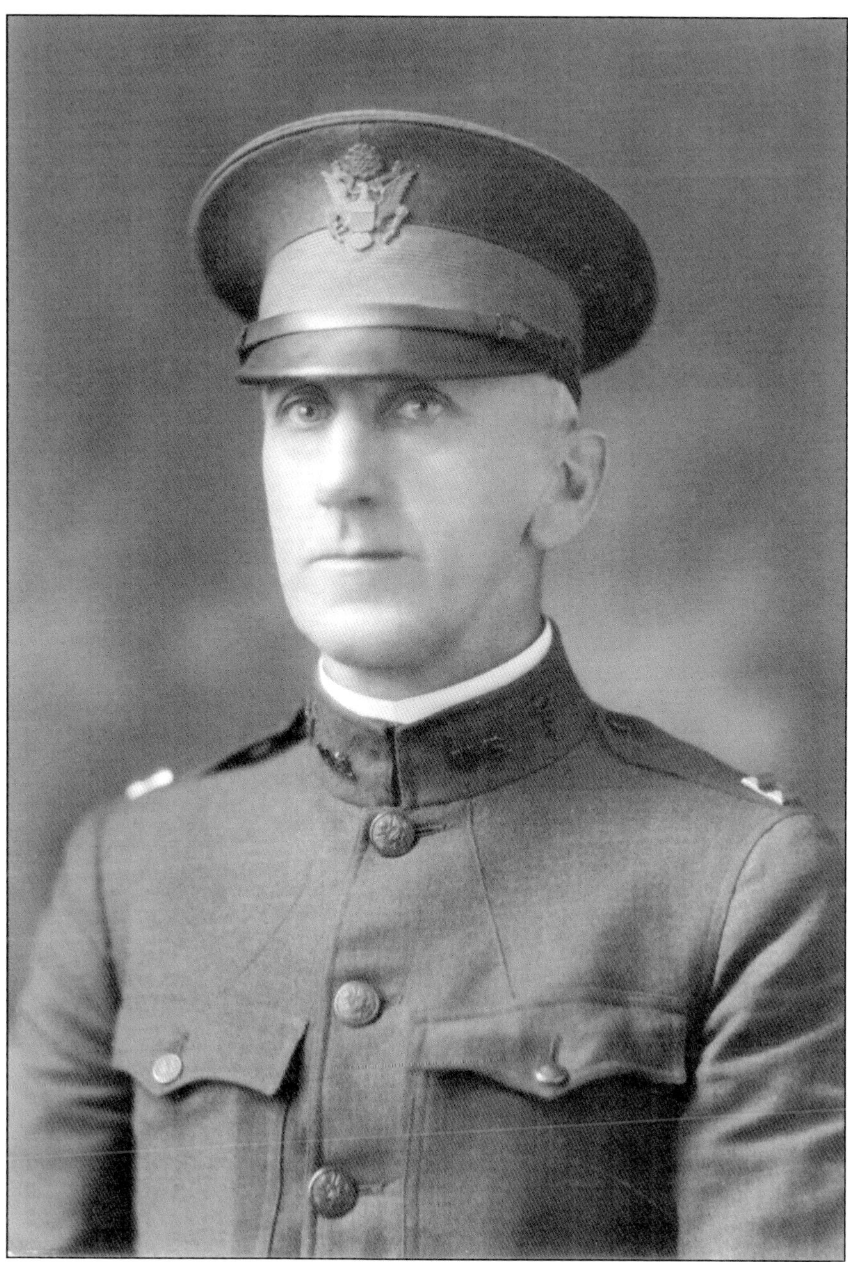

Charles E. Harris, MD. Dr. Charles Harris arrived in Hyannis in 1898 and was a practicing physician up until he died in 1947. He played an active role in establishing the Cape Cod Hospital in Hyannis. Several years before the new hospital was built, he hosted circus fundraisers in his backyard, where local residents dressed up as animals and clowns to entertain the guests. Once the new hospital was built, he worked to establish an X-ray department and served as its first chief. During World War I, he served as a captain in the Army Medical Corps. Locally, he was a member of the Federated Church, trustee of the Hyannis Public Library, held a membership in the Rotary Club and the chamber of commerce, and was a founding member of the Hyannis USO. His family donated his photo albums to the Barnstable Historical Society, and some of those images appear in this book.

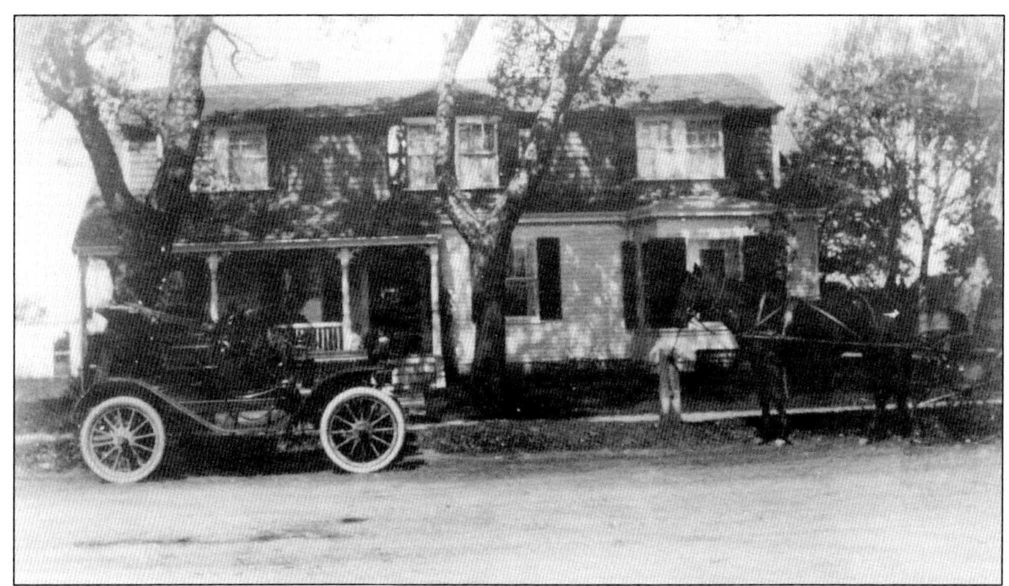

Charles E. Harris Home. Doctor Harris practiced medicine from his home on Main Street in Hyannis. He also made house calls. Alvah Bearse, in his book *Physic Point: Memoirs of Hyannis 1914–1929*, wrote of an influenza outbreak: "Like many of my friends, I was very ill. I was attended at home by Dr. Harris; the physician who brought me into this world now plied his skill to keep me here."

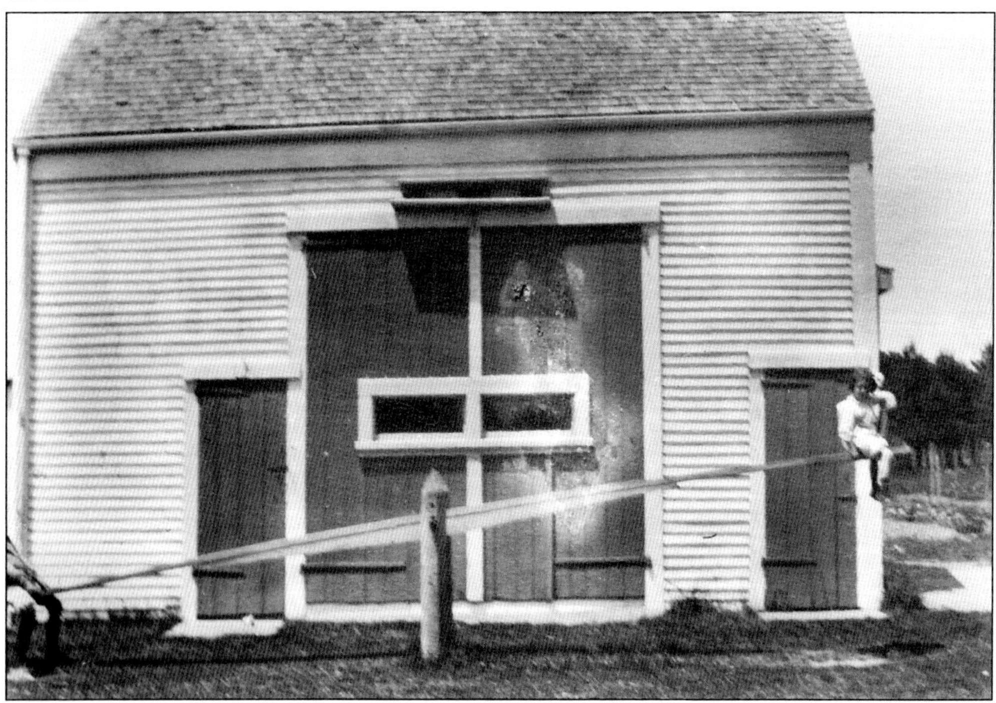

Harris Barn. This photograph shows the barn in the backyard of the Doctor Harris residence. It was renovated sometime in the 1920s in order to turn it into the first location for Lorania's Toys, a shop on Main Street. Behind the Harris barn was a grove where the doctor allowed others to hold fundraisers for the community.

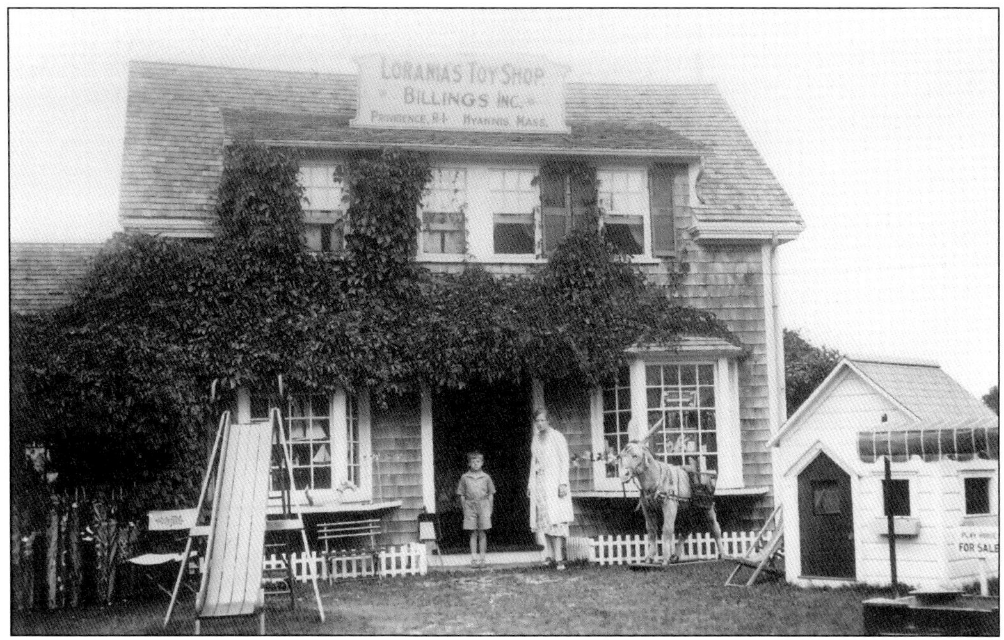

LORANIA'S TOY SHOP. Pictured about 1930, Lorania's was started by Mr. and Mrs. Edward Billings of Providence, Rhode Island. Their daughter Marion Billings was the manager of the shop. In the summer of 1930, Marion married John Smith of Hyannisport. Dr. Charles Harris and his wife attended the wedding.

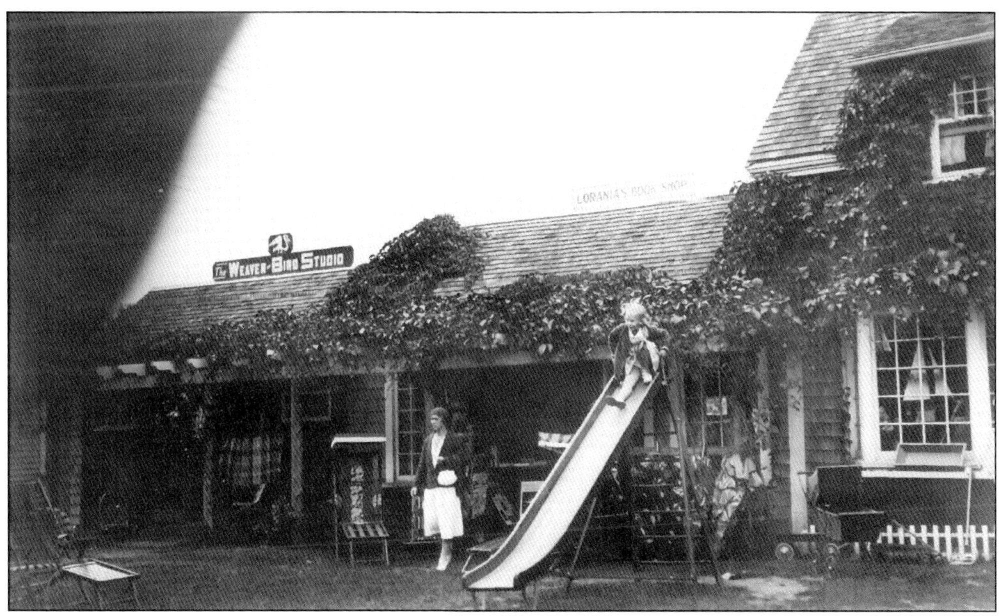

LORANIA'S. An expanded Lorania's is pictured here with a new bookstore and weaver's shop. The weaver's shop specialized in handmade afghans and throws. The space above the main store was remodeled into separate apartments.

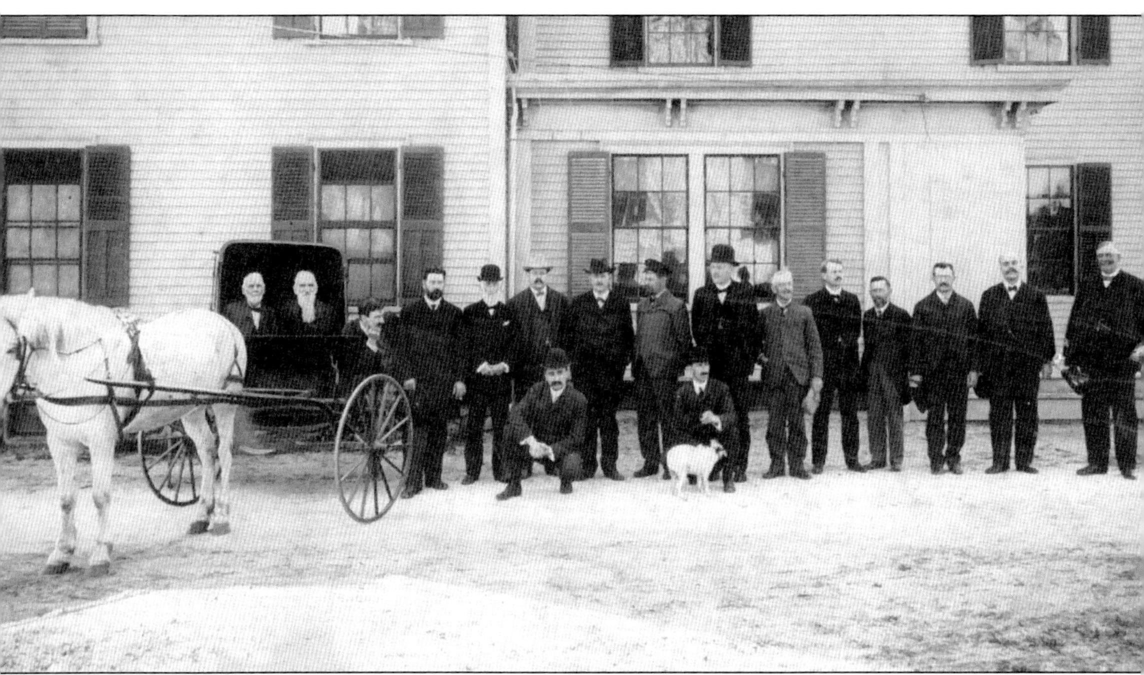

The Medical Men of Barnstable. This photograph is believed to have been taken outside the Iyannough Hotel, where the doctors of Barnstable gathered for regular meetings. Although socializing was part of the reason for the meetings, the doctors also met for discussions and presentations on various medical matters. In this way, they were able to keep current with new medicines and procedures. The 12 men standing are, from left to right, Doctors Baker, Millikin, Doane, Higgins, Binford, Hart, Haskins, Cummings, Kinney, Davis, Osborne, and Harris. Doctor Harris's dog Pinch is also pictured. According to records, one of the two doctors seated in the carriage should be Samuel Pitcher, formulator of Pitcher's Castoria. This medicine was patented in 1868 and later sold to Charles Fletcher in 1871, when it was renamed Fletcher's Castoria.

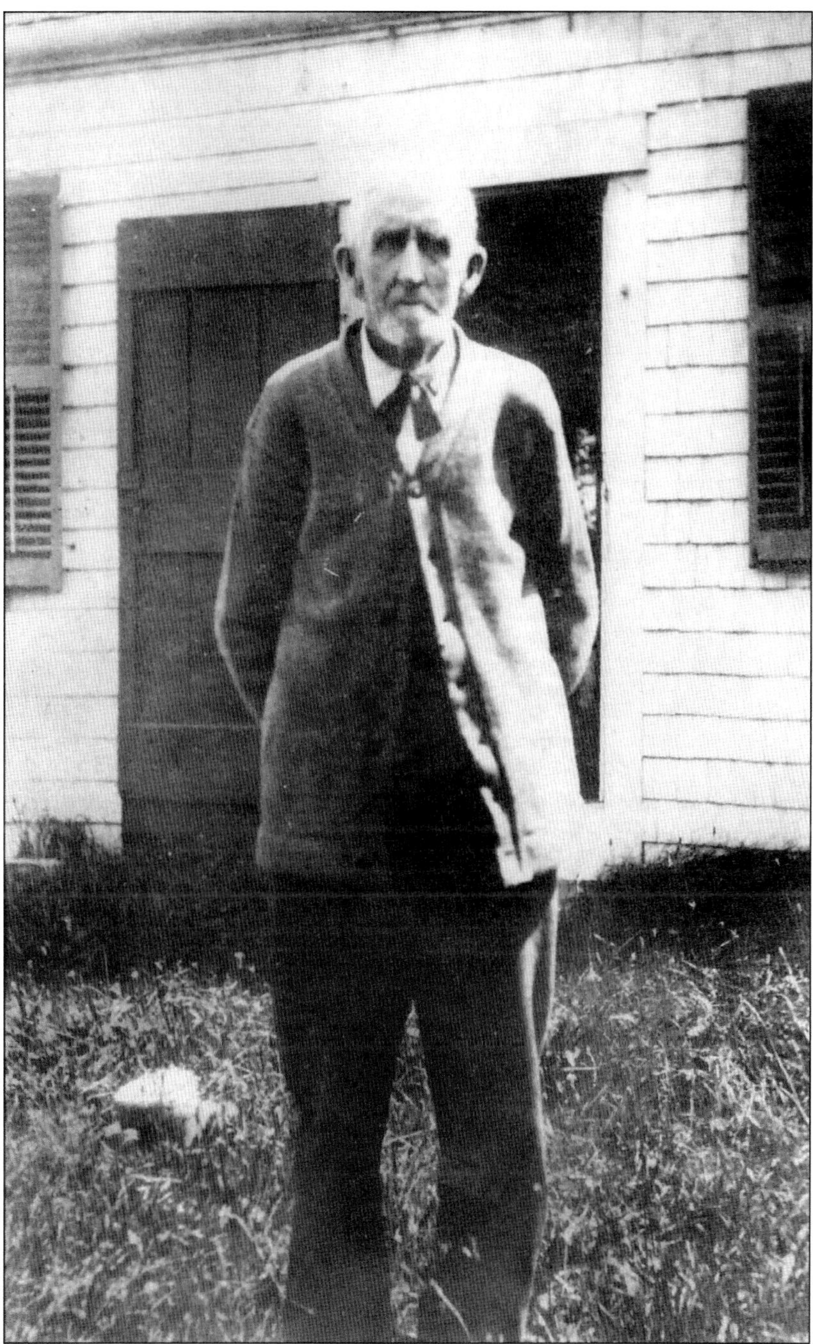

AURIN B. CROCKER, HYANNIS. In the course of a very long life, Aurin Crocker owned salt works, was proprietor of a livery stable, postmaster in South Hyannis, and for 40 years, was in charge of the US Signal Service Station. In addition, he was a marine correspondent for the *New York Herald*, *Associated Press*, and the *Barnstable Patriot*. Crocker reminisced about the "old days" in Hyannis in his writings. He would often remember details about the town, including the old stage line that picked passengers up in Sandwich in the 1840s in order to bring them to Hyannis. In those days, there were about 200 ship captains living in town.

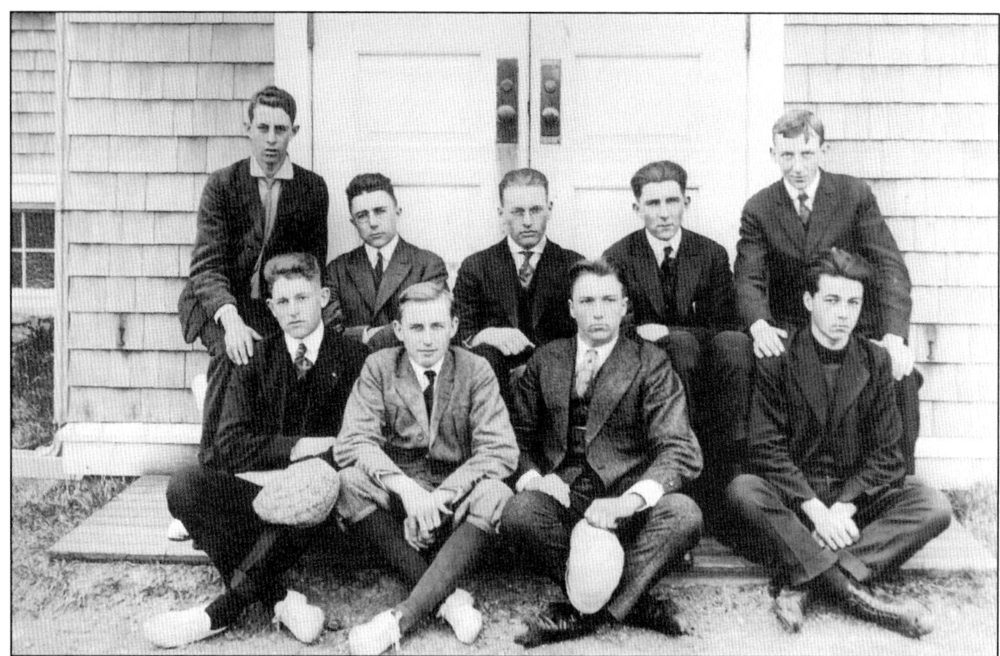

Barnstable High School Baseball Team. Pictured about 1916 are, from left to right, (first row) Russell Starck, Hugh Ferguson, Nelson Bearse, and Fred Nute; (second row) Robert Elliot, Stuart Bradford, Carl Starck, Ray Maher, and Carroll Stevens. Barnstable lost the championship to Yarmouth in 1916 but came back to win the cup in 1917.

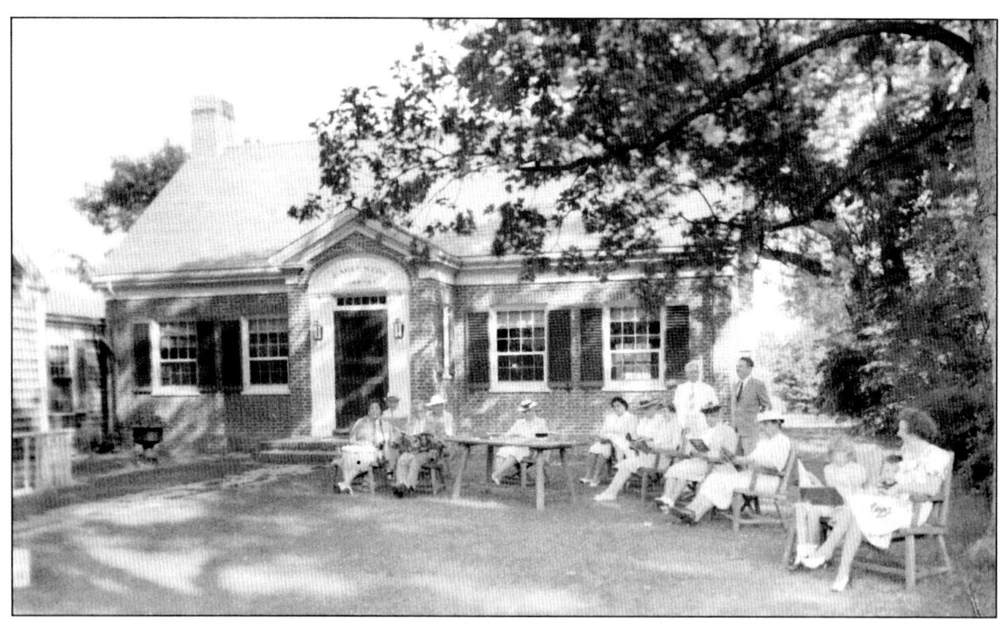

Hyannis Public Library. This 1939 photograph shows the new Eagleston Library addition. Edward L. Eagleston left a substantial bequest to the library (incorporated in 1902) in order to build a new addition bearing his name.

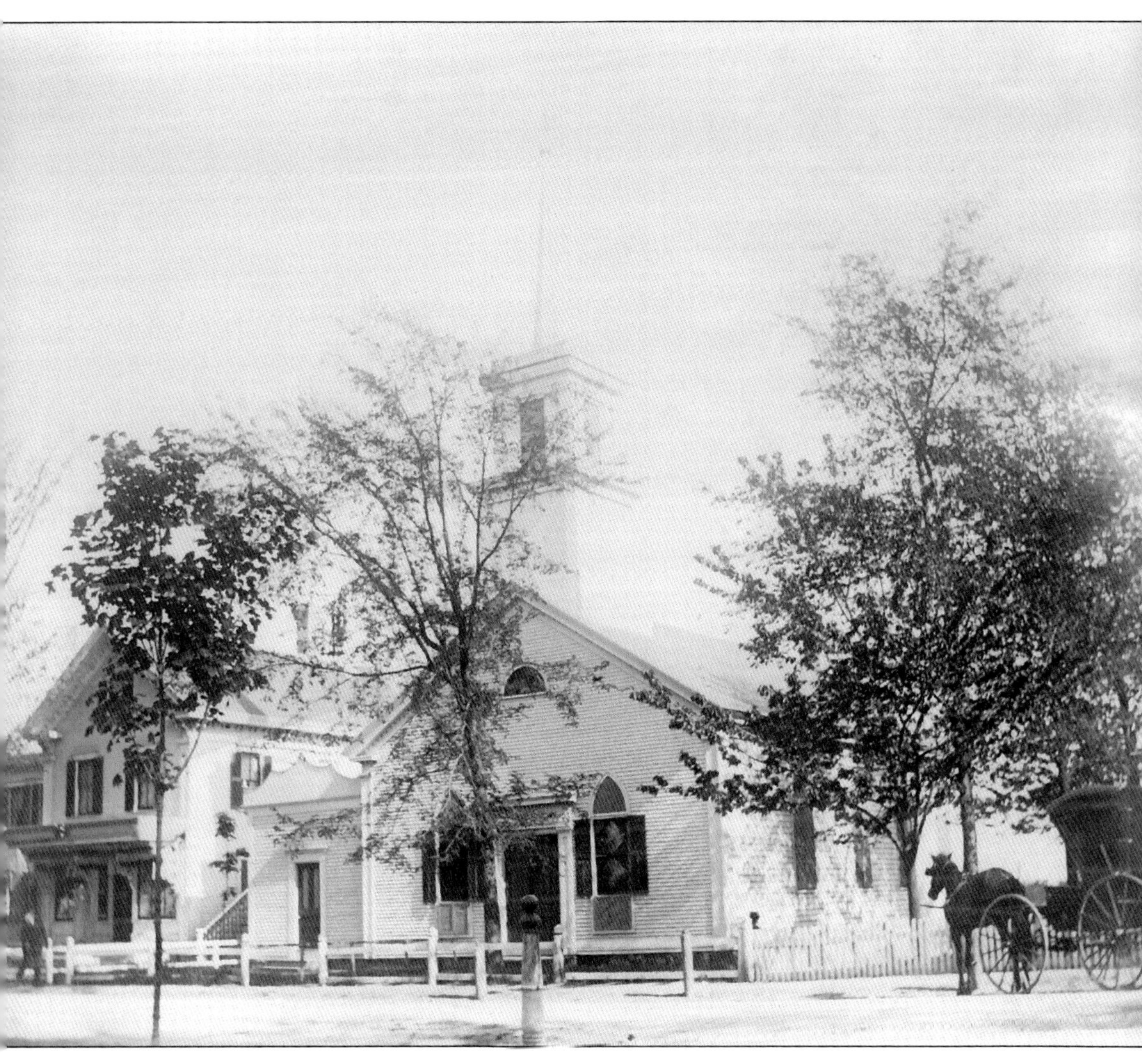

FEDERATED CHURCH, MAIN STREET. The Federated Church was a combination of the old Methodist, Congregational, and Universalist churches. By 1830, the church pictured here was built and then replaced by a succession of two buildings constructed in 1847 and 1873. Both were destroyed by fire. By 1917, the Congregational and Universalist Churches combined at this location. The old Congregational Church was left as a recreational building and was later remodeled into the Church Bell Apartments. Alvah Bearse, author of *Physic Point: Memoirs of Hyannis 1914–1929*, recalled spending many pleasurable hours in his youth playing on a basketball team in this building.

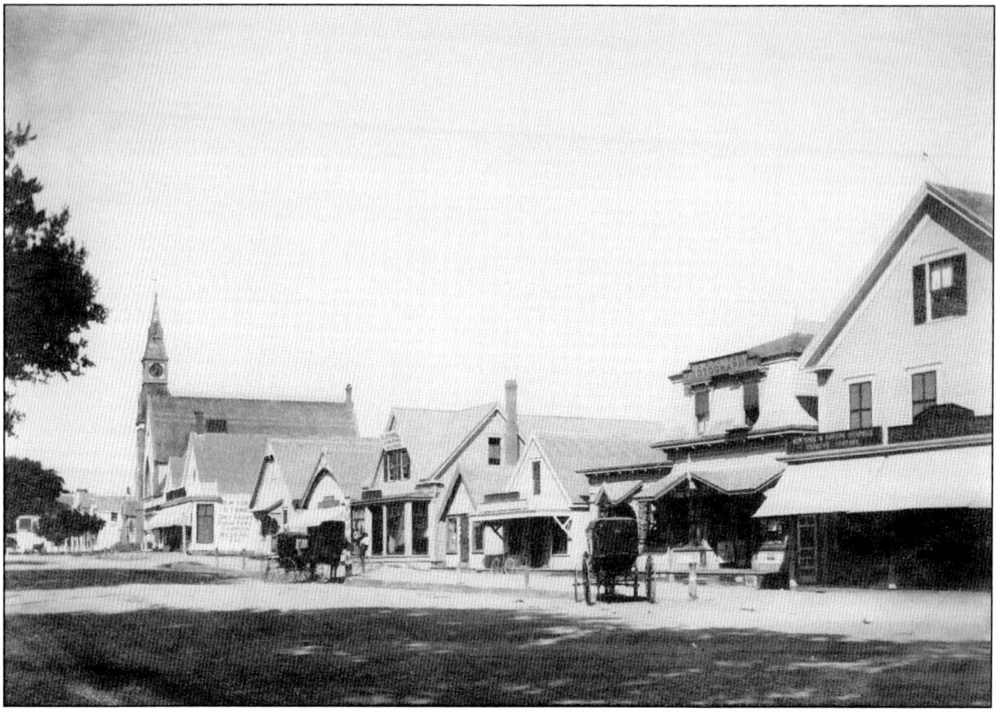

Baptist Church, Hyannis. In 1772, the Baptist Society formed a church in Hyannis. A new house of worship was built on Main Street in 1825 with a very distinctive bell tower that included a clock. This clock has been visible to all who come to the village. Branches of the church were established in Chatham, Bass River, Falmouth, Mashpee, and Barnstable Village.

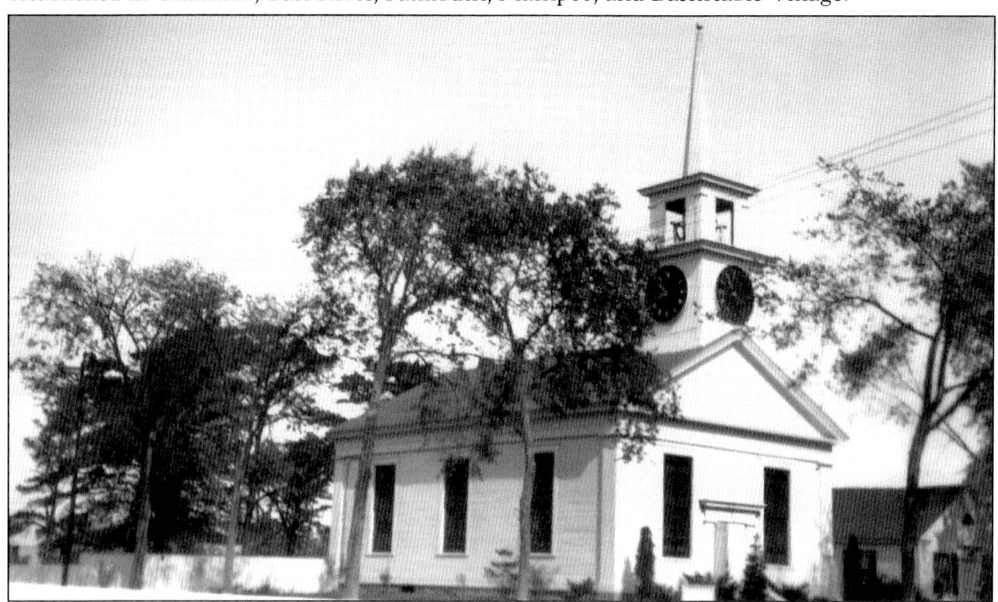

Baptist Church Vestry. Five members of the church were licensed to preach and went on to help establish other Baptist churches in Barnstable County. The church had its own circulating library of 350 volumes before the public library was established. An ell was added in 1866; an education wing was added in 1938.

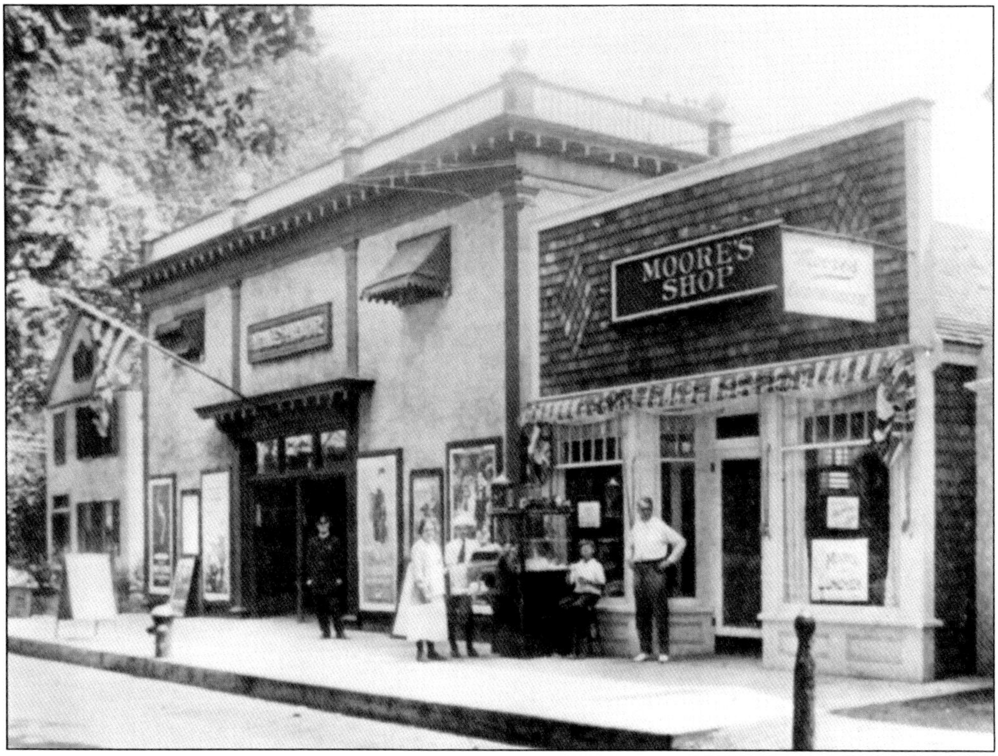

Idle Hour and Moore's Shop. The Idle Hour was a popular destination. It was opened as a "photograph play" theater and graduated to silent films. There were two shows a night for 10¢ with matinees on Wednesday and Saturday afternoons for 5¢. Moviegoers could go next door for popcorn and ice cream at Moore's. The movie theater burned down on Christmas Eve 1971.

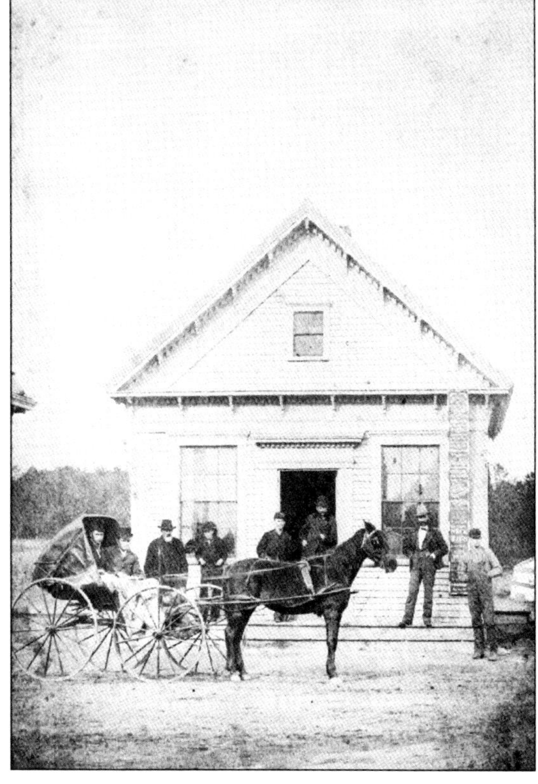

Joshua Sutton's Store. Many stores have come and gone in Hyannis over the years. According to records at the Barnstable Historical Society, this was one of the earliest store buildings in Hyannis, pictured here in 1877. It was situated on the north side of Main Street on the corner of Center Street.

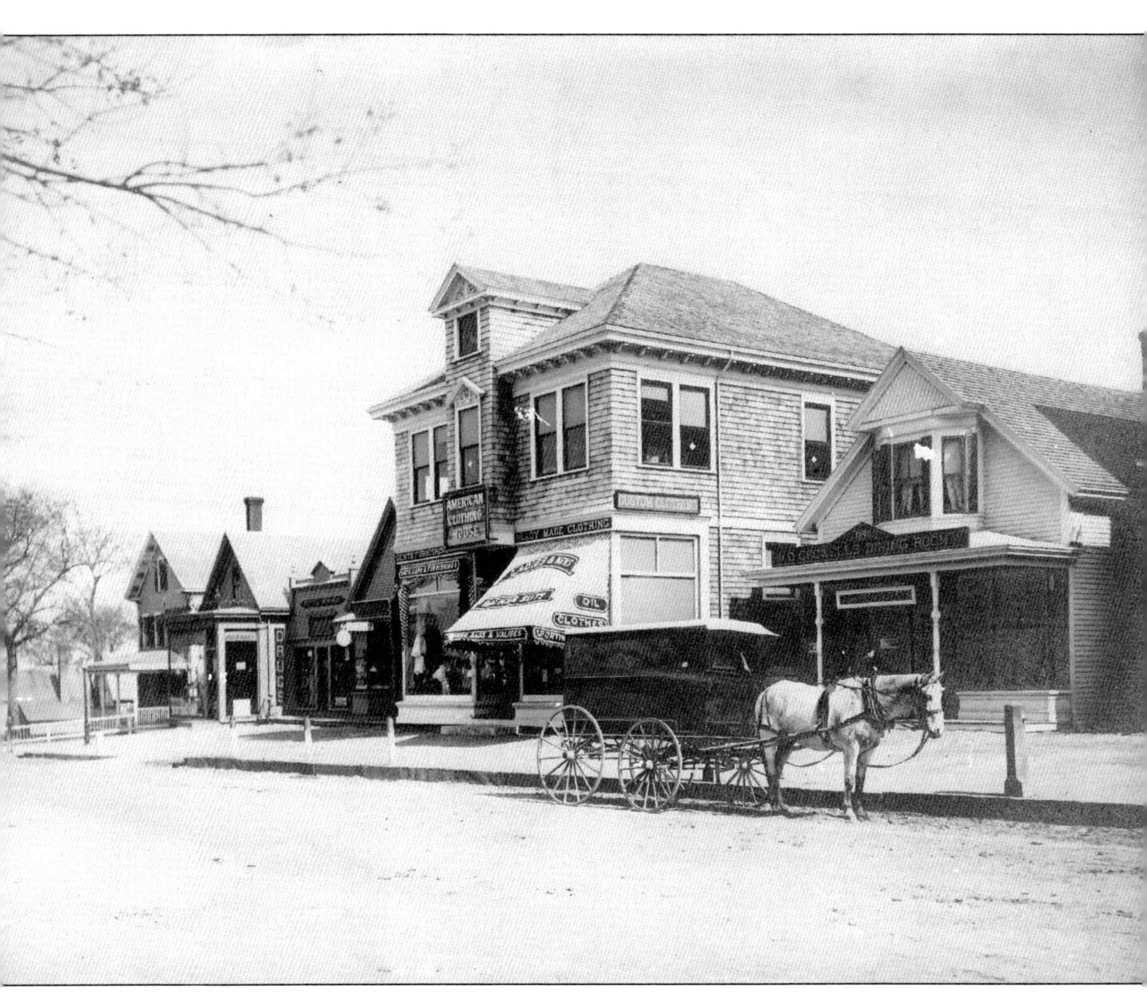

Business Section on Main Street. This photograph shows Crowell's Dining Room, the American Clothing House, a bicycle shop, and a drugstore. Louis Arenovski established his clothing house in 1885 and claimed to have the largest, finest, and most complete stock of men's, boy's, and children's clothing. The carriage on the street was used by George W. Nickerson, a traveling candy salesman. Arenovski was an active citizen in the Hyannis community, with memberships in several different organizations, including the yacht club, and was generally involved in planning committees for celebrations and community improvement.

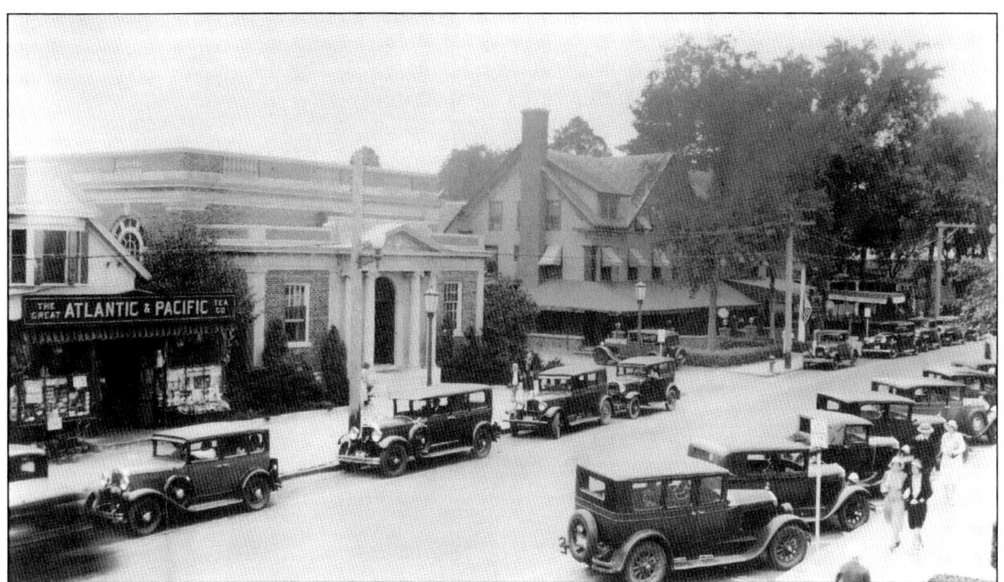

Ocean and Main Streets. The south side of Main near the corner of Ocean and Main Streets is shown in this 1930 photograph. From left to right are the Atlantic and Pacific Tea Company, Hyannis Trust, and the Ferguson Hotel, which were bought by Hugh Ferguson Sr. in 1915.

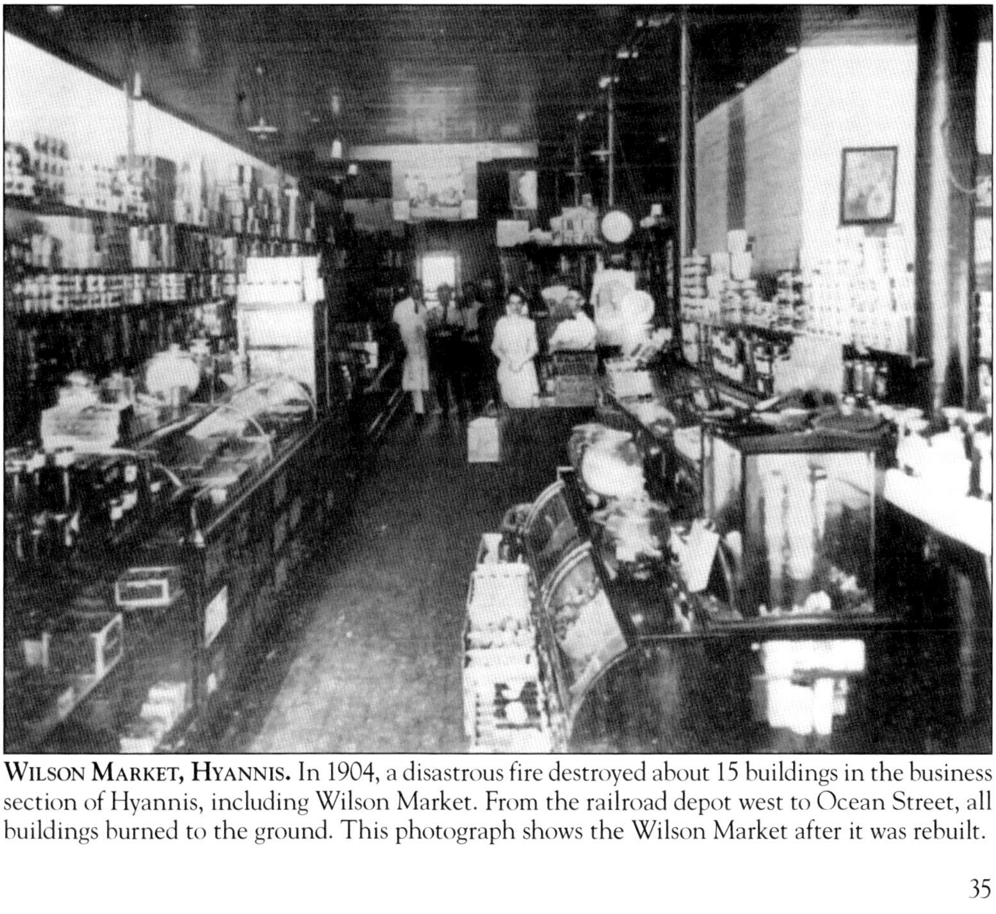

Wilson Market, Hyannis. In 1904, a disastrous fire destroyed about 15 buildings in the business section of Hyannis, including Wilson Market. From the railroad depot west to Ocean Street, all buildings burned to the ground. This photograph shows the Wilson Market after it was rebuilt.

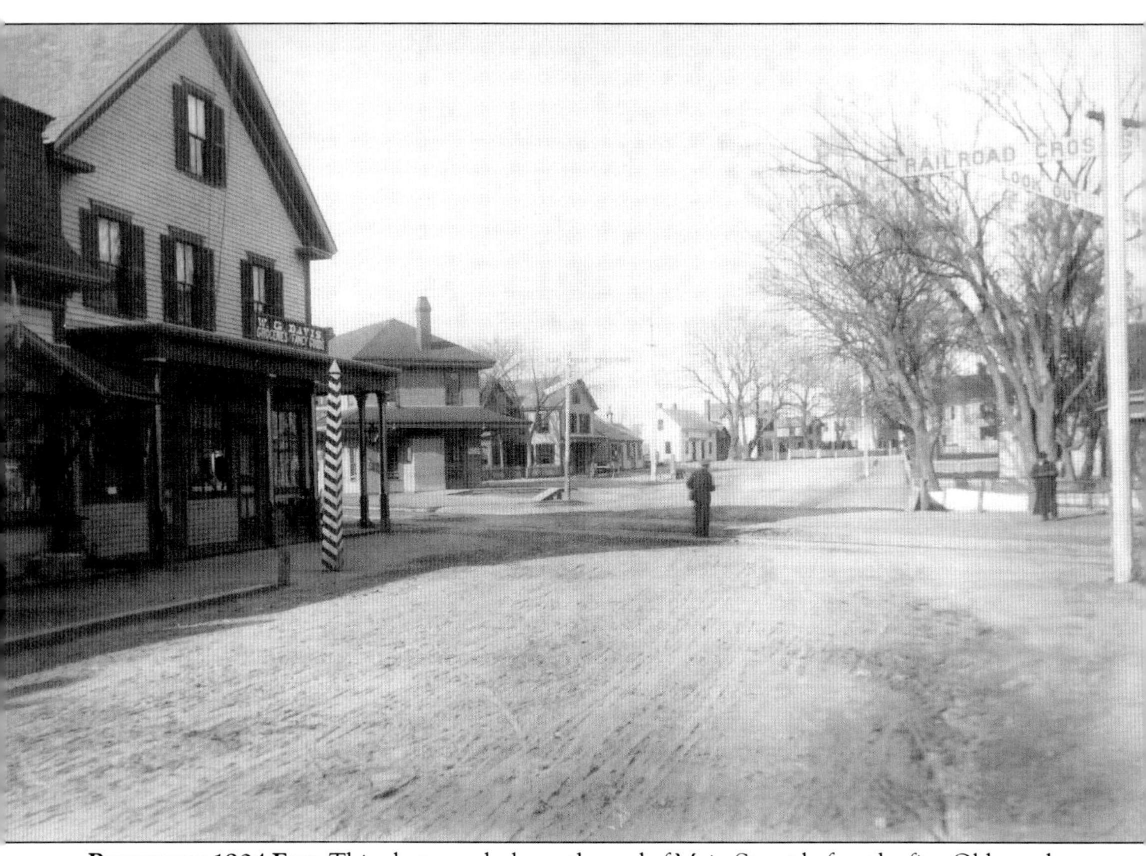

BEFORE THE 1904 FIRE. This photograph shows the end of Main Street before the fire. Old wooden buildings, along with wood stoves and fireplaces, were susceptible to fire. A.B. Nye & Co. (in the locus of the fire) saw its building burn three separate times. Fire was a constant threat to these buildings, and many would be rebuilt incorporating fire-prevention designs.

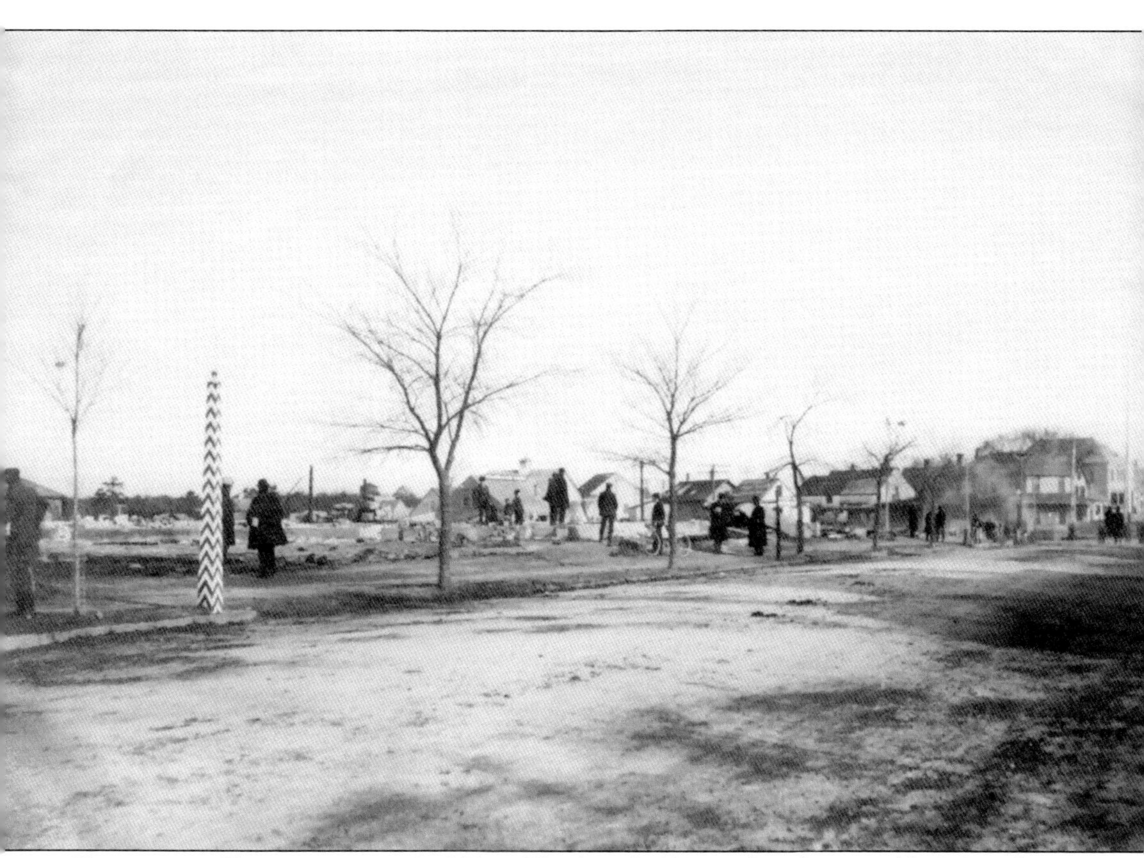

DEVASTATION FOLLOWING THE 1904 FIRE. The fire of 1904 was first discovered by L.P. Wilson, who realized both his and Baker's stores were burning. Wilson and his family lived over their store and barely escaped, losing all their possessions in the fire. The railroad tracks and street were between the fire and the depot, sparing the latter from burning. Even though the fire district was created by voters at that point, the wooden buildings were often quickly consumed by these raging conflagrations before they could be put out.

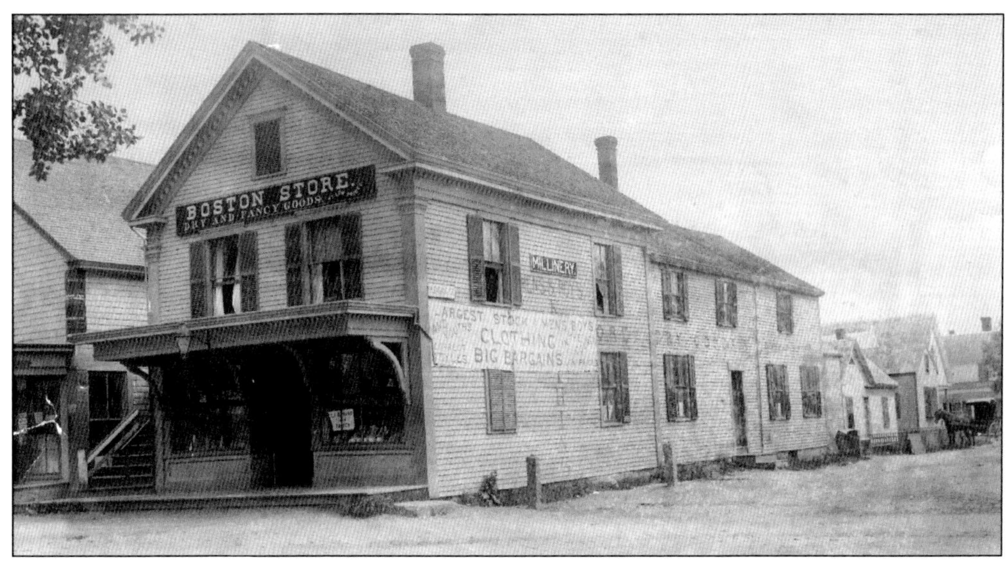

1892 Fire, Hyannis. A large fire completely wiped out the "business corner" on the intersection of Pleasant and Main Streets. On the burned block were the Boston Store, the Cash and Bradford store, the Joyce Taylor grocery store, and Augustus B. Nye's paint store. The cause of the fire was determined to be a defective chimney in the Boston Store. It was discovered in the morning when smoke was spotted coming out of the second floor of the Boston Store. P.M. Crowell was able to enlist the help of the gathered crowd in carrying merchandise out of the stores and into the street. He was also able to get help saving his nearby home as well. Local voters would later create a fire district in 1896.

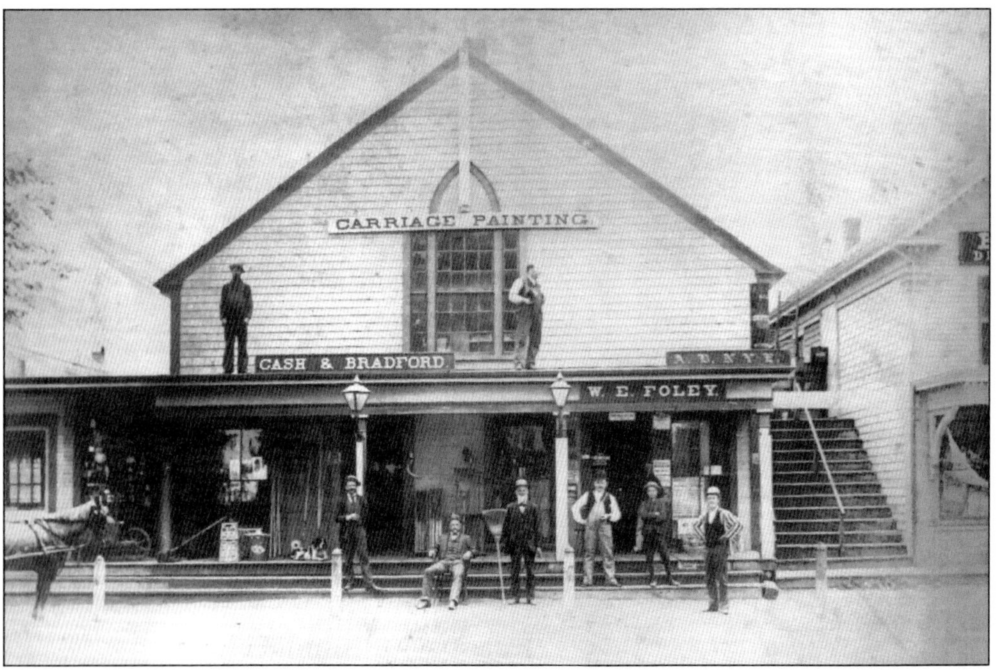

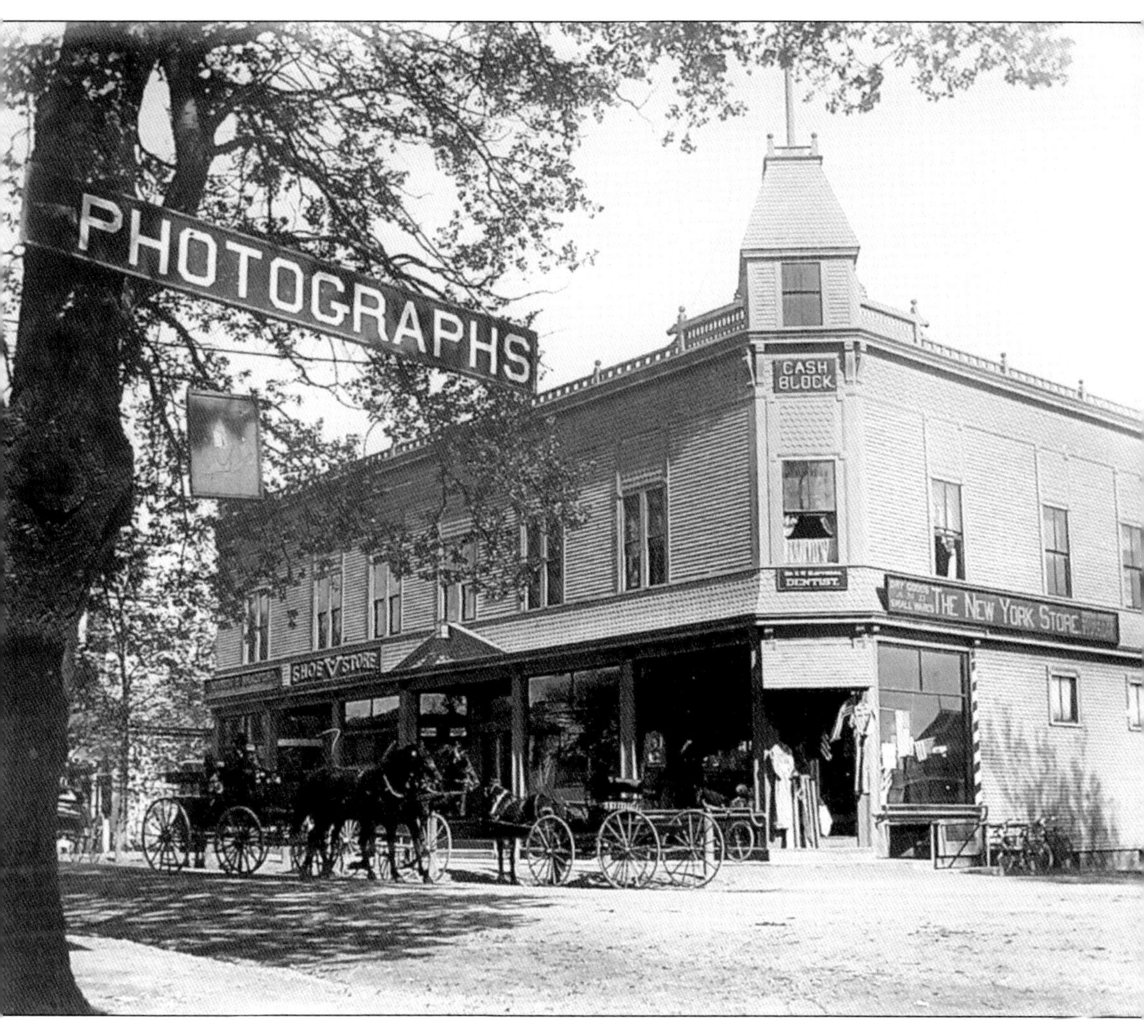

The New Cash Block. Like a phoenix rising from the ashes, a new commercial building was built where there had been but a smoldering pile the year before. The New Cash Block (pictured in 1893) opened in 1893 to a gala ceremony with music provided by the 20-piece Hyannis Cornet Band. The new building had steam heat and a metal roof with a large tank of water for both everyday use and fire prevention. This photograph was taken by S.A. Putnam, who had a shop across the street. In the new building were the New York Store, a dentist's office, a shoe store, a millinery, and Myron Bradford's hardware store. This building stood the test of time and is still standing to this day. Bradford's hardware store is credited as the oldest business in Hyannis.

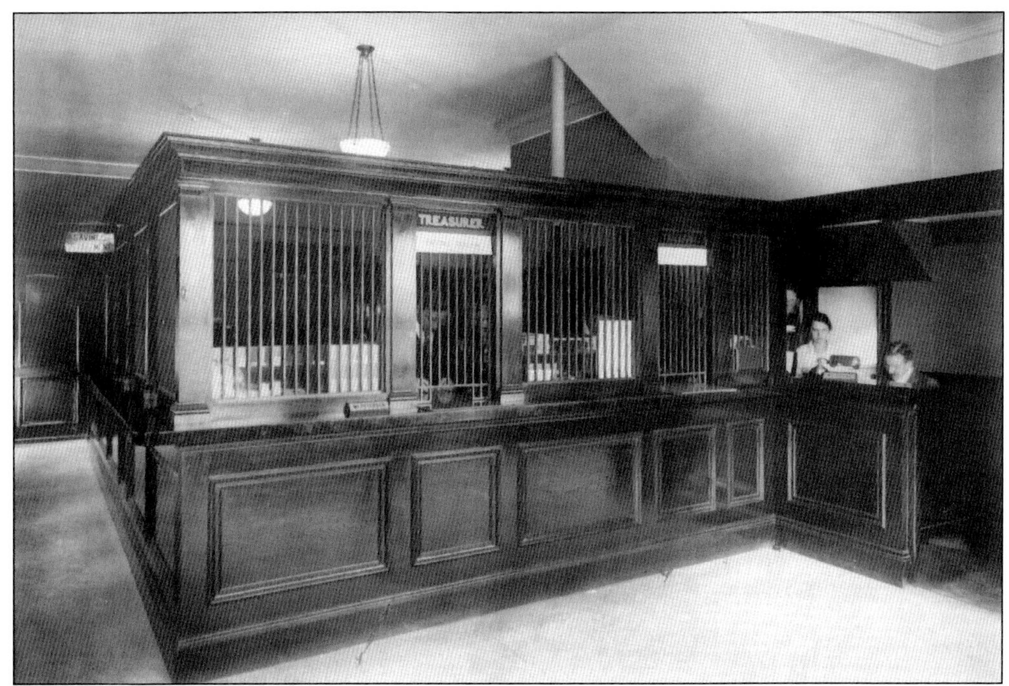

THE HYANNIS TRUST. The old Hyannis Trust became the Cape Cod Bank & Trust, which operated for years as a local bank. This interior photograph was taken in 1919 when it was on the north side of Main Street close to the railroad depot. Pictured here from left to right are (behind the cage) William Peterson and Roger Tillson; (behind the counter) Irma Taylor and Walter B. Chase.

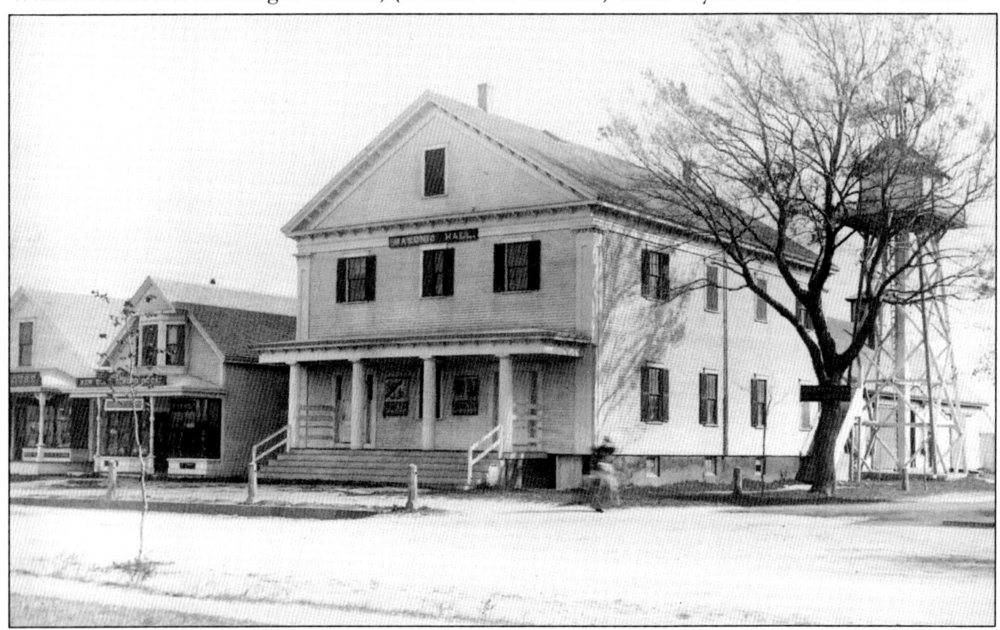

MASONIC HALL. The fraternal lodge Ancient Free and Accepted Masons was chartered in 1801, and by 1855, a Masonic hall was built on Main Street. It was considered the center of social life in Hyannis with lyceum talks, plays, concerts, and balls. At one time, a private school was located upstairs.

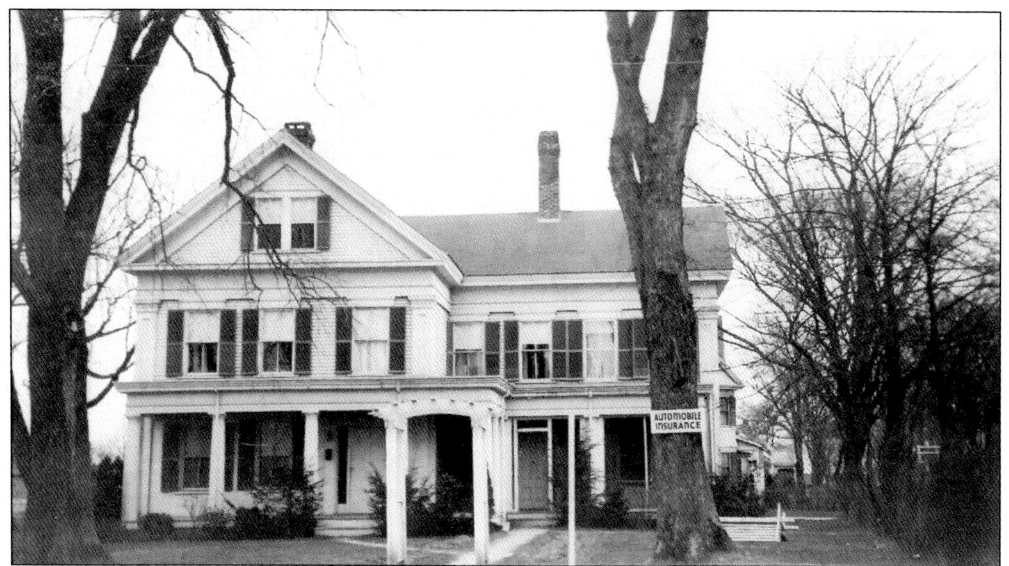

ASA BEARSE HOUSE. Asa Bearse was a Cotuit merchant with Hyannis roots. His grandfather was Moses Bearse, a carpenter who lived on Main Street in Hyannis. Asa Bearse was at sea for 17 years, 14 of which were spent as a captain. Dr. Charles Harris took this photograph in 1930.

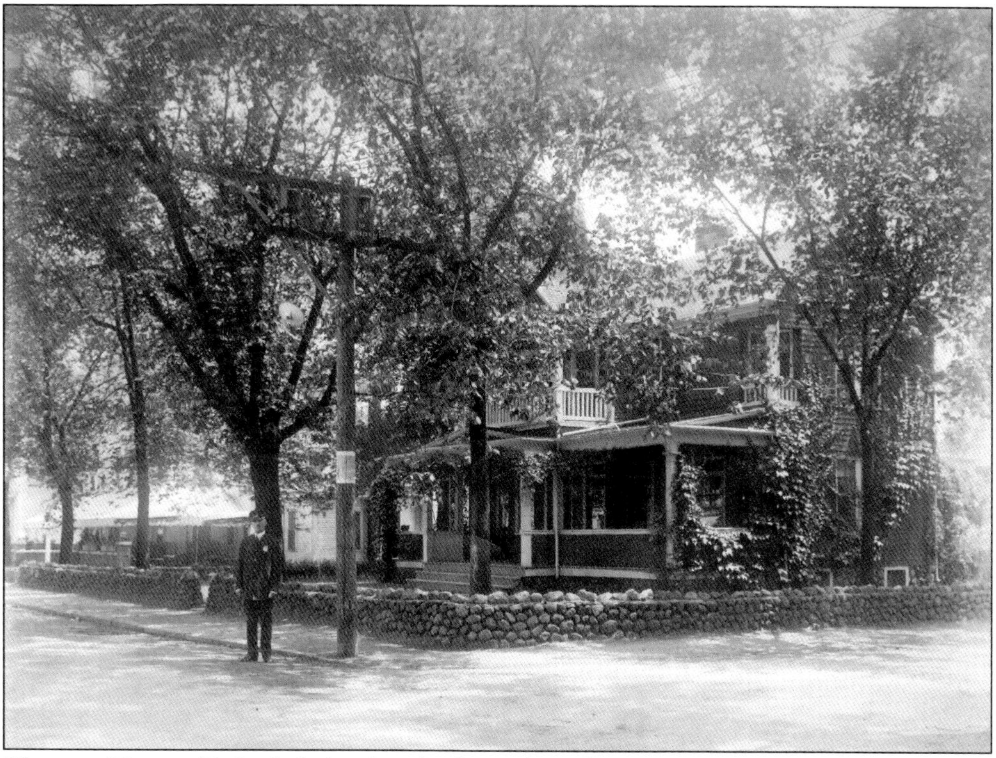

WAYSIDE. Thomas H. Soule Jr. lived in this house he called Wayside on the corner of Main and South Streets. He was the owner of the Iyanough House for many years.

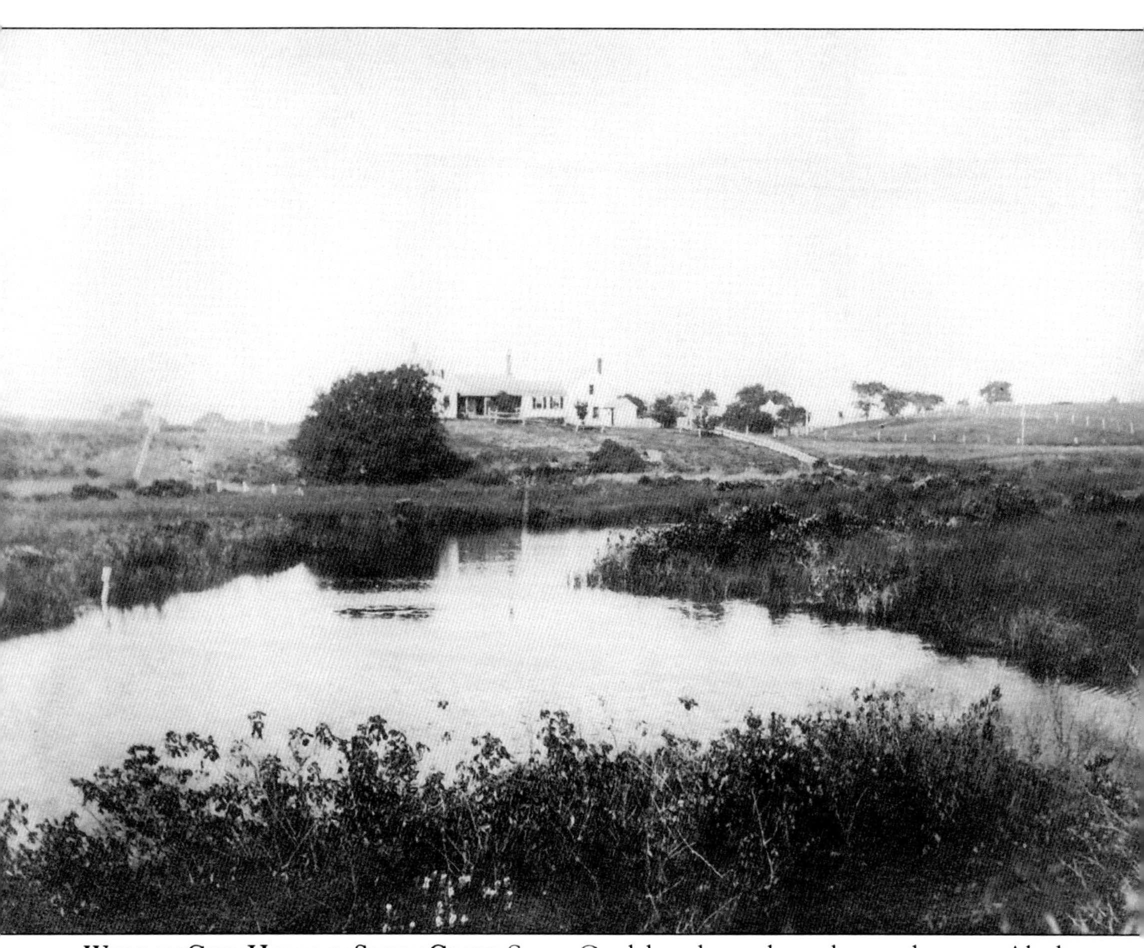

WINSLOW GREY HOUSE AT SNOWS CREEK. Snows Creek has changed greatly over the years. Alvah Bearse stated that the best swimming hole in Lewis Bay was a spot halfway between the creek and the southern tip of Dunbar's Point. This bucolic view was somewhat spoiled by the railroad track that would later be built to access the train wharf.

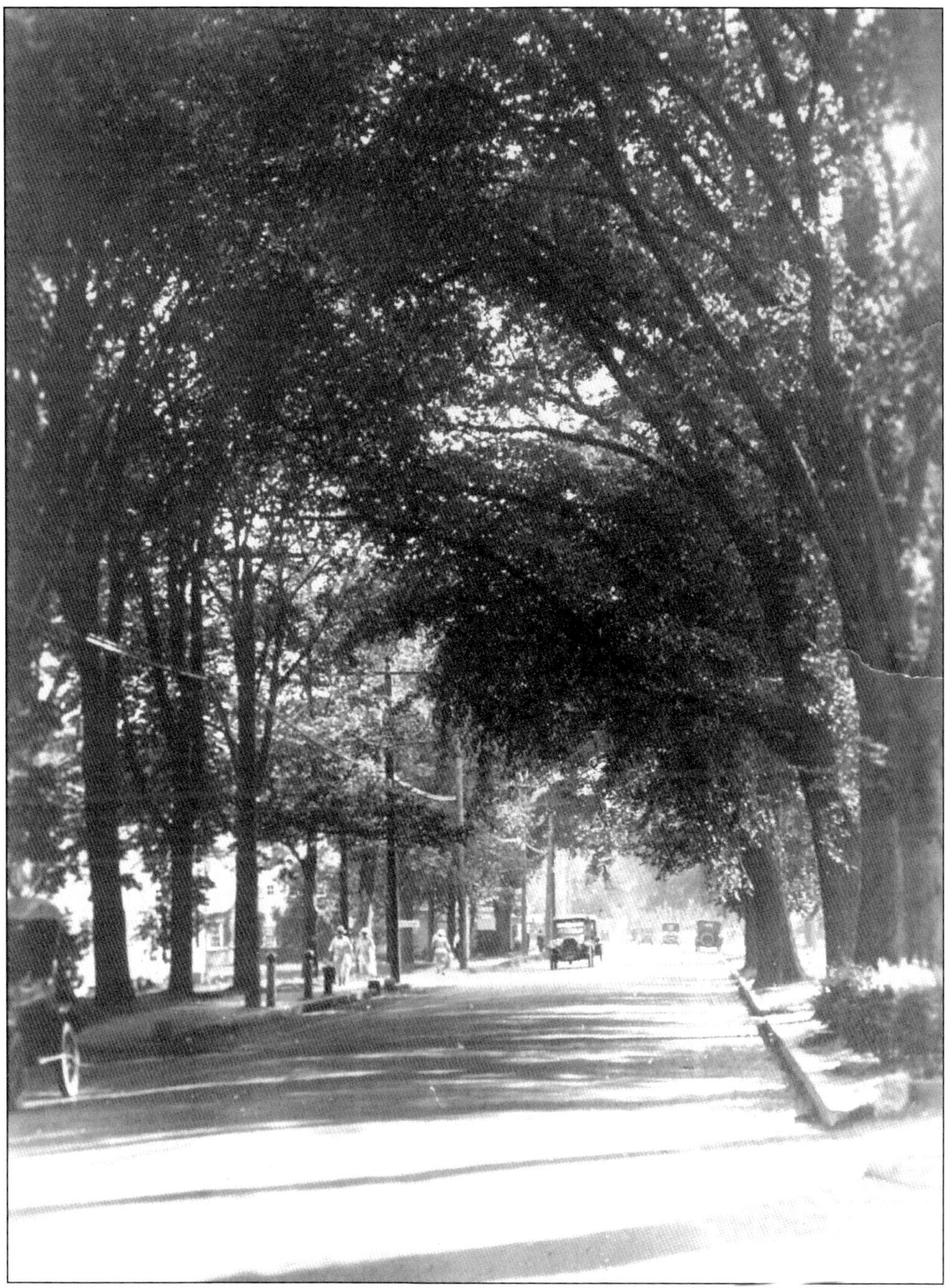

MAIN STREET LOOKING WEST. This photograph of Main Street was taken looking west from what is now known as the 500 block area. This portion of Main Street, while still very residential, shows W.C. Woodbury's tailor shop, which he operated until the 1920s. Approximately where the photographer was standing, or somewhere behind him, on the corner of Main and Sea Streets, was the location of an early hospital in Hyannis. It was staffed by a local nursing organization and was not considered a full-service hospital. Presumably, it closed around the time the newer Cape Cod Hospital opened.

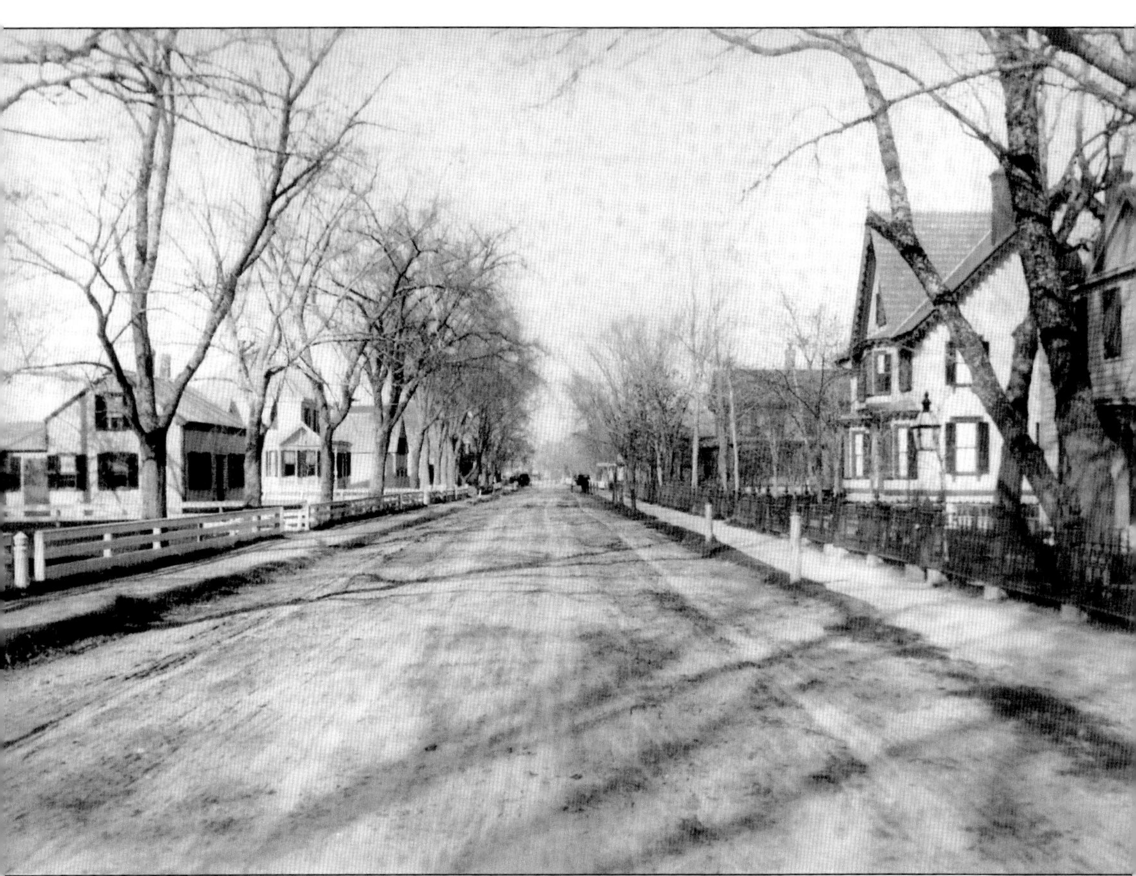

MAIN STREET TOWARD WEST END. This photograph was taken from the residential portion of Main Street looking west toward the railroad depot and the business section of town. By the 1960s Main Street lost its last residence, and the entire street was devoted to businesses. The last residence was the Charles Harris home, which was converted to commercial use by 1968.

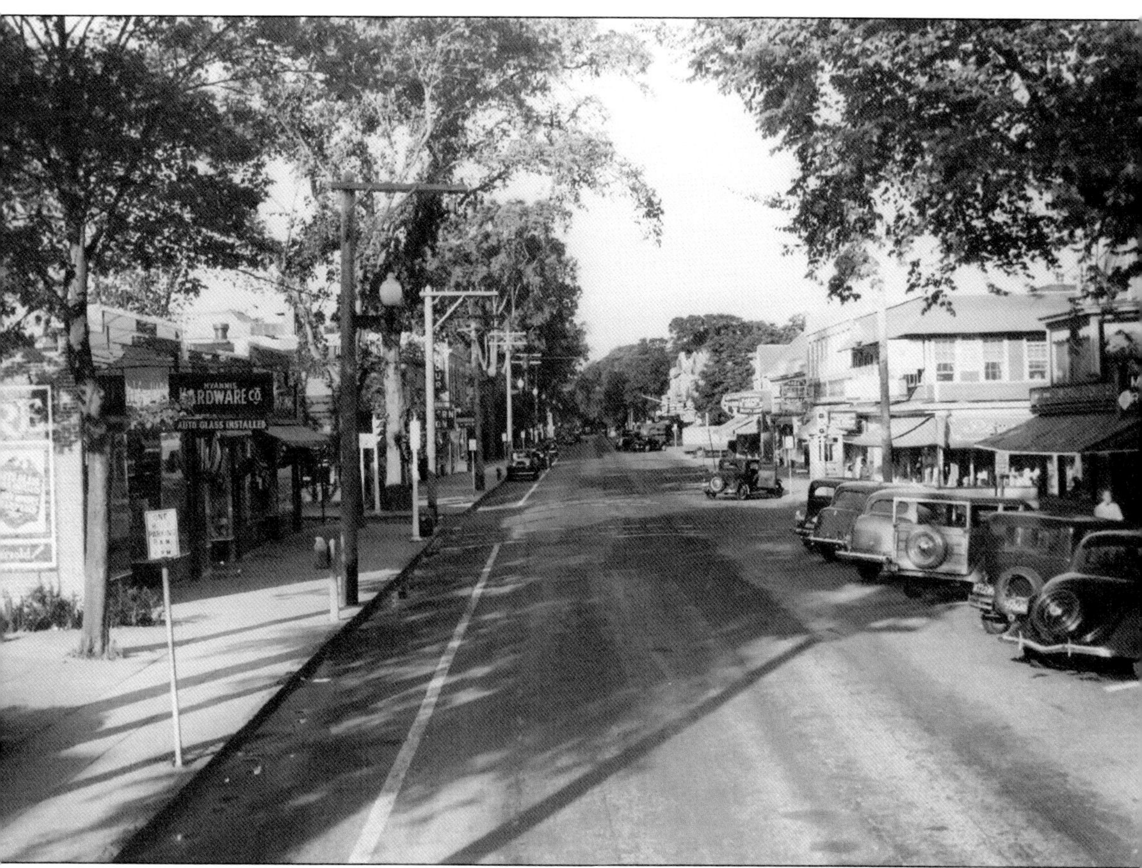

MAIN STREET LOOKING EAST. As development on Main Street continued, sights like this were very common as older homes made way for newer commercial buildings. This 1936 photograph shows a vacant lot on the south side of the street as well as the intersection of Main and Ocean Streets. The vacant lot is the former location of the Ferguson.

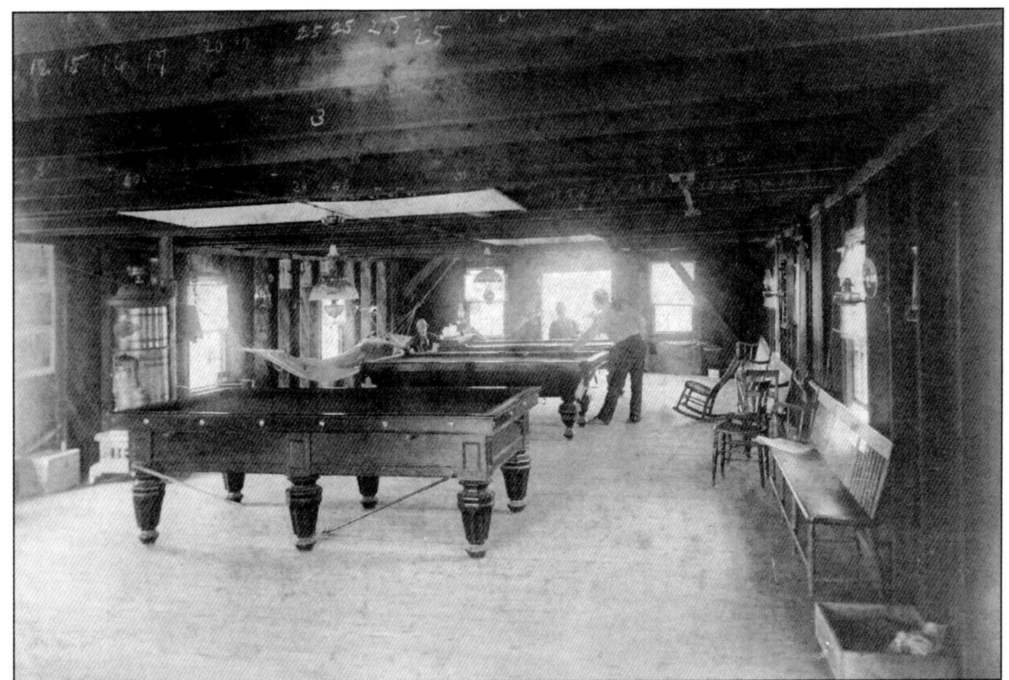

SATURDAY NIGHT CLUB. This club was founded by Charles Gibbs in an old sail loft on Pleasant Street in 1889. Its original location was a place for men to congregate and socialize. It burned down later that year and the club continued to meet at different locations. In 1927, a new club was built on Main Street.

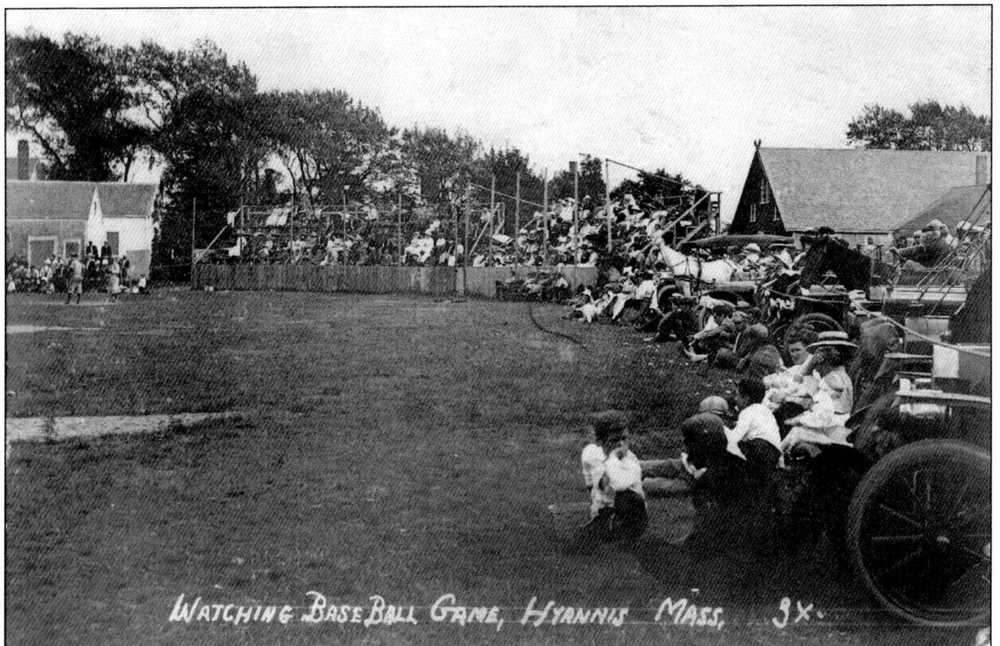

HYANNIS BASEBALL. Baseball was such a popular sport in Barnstable that a field was used just off Main Street for summer games. Baseball has been played as a team sport in Barnstable since 1885. Many players have gone on to professional teams after playing in these summer leagues.

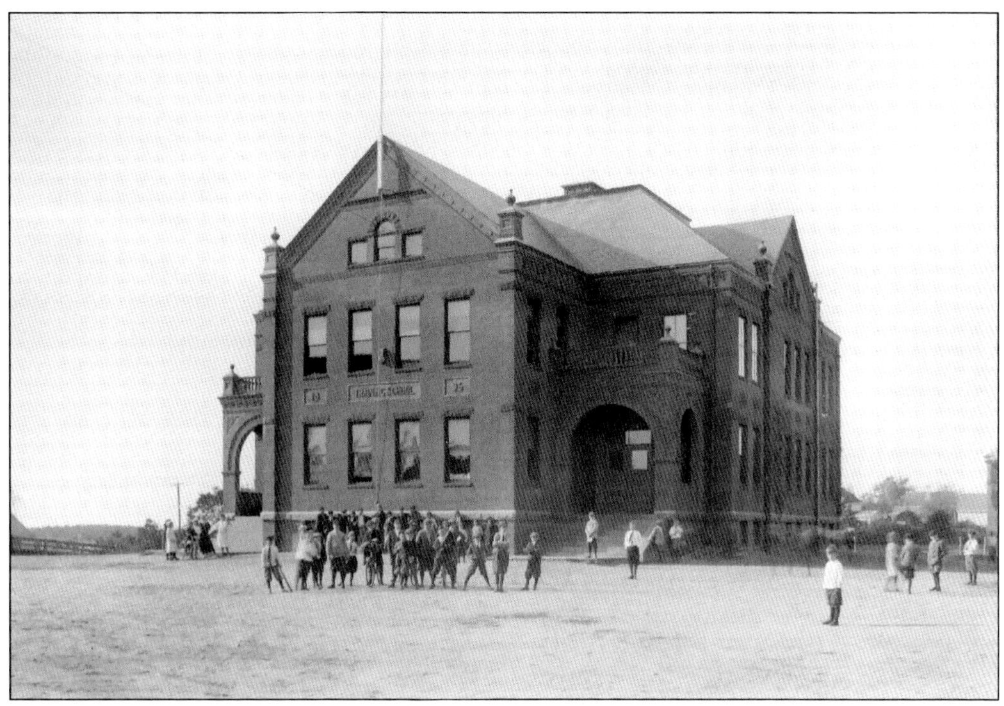

HYANNIS TRAINING SCHOOL. In 1895, the new training school was built on the west side of Ocean Street and was designed to be the town's combined elementary school and training school for teachers. It burned down in January 1896. It was quickly rebuilt by November of the same year.

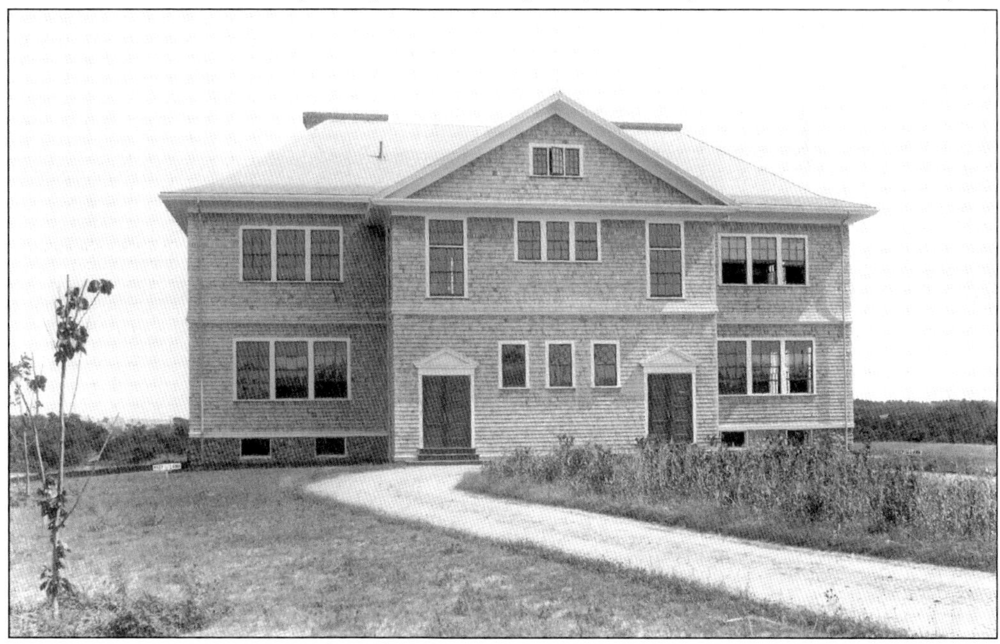

BARNSTABLE HIGH SCHOOL. The old high school was constructed in 1905 and sat at the end of High School Avenue on the south side of Hyannis. Starting in the 1870s, the location of the high school changed several times until it finally came to rest on High School Avenue. In 1957, it moved to its current location on West Main Street.

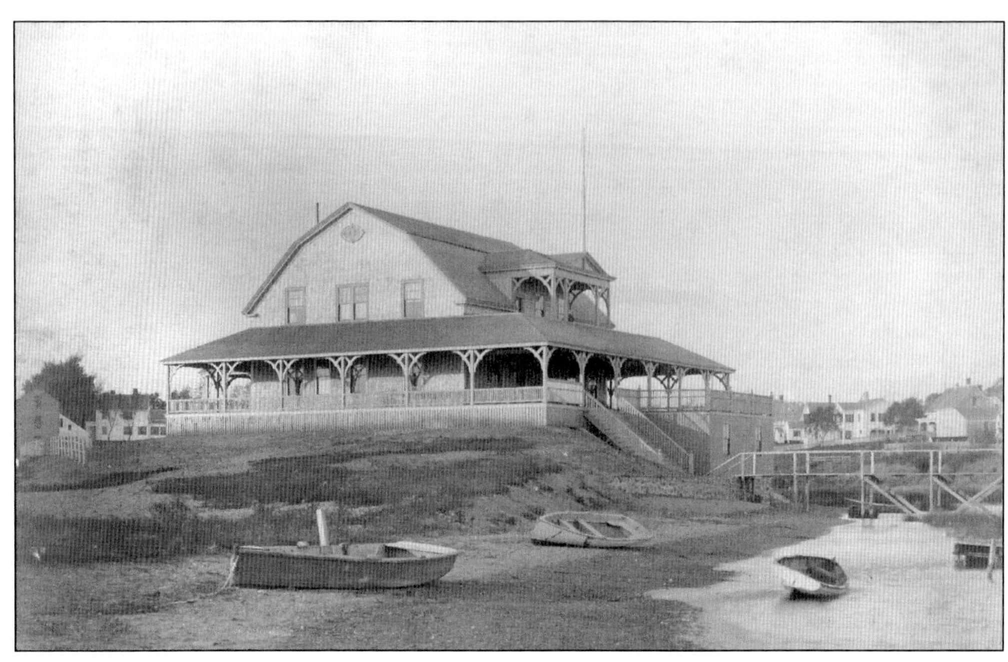

Hyannis Yacht Club. This yacht club was located on Pleasant Street in Hyannis. It opened in August 1896 with a gala celebration of 500 people. There was music and dancing to an orchestra and brass band. The club featured a wide porch offering great views of the water; a bowling alley and lockers for boat equipment in the basement; a parlor, three card rooms, a billiard room, and a kitchen on the first floor; and a banquet room that could seat 150 on the second floor. By the early 1900s, the club became insolvent and was open infrequently. By 1921, the old clubhouse was the site of an artificial pearl factory run by Edward Petow, a French chemist. The yacht club relocated to Ocean Street and reopened in 1927.

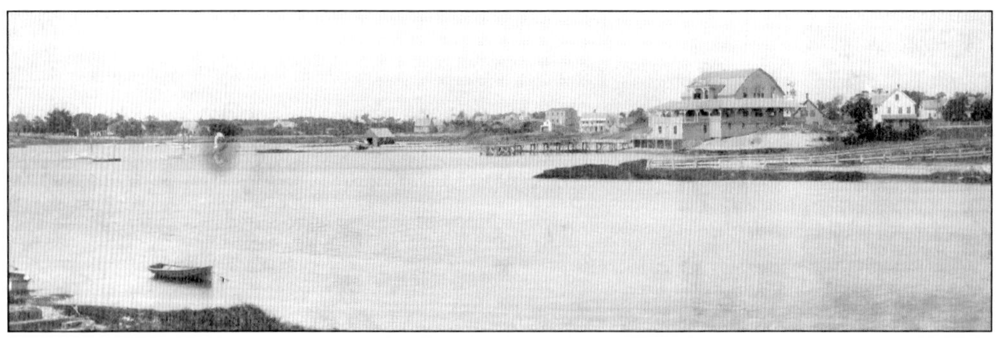

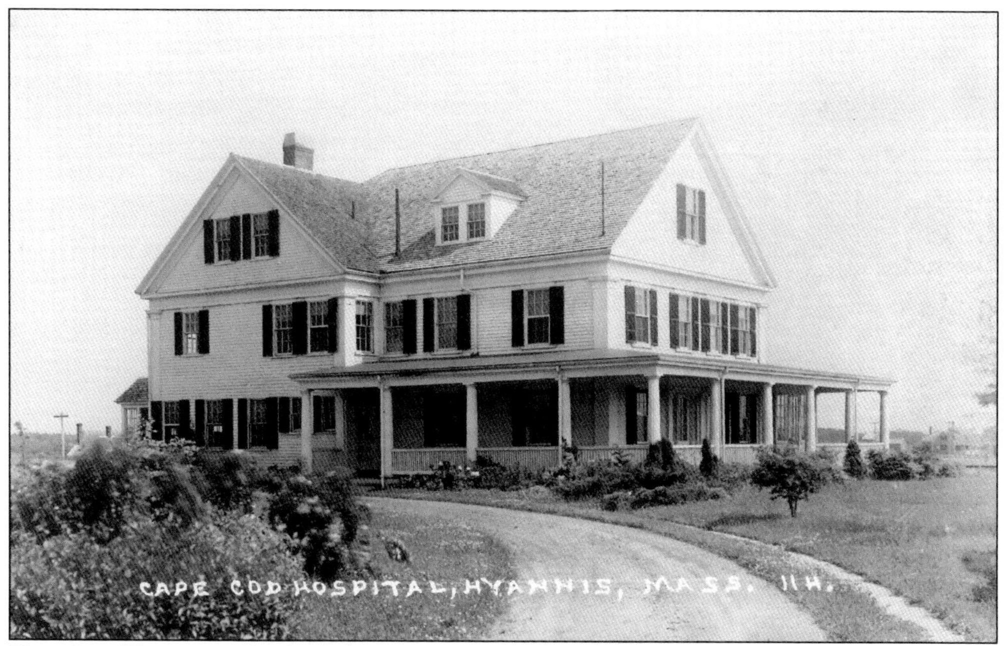

Cape Cod Hospital. Charles Ayling, a summer resident and Boston banker, recognizing the need for a local hospital, helped to raise $35,000. The summer home of Dr. E.F. Gleason was purchased and opened as the new hospital in 1920.

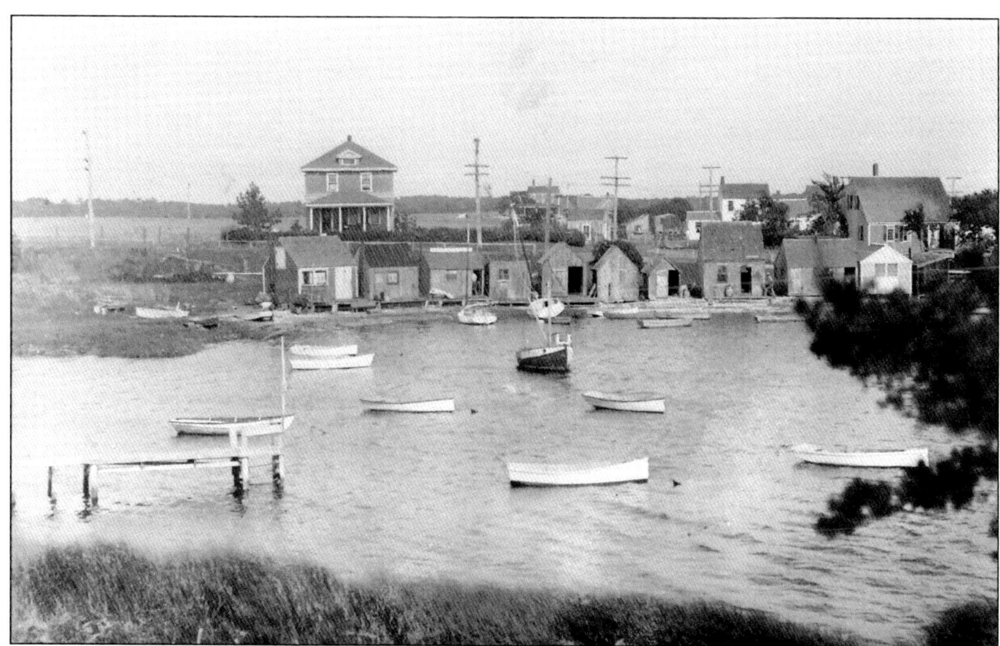

Fish Shanties, Pickering Cove. This photograph shows picturesque fish shanties lining the shore of Pickering Cove in Lewis Bay. Shanties were places where fishermen could store their equipment and dry fish.

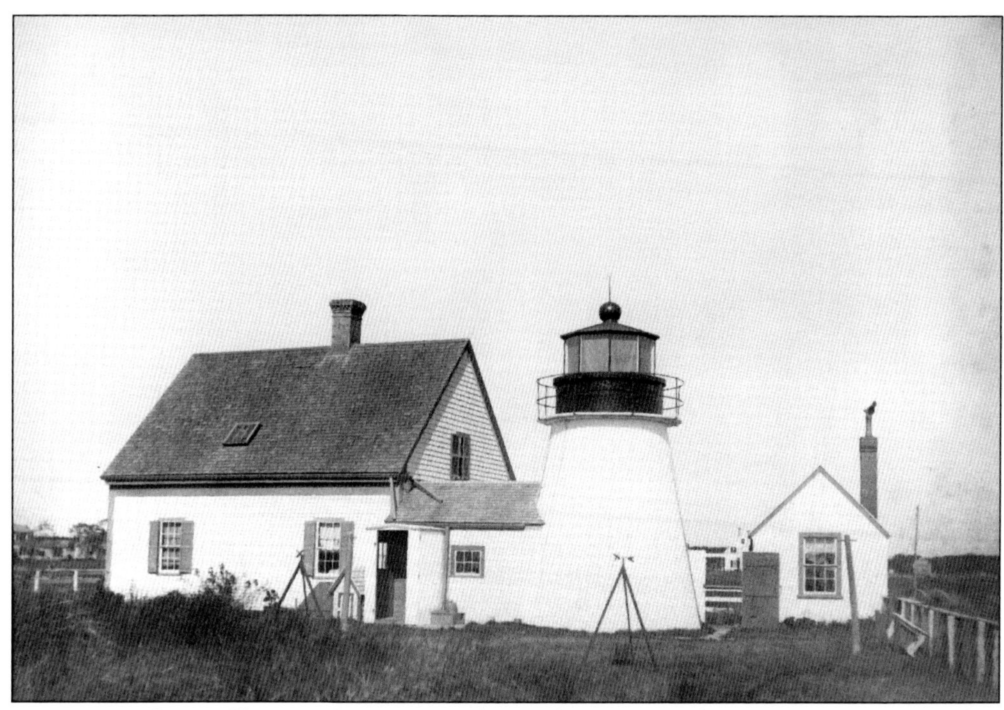

LIGHTHOUSE, SOUTH HYANNIS. In May 1849, the South Hyannis Light lit up the water for the first time. Daniel S. Hallett was its first keeper. His instructions were to "light the lamps at sundown . . . and extinguish them at sunrise."

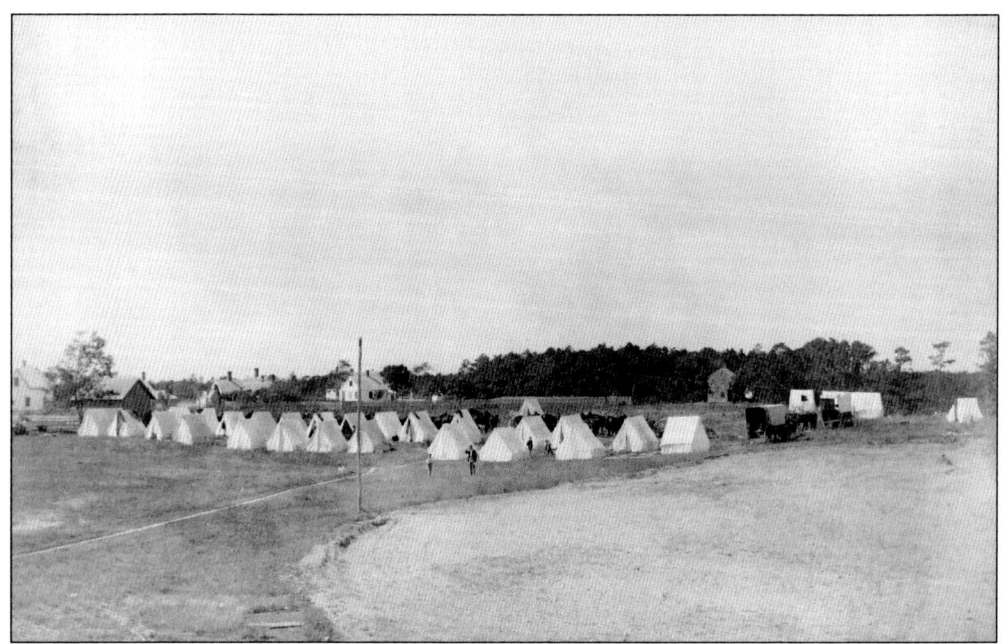

MILITARY CAMP, HYANNIS. Battery B of the 4th US Light Artillery camped in Hyannis on September 9, 1893, on what was known as Aunt Emily's Hill. The area, which is near the transportation center, was later known as Elm Street.

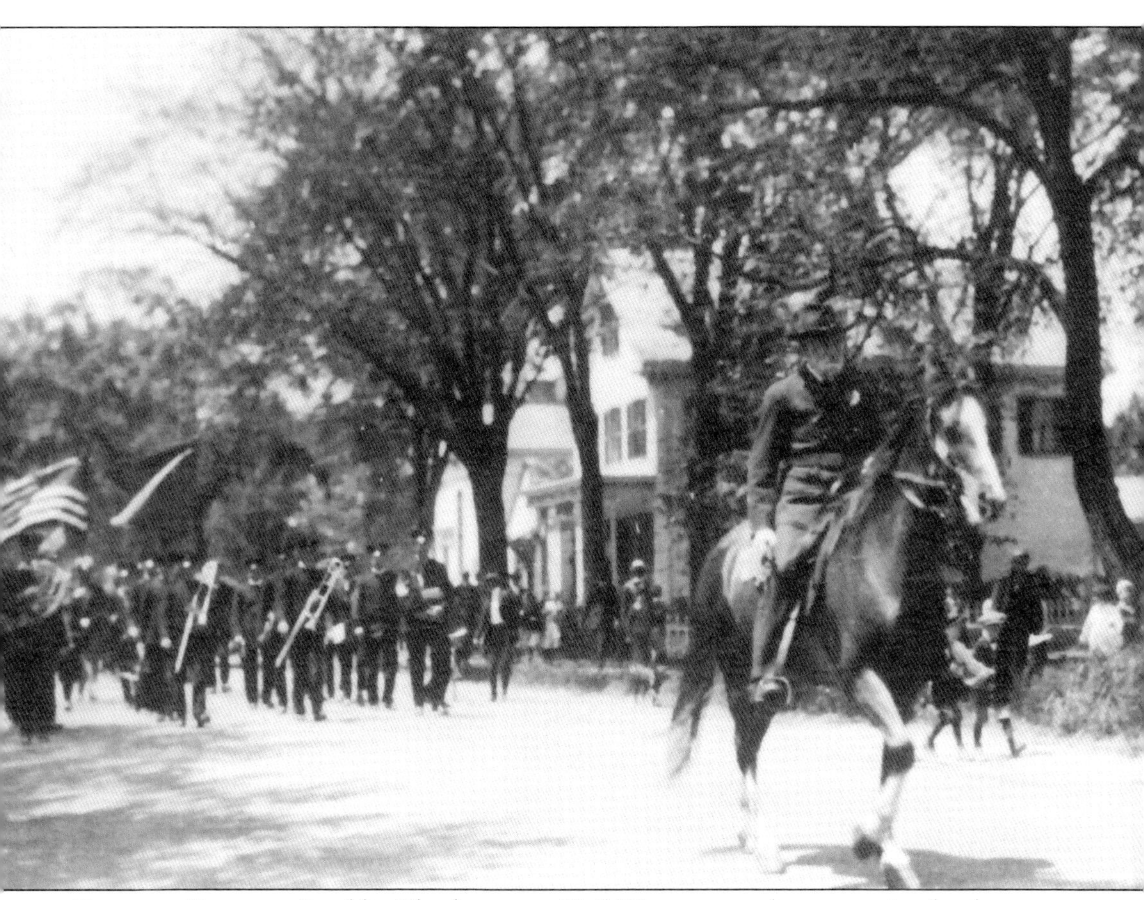

FRANKLIN THACHER. Franklin Thacher was a Civil War veteran who never missed a chance to lead the Memorial Day parade in his Grand Army of the Republic uniform. In 1861, he left his job as Yarmouth Bank clerk and enlisted in Company E, 5th Regiment, Massachusetts Volunteers. On his return, he worked in the insurance business for the Barnstable Mutual Insurance Co. and was also the treasurer for the Hyannis Savings Bank. Thacher was married twice, first to a woman named Mathews and then to Eleanor Pratt, whose father was Capt. Allen Knowles. From this second marriage came Franklin G. Thacher, Winslow K. Thacher, Eben A. Thacher, and Carrie G. Thacher, who later married Dr. Charles E. Harris. In 1921, the *Barnstable Patriot* said of Thatcher: "One familiar with Memorial Day and its observance in Hyannis, cannot recall the exercises without seeming to see a figure in uniform riding in soldierly fashion on a favorite horse. And in all the processions on public occasions the marshal leading the way was Mr. Thacher." Franklin Thacher led the parade welcoming back Barnstable's native sons who went off to serve in World War I.

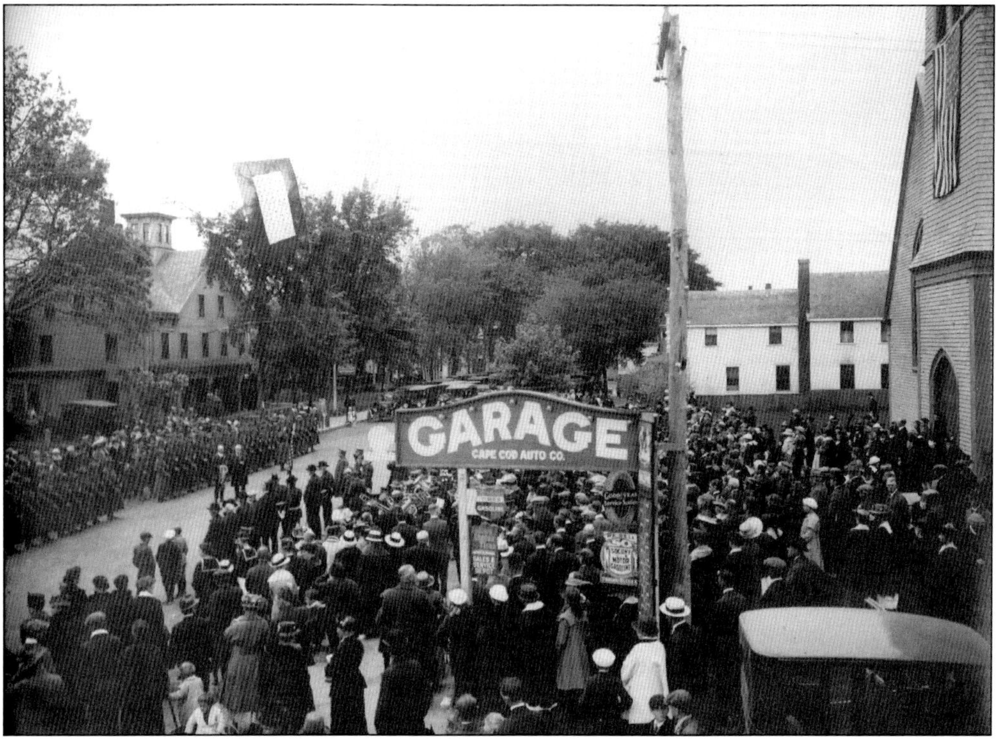

MEMORIAL DAY. This 1918 Memorial Day parade was held in Hyannis at the height of World War I. A service flag was unveiled with 65 stars. Names and ranks were read by Clarence M. Chase, town clerk, and the flag was unfurled by selectman Alex G. Cash. Franklin Thacher is standing in the street in line with other Civil War veterans.

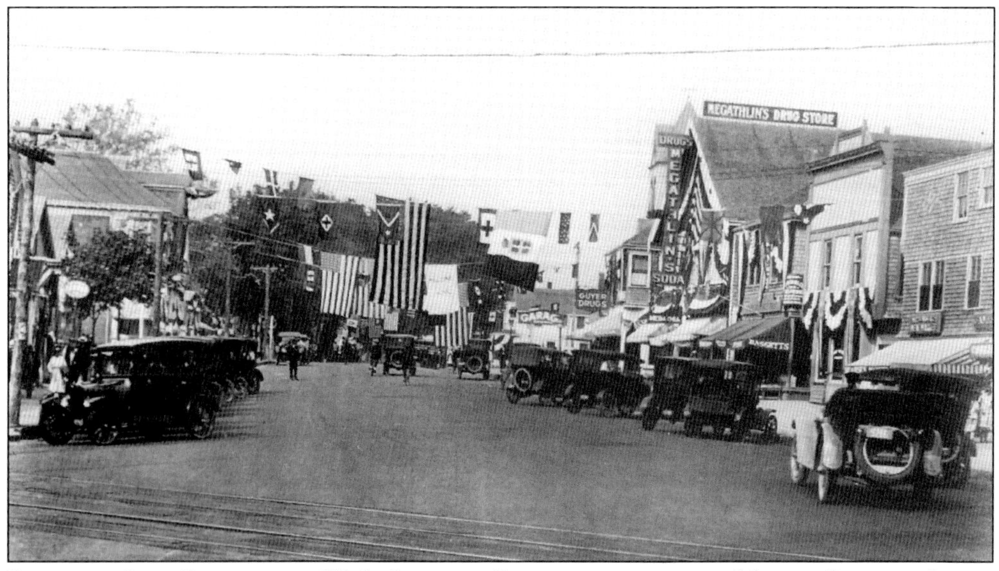

FOURTH OF JULY CELEBRATION. With the war in Europe over, veterans of the conflict came home. In Barnstable, the people organized a huge welcome back parade in 1919. A stand was erected in Depot Square for speeches with a formal flag raising. A baseball game was scheduled, and a clambake for 800 was served. Tickets for the clambake were only $2.

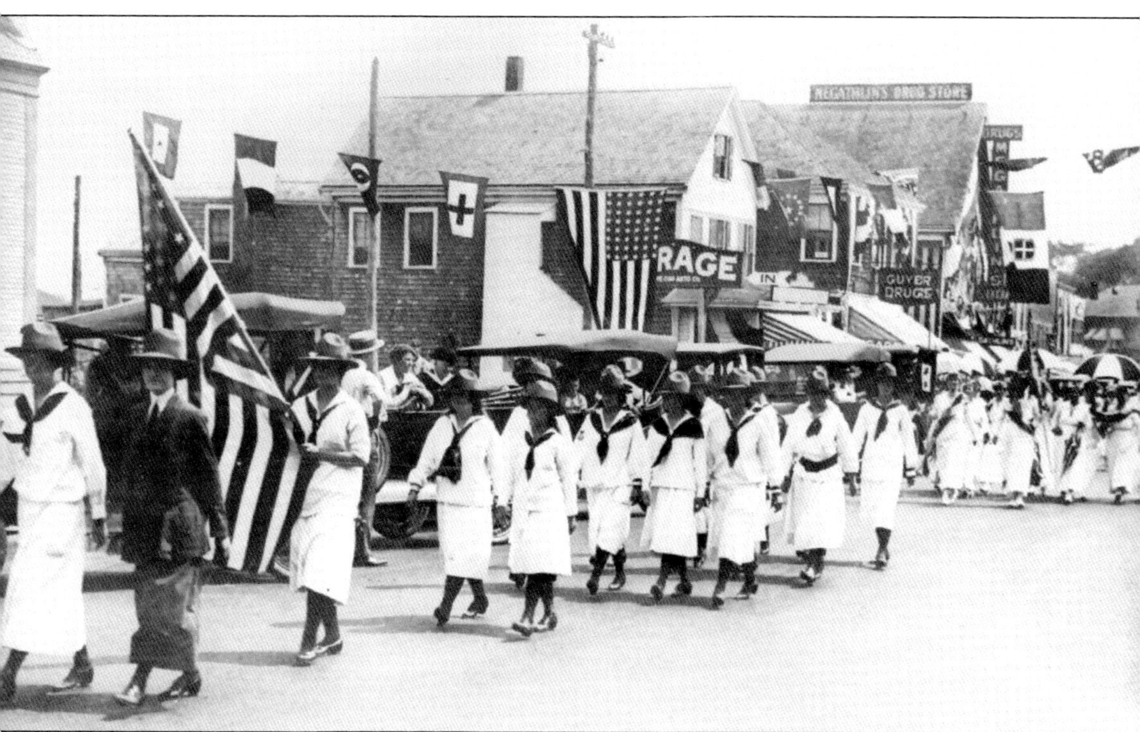

Girl Scouts Welcome Home Parade, 1919. In the early 1900s, many youth groups came and went in town. This local Girl Scout troop was organized a year before the parade on Main Street and had received new uniforms just days before the parade. The scouts at that time were involved in public events, participated in outdoor hikes, and attended Girl Scout camps in the summer months.

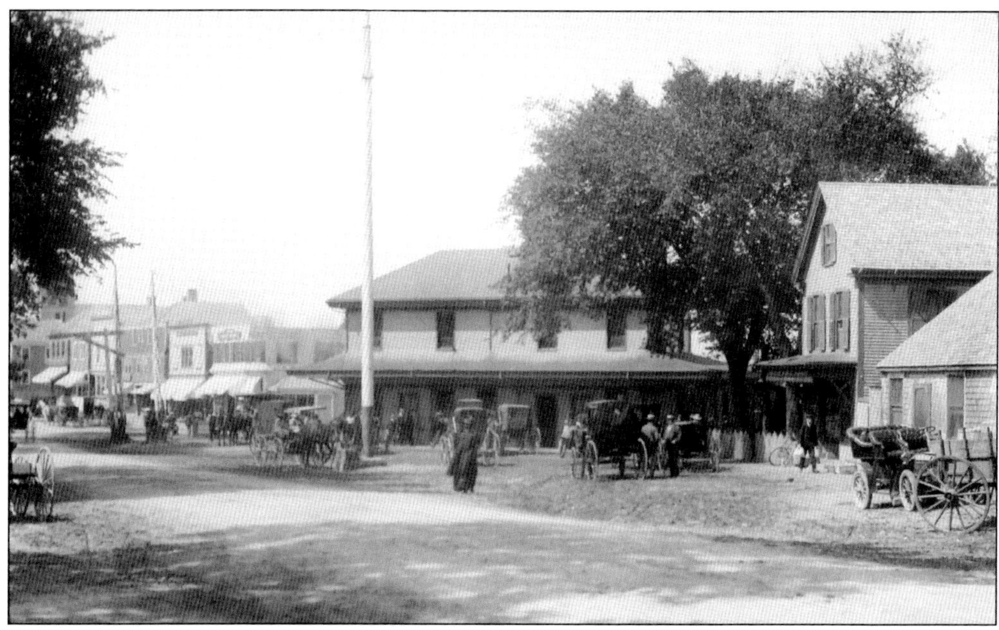

TRAIN DEPOT, HYANNIS. The first train to reach Depot Square in Hyannis, on July 8, 1854, was greeted by a jubilant crowd of thousands cheering and firing salutes by cannon. A large crowd boarded the train in Barnstable so they could arrive during the celebration. The depot is pictured in the 1890s.

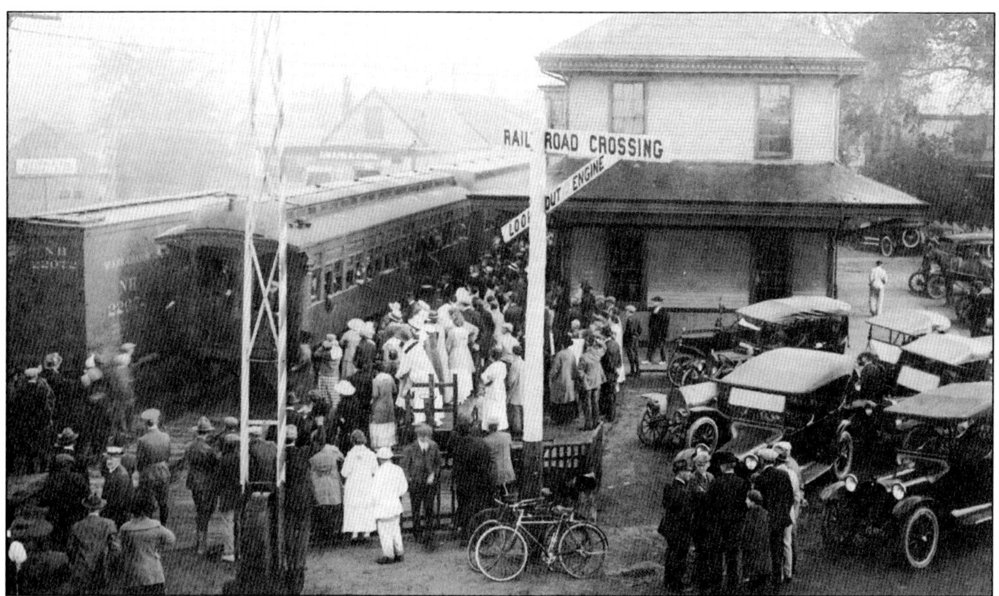

SOLDIERS DEPART, HYANNIS. This photograph shows soldiers leaving Hyannis by train for their duty stations. Approximately 250 soldiers answered the call of duty from Barnstable. Four did not return, having been killed in action. (Courtesy of the *Barnstable Patriot*.)

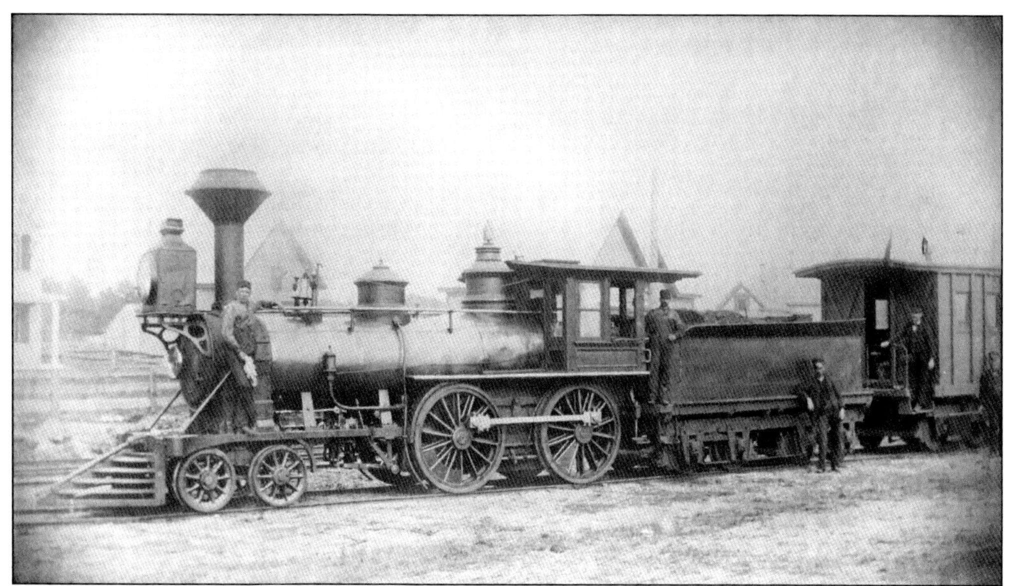

Locomotive Engine, Barnstable. This locomotive, type 4-4-0, was a commonly used engine due to its stability on the uneven roadbeds in the United States. In 1940, A. Howard Crocker, a railroad man whose recollection went back to the 1880s, stated that he recognized conductor Ezekail Taylor standing on the steps.

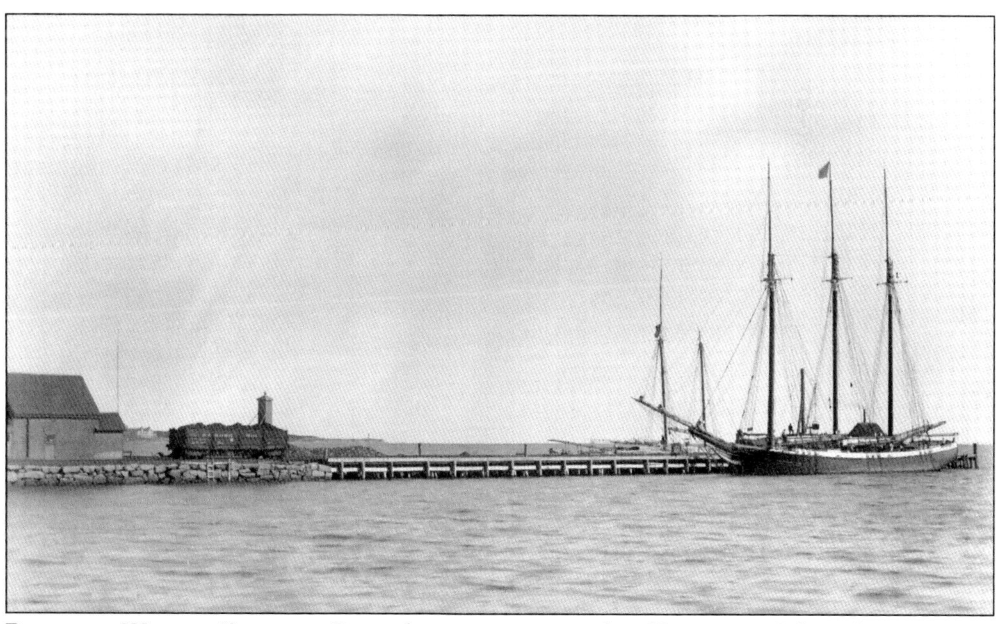

Railroad Wharf, Hyannis. Once the train connected to Hyannis in July 1854, a spur was constructed to a newly built train wharf in Hyannis Harbor by autumn of the same year. Steamer service commenced to Nantucket as soon as the wharf was finished. Coal was a common cargo to Hyannis. In the photograph stands a carload of coal waiting for its engine.

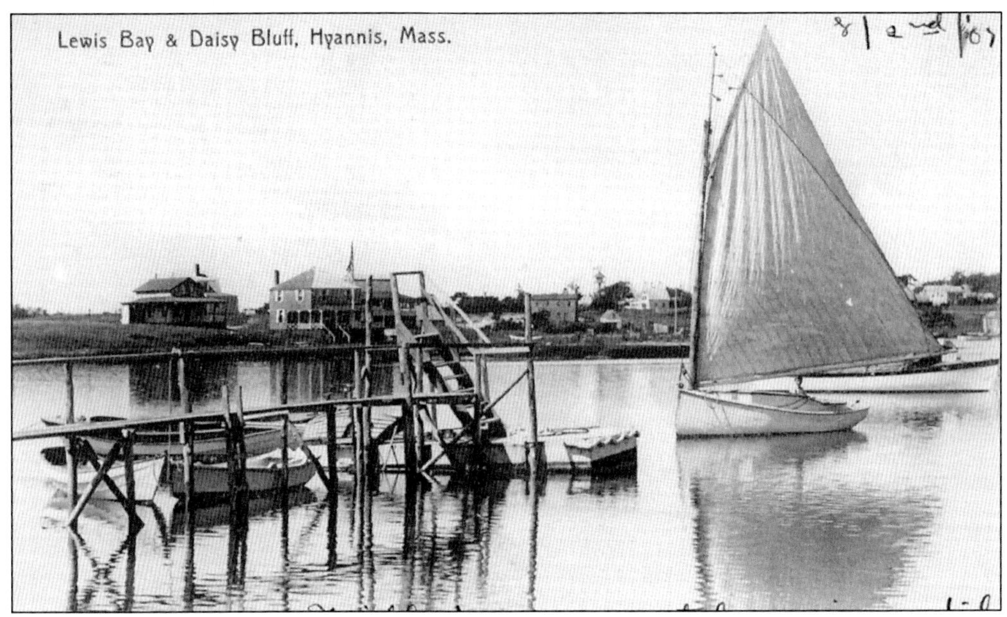

Lewis Bay. This view of Lewis Bay shows Daisy Bluff in the background, still relatively undeveloped. Alvah Bearse described Lewis Bay as a perfect place for a young man to explore the waterfront.

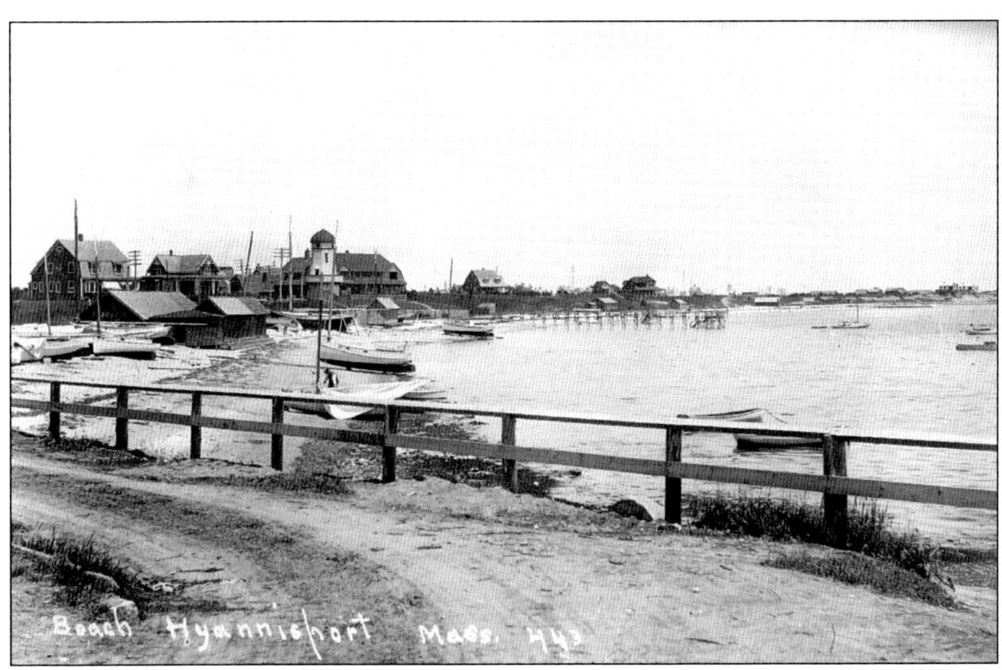

Hyannisport Beach. This early 1900s photograph shows limited development on shore. Many of the sailing vessels are catboats, still produced locally.

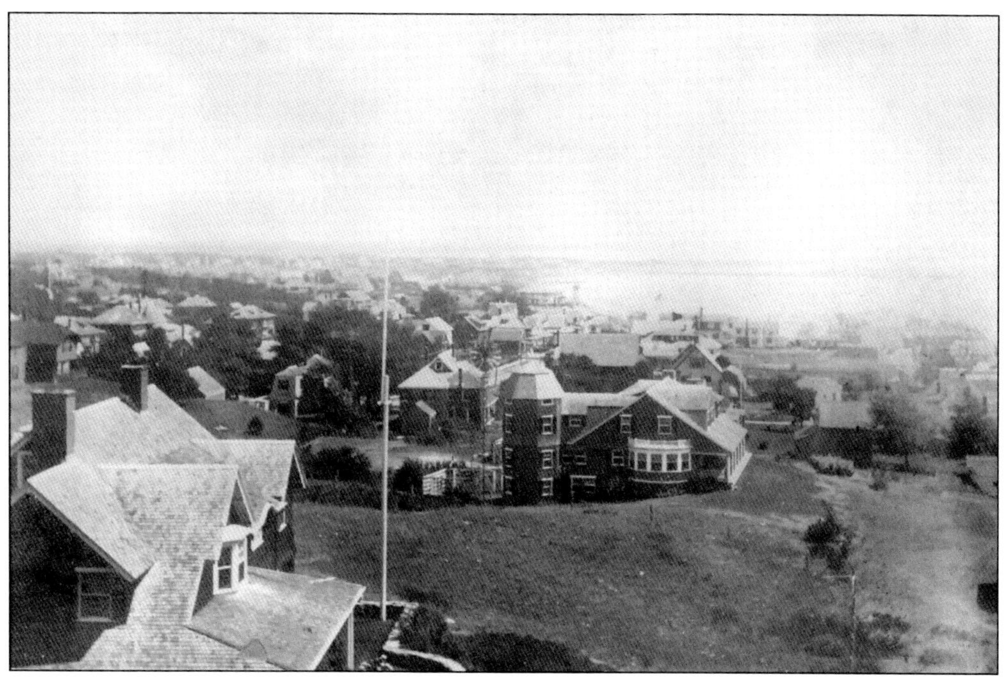

View From St. Andrews. St. Andrews Episcopalian Church was built on land donated in 1904 by Augusta Whittemore of Cambridge. Construction began in 1906 and was completed in 1911. Bishop William Lawrence officially consecrated the church that year.

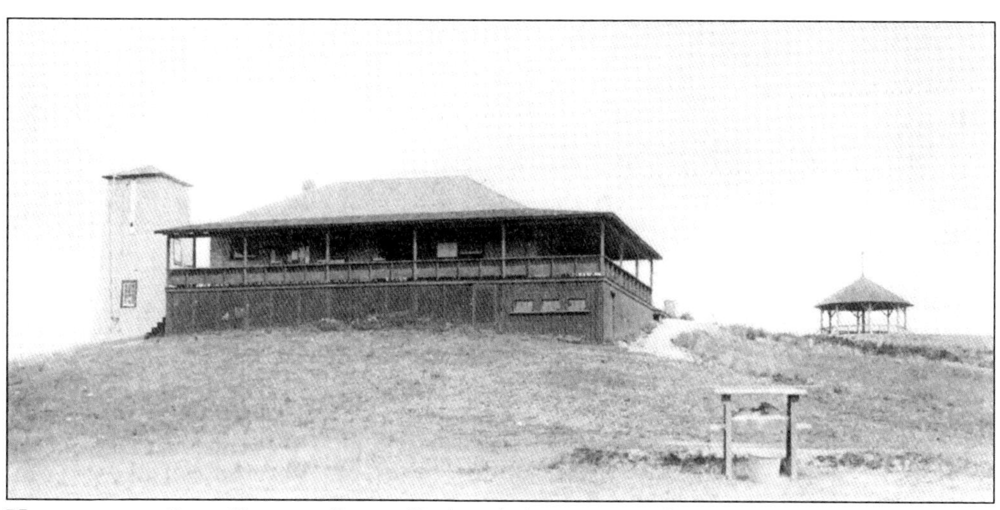

Hyannisport Golf Course. Originally founded in 1897 as the Hyannisport Golf Club, the organization changed its name to the Hyannisport Club in 1909. The first nine holes were designed by John Reid, a famous Scottish architect. The club offered sweeping views of the water and Squaw Island.

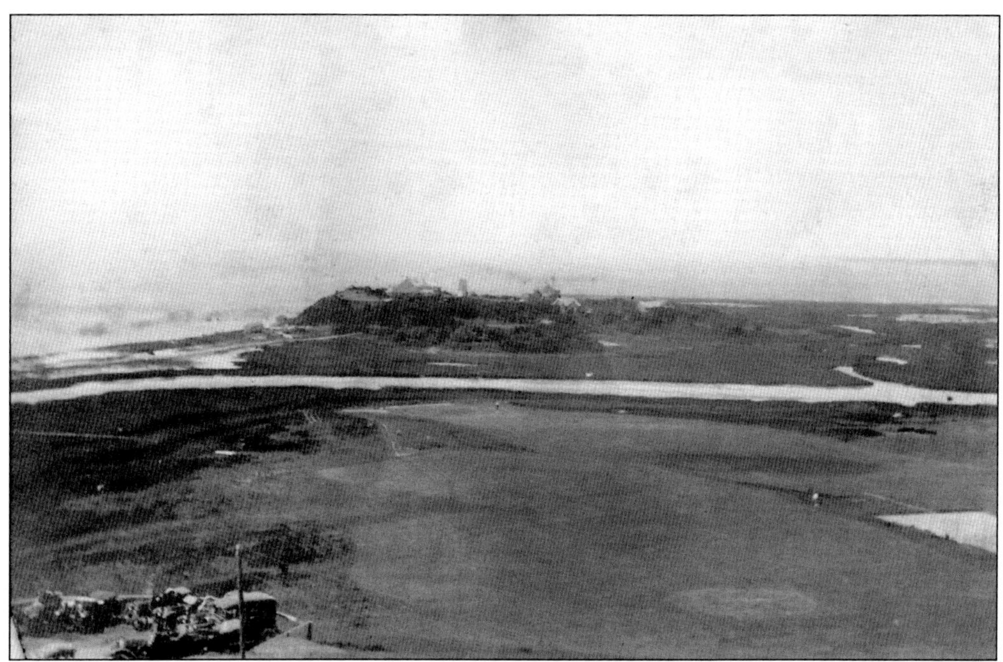

SQUAW ISLAND. Squaw Island is seen from Saint Andrews by the Sea, located on Sunset Hill. Squaw Island was town-owned land, reserved for hunting and fishing. In 1872, a vote was taken at town meeting to sell or lease the land on the island. Development of the island took place after that.

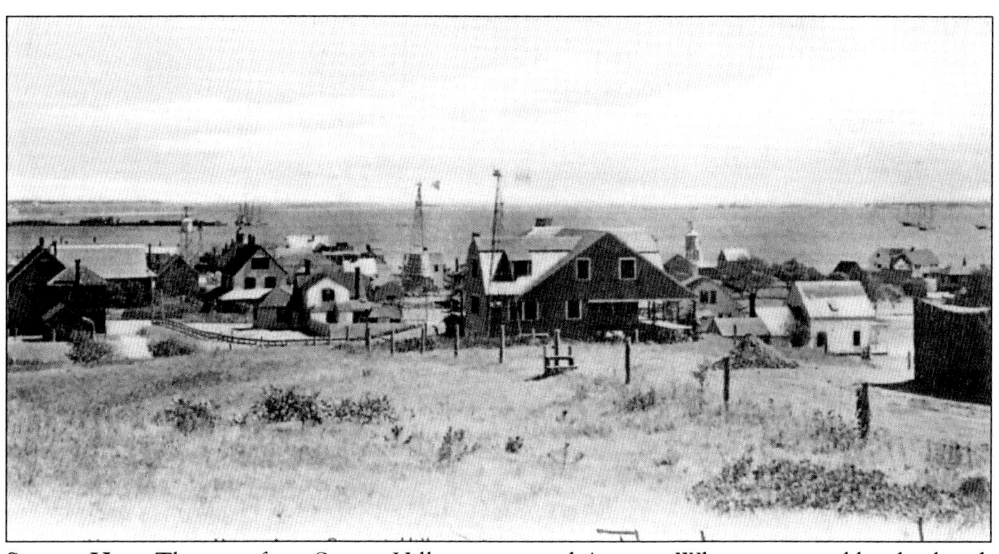

SUNSET HILL. The view from Sunset Hill so entranced Augusta Whittemore and her husband, E.F. Whittemore, that they purchased the land. When her husband died, she buried his ashes on the hill.

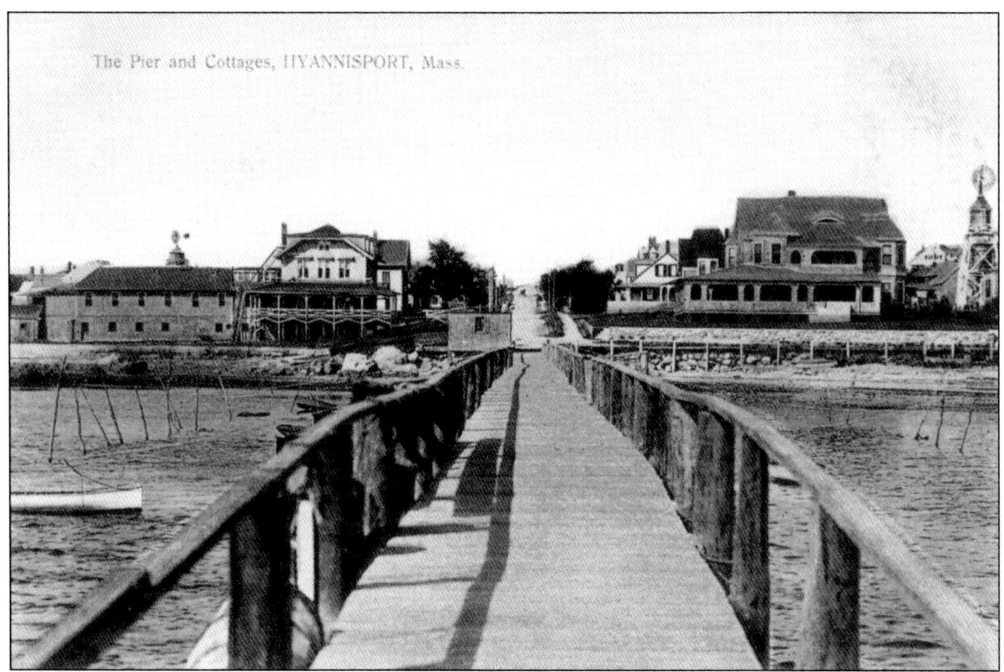

HYANNISPORT PIER. In 1872, the town sold 1,000 acres to the Hyannis Port Land Company, including Squaw Island and other land along the shore up to and including what would later be Craigville Beach. The total cost of the purchase was $100,000. It laid out Hyannisport, which remains pretty much the same to this day, with hotels and cottages on the shore. The company got into financial trouble in the winter of 1878–1879, and banks took over its holdings. The pier pictured here was originally designed to be a long pier out into the water, the end of which was anchored on a sunken schooner. Boats were also moored around the pier, which was eventually washed away in a violent storm.

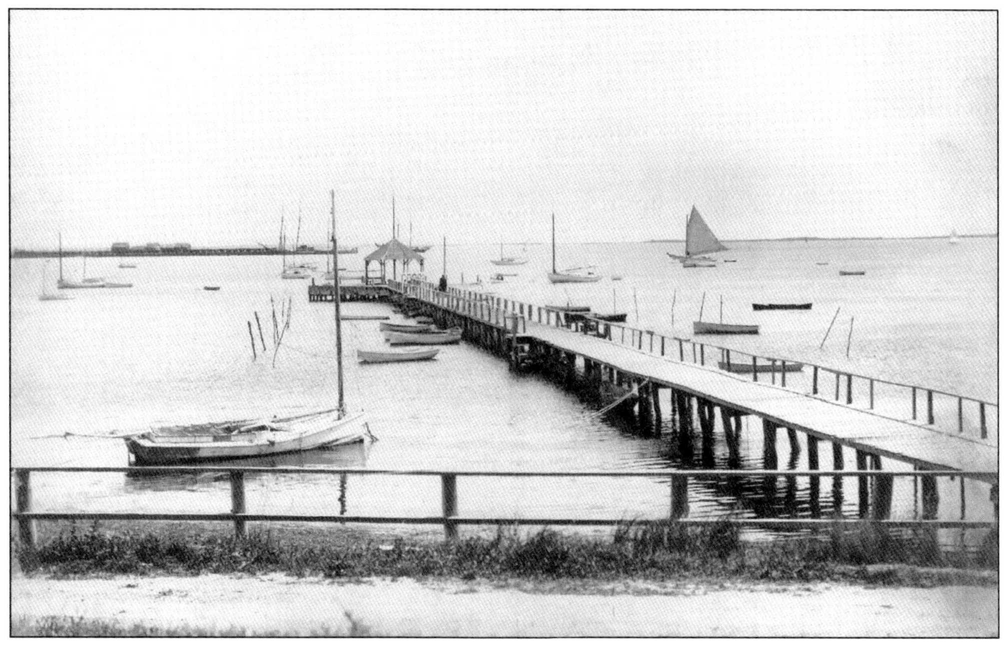

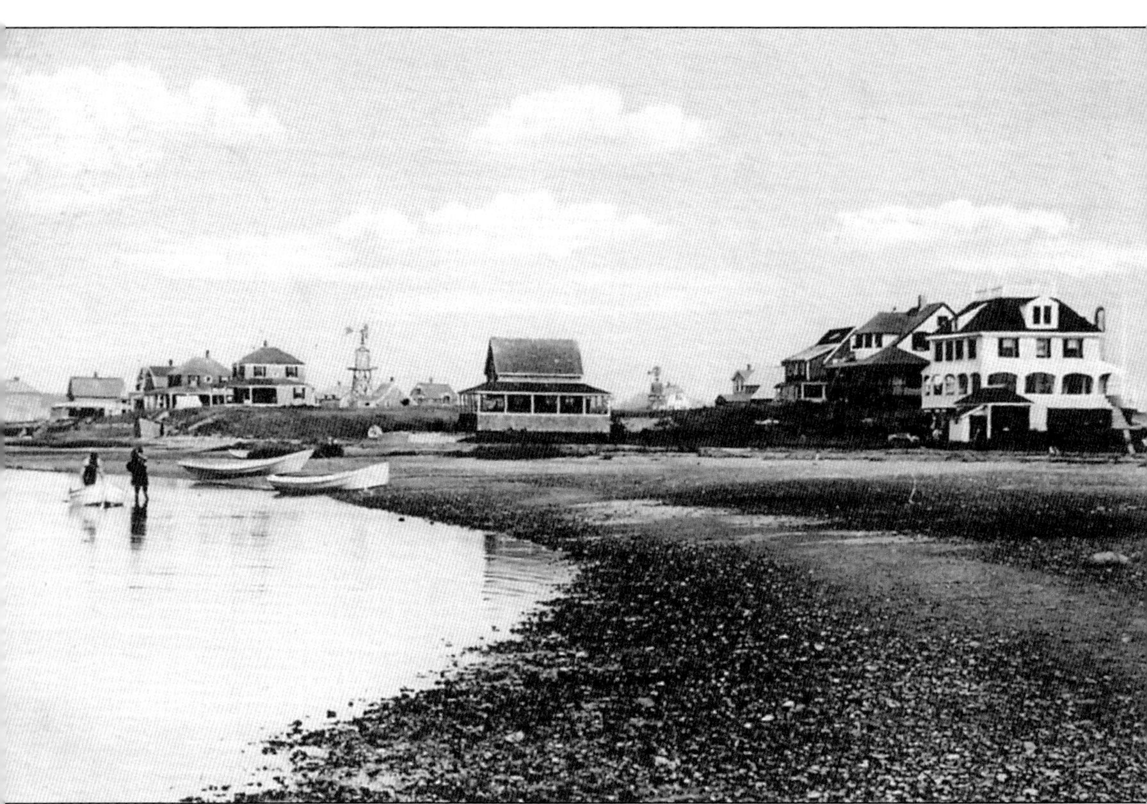

THE NOT-SO-HYANNIS, HYANNIS PARK. Adjacent to Hyannis Harbor and Lewis Bay is the area known as Hyannis Park. This area is not in Barnstable but is part of Yarmouth. According to Yarmouth historian Duncan Oliver, this area was called Yarmouth Meadows. As he writes: "Before the Civil War this area was called Yarmouth Meadows. Later it became the Burt Farm, and the Hyannis baseball team played games there. A marine railway was built and assisted in the repair of ships. Speculators after the Civil War thought this could be a prime area for summer folks and it was bought by the Hyannis Land Company. In 1893, a group of Brockton investors bought the land and the term Hyannis Park started to be used."

Three

Hotels and Resorts

After the Civil War, the lively maritime era was on the decline, although coasting ships still held their own for several decades. Steam ships displaced deep-water sailing ships. Larger schooners were built to compete with the railroads, but eventually the rail lines, aided by steam tugs with the ability to haul large groups of barges, finally replaced the coasters. Hyannis shipmasters began to disappear in the 1870s and 1880s, as sailing opportunities declined and the young stopped following their elders to the sea. Historian Donald Trayser said: "After flowing for three quarters of a century, the tide of maritime had ebbed. Hyannis and other south shore villages saw dark days on the horizon, but by this time the summer people had come."

Here and there around Barnstable, a trickle of city dwellers was already summering by the sea. By the 1870s, that trickle turned into a flood as the Hyannis Land Company was formed in the winter of 1871. This land company was responsible for a huge promotional effort in selling real estate in and around Hyannis and the shore on the south side of the town. The Iyanough house was purchased by the land company so that parties of buyers could be brought to the area, wined and dined, and sent out by carriage to review potential purchases, with parcels and streets all staked out. Newspapers like the *Barnstable Patriot* proudly proclaimed the benefits of summering in Barnstable. Between 1870 and 1900, the whole fabric of business and social life changed, for tourism and development were on the rise.

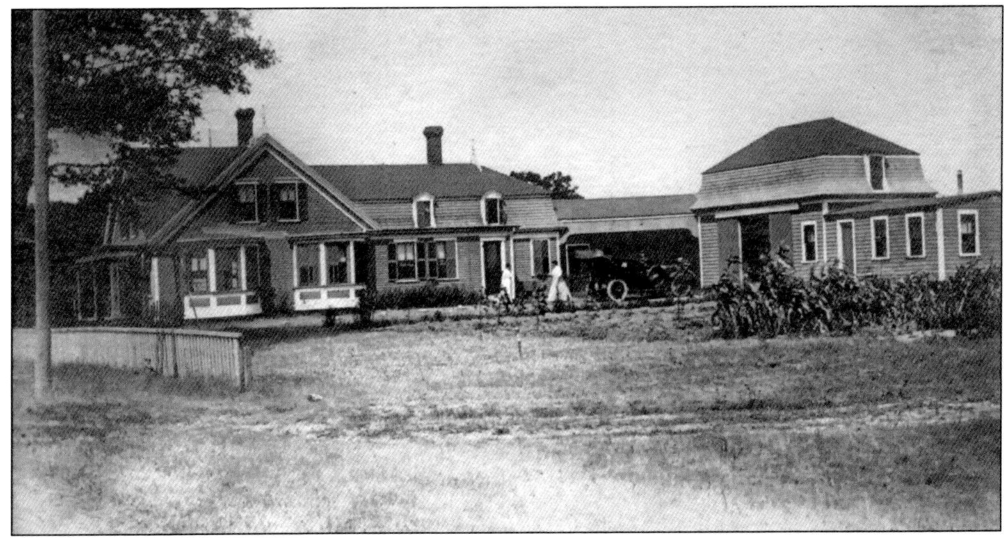

Cahoon House. The Cahoon House was typical of early accommodations in Hyannis. Alvah Bearse wrote in *Physic Point: Memoirs of Hyannis 1914–1929* that many residents of Hyannis made extra money by taking advantage of the summer trade. Some rented rooms in their houses or provided a service of some kind, such as transportation or food. Eventually, many old sea captains' houses were renovated into inns.

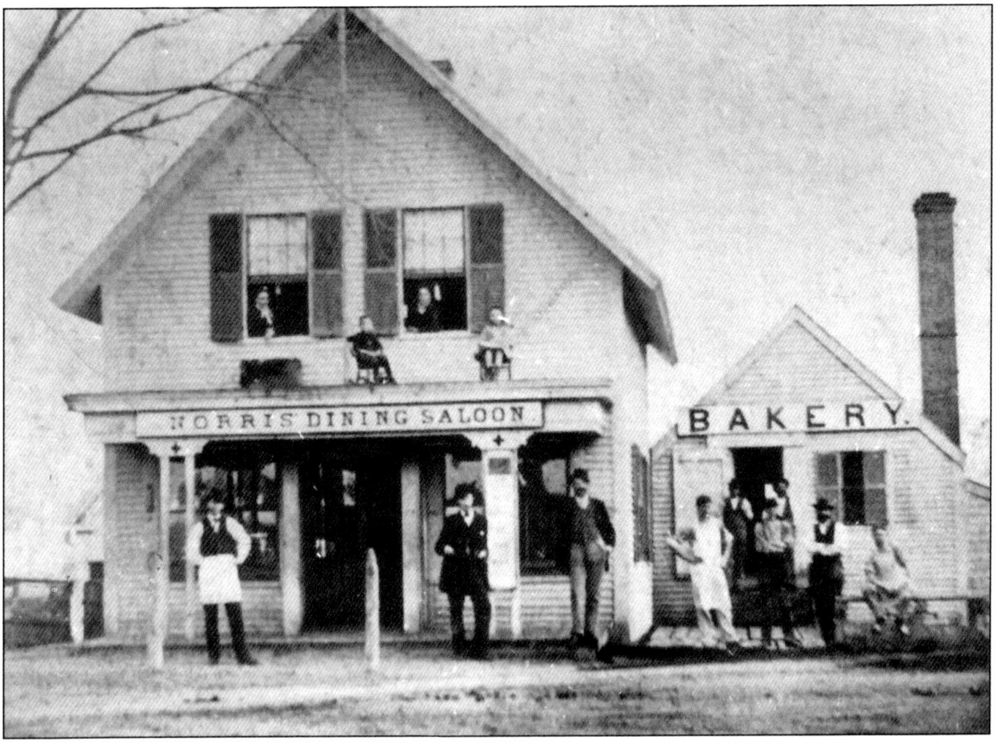

Norris Dining Saloon. The Norris Dining Saloon was opened in 1876 by Capt. John Norris, who had purchased the restaurant from a Captain Burgess. The *Barnstable Patriot*, commenting on the new management, stated: "He is filling up with new goods and everything is in tip top order. John Osborne of Boston will be pleased to wait upon all who may call."

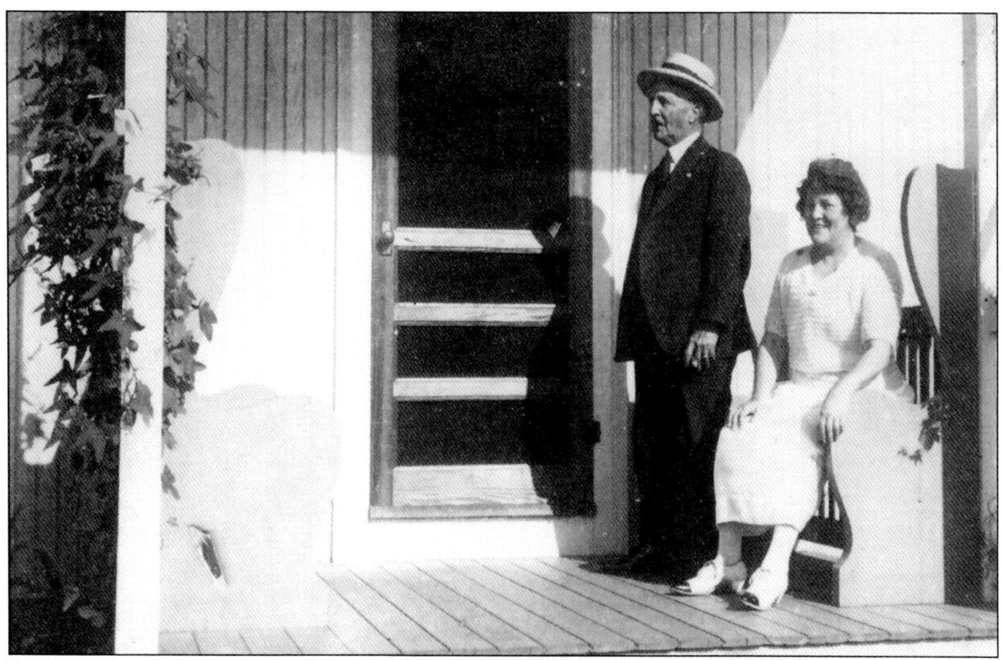

Lewis Bay Lodge. In 1666, native Sachem Kennecompsit sold John Lewis a parcel of land on the north side of what became Lewis Bay. His descendants would later build the Lewis Bay Lodge as a business catering to the tourist trade. John and Helen Lewis are pictured above at an entrance to the lodge. As the photograph below shows, the lodge offered an uncomplicated view of the relatively undeveloped bay. Helen Baxter managed the lodge, which was only open for the summer months. It featured meals on the "American plan," with chicken dinners starting at 50¢. Generally considered sedate, the lodge saw some excitement in the summer of 1929, when the lodge secretary almost drowned while swimming nearby.

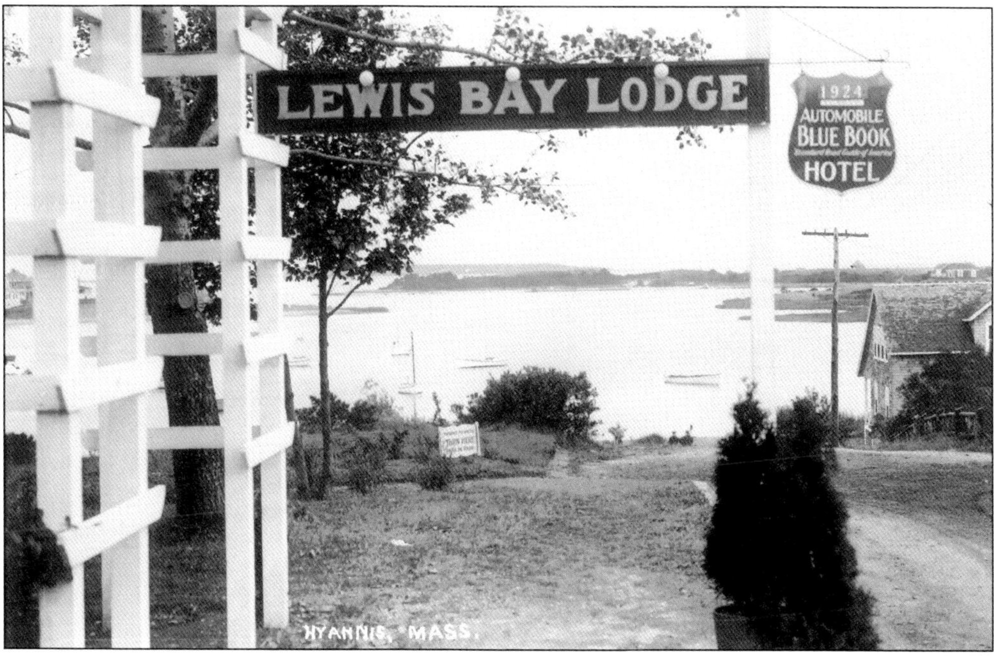

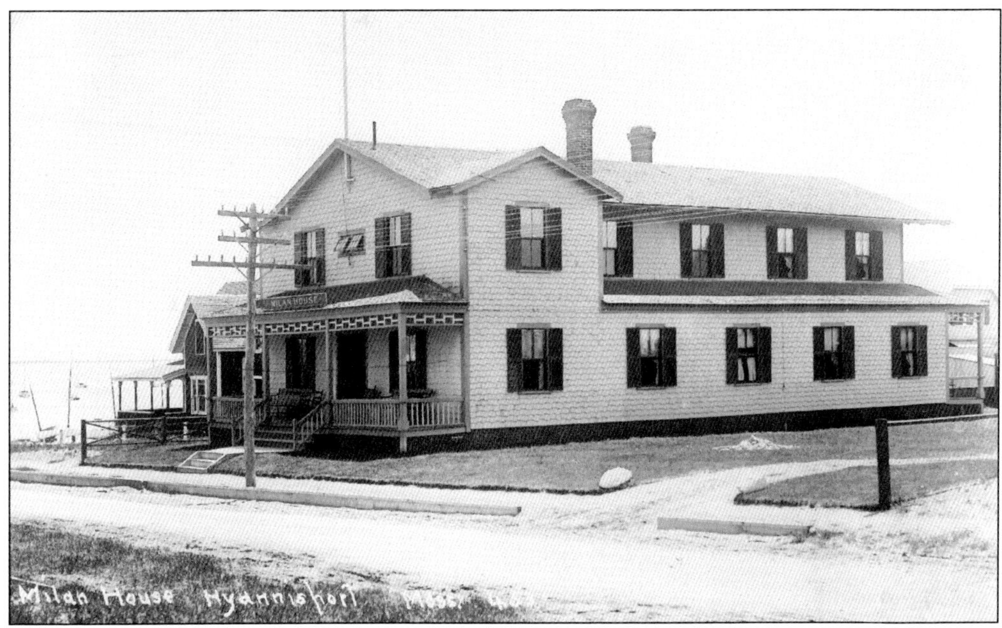

MILAN HOUSE, HYANNISPORT. The Milan was formerly known as the Pavilion before it changed ownership in 1896. The J.K. & B. Sears Co. sold the house to a Dr. M.B. Milan, who ran it as the Pavilion for one season before changing its name to the Milan House. It would remain as such until 1926, when it was sold to Norman Nagle, who changed the name to the Breakwater Inn.

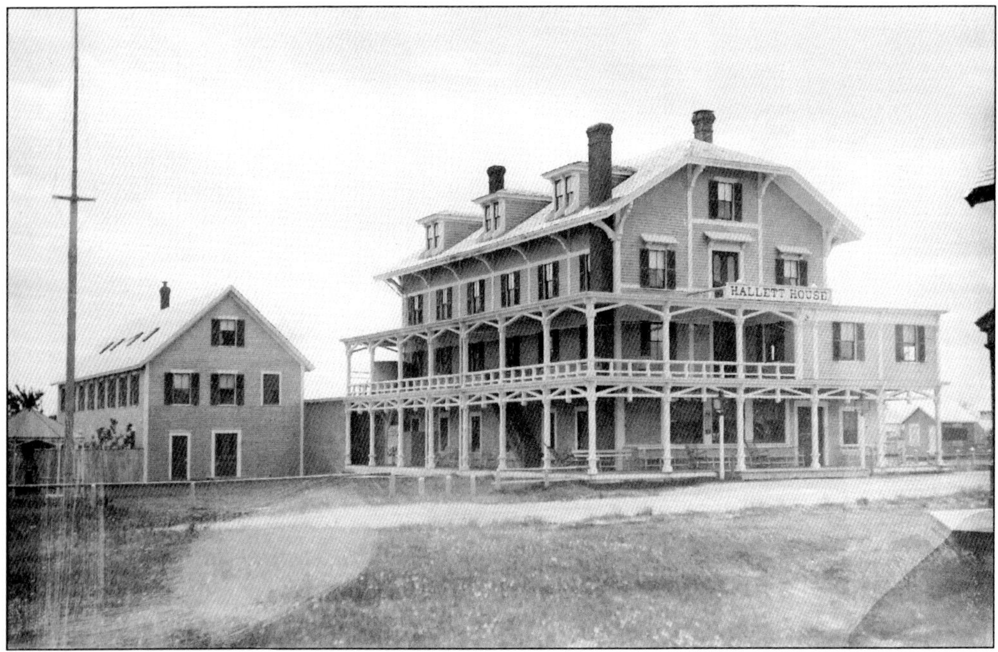

HALLET HOUSE, HYANNISPORT. The Hallet House was built by Gideon Hallet in 1872 and opened its doors in 1873. Considered one of the finer establishments in Hyannisport, it was billed as a place for those with "simpler" tastes who enjoy quiet and rest. It caught fire during the summer season of 1905 and burned to the ground. Many guests lost all the possessions they had brought along for their summer vacation and were temporarily taken in by those renting cottages.

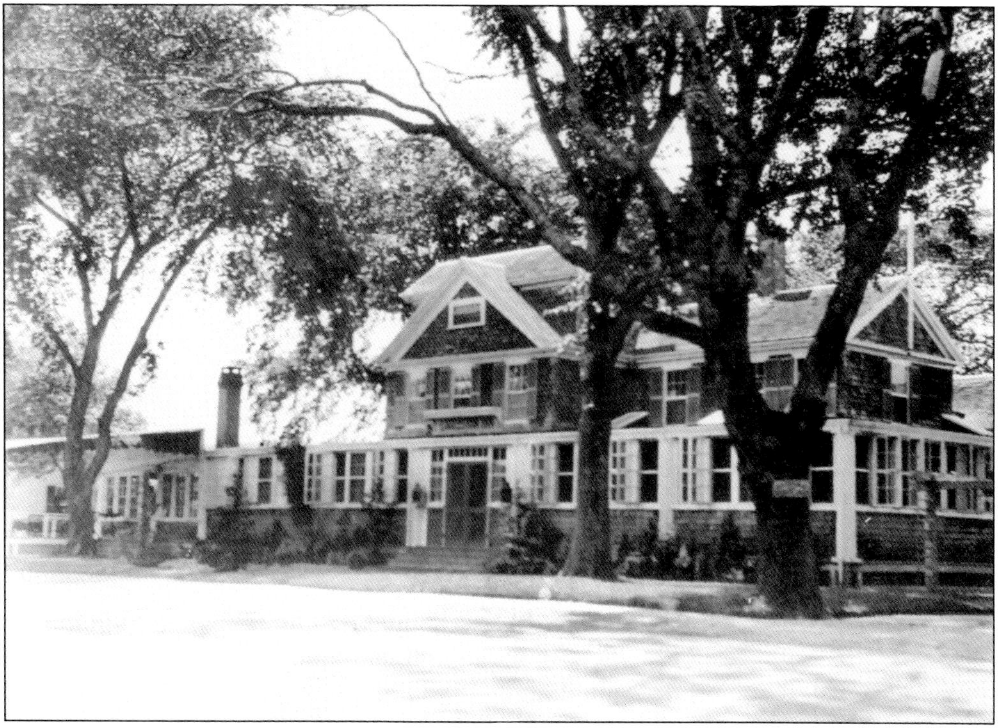

EAGLESTON INN, HYANNIS. The Eagleston Inn was originally a sea captain's house, owned by John W. Baker, which was converted into a hotel during World War I. The hotel had quite a reputation for elegance. People went to dinner in formal evening dress, and there were many Rolls Royce and Pierce Arrows lining the street with uniformed chauffeurs. The hotel was bought by the Eagelston family in 1917 and sold to Morgan Dada in 1920. Dada was an experienced hotel manager from Boston who ran the hotel until 1936 when it was again sold, this time to Carl Holm. The hotel closed during World War II and reopened in 1945.

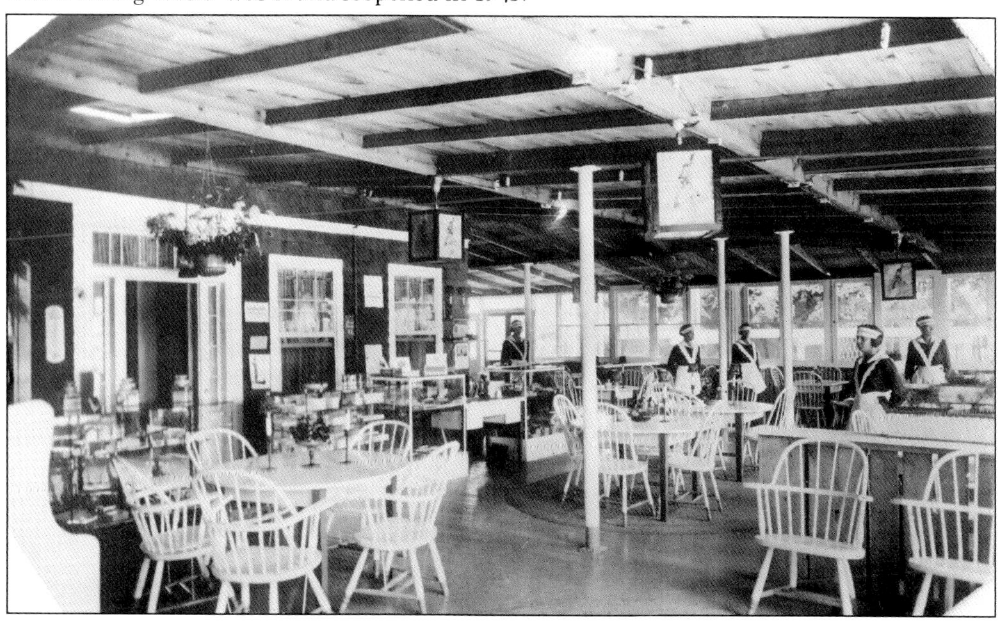

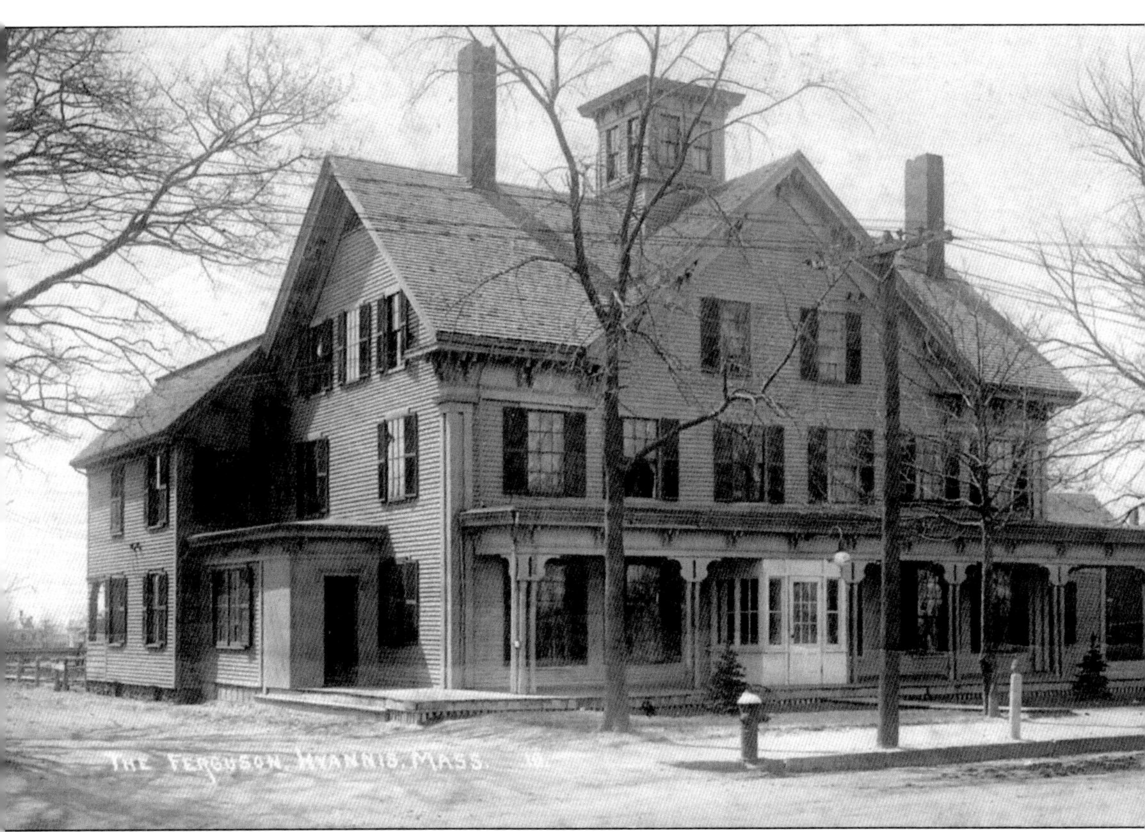

THE FERGUSON, HYANNIS. This hotel, known as The Ferguson, had a reputation for excellence. It was originally known as the Iyannough House, owned and operated by the very popular Thomas Soule Jr. of Hyannis. Soule had purchased the Iyannough House from The Hyannis Land Co., which operated it for a brief period of time. According to an article published in the *Barnstable Patriot* in 1874, the hotel was congratulated for the fine food that was served to the local Masons. Soule Jr. also continued in this fashion to offer fine food and lodgings. As part of the times, the Iyannough had a livery stable with teams that were advertised as being "let out" for reasonable prices. When Hugh Ferguson bought the inn in 1915, he had to update it by replacing the stable with a garage, which required a special permit from the town. When the Iyannough was sold in 1915, the Soule family moved down the street to a family-owned house called the Wayside.

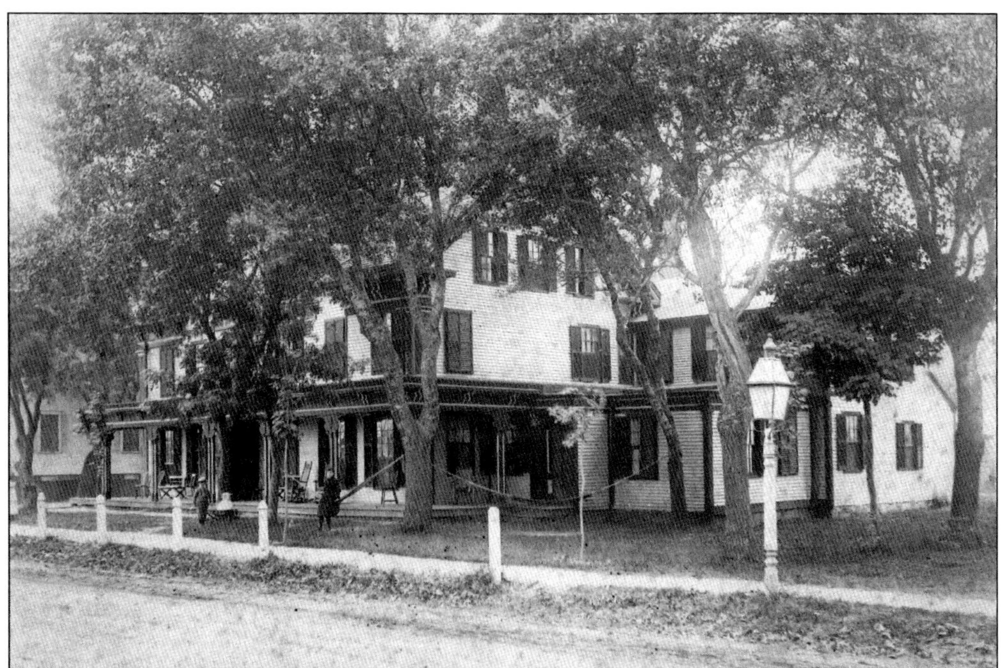

Hyannis Inn. Hyannis Inn was one of only two year-round hotels that operated in Hyannis. It was the type of inn that accommodated local groups, providing meeting rooms and fine food. Dr. Charles E. Harris and the local medical society were in the habit of meeting at the inn, sharing new medical information over a meal. The inn served steak, chicken, and lobster dinners.

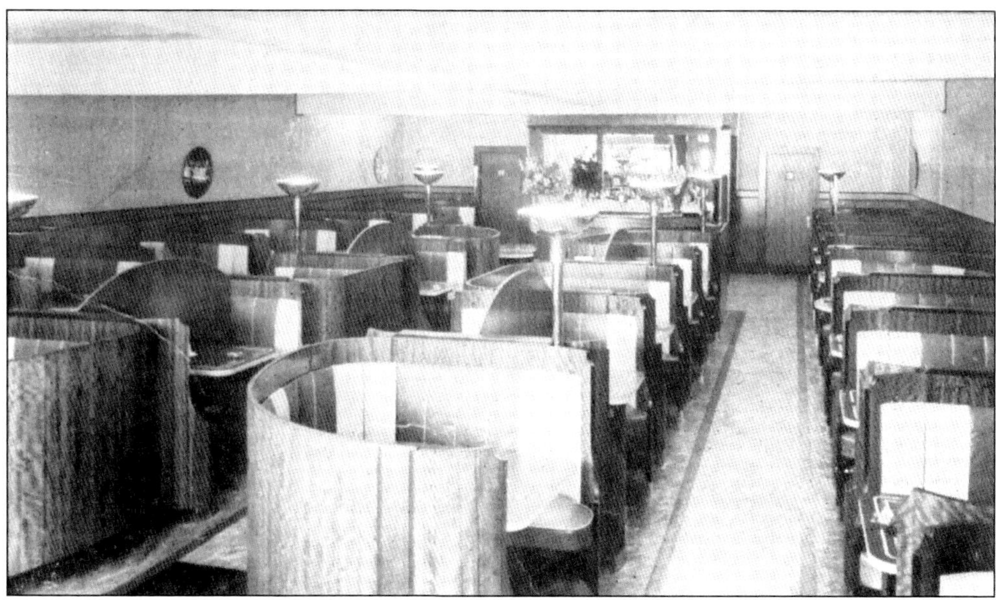

New York Restaurant, Hyannis. The New York Restaurant was located by the Idle Hour movie theater in the business district of Hyannis. Offering fine food in thoroughly modern surroundings, the restaurant profited from a very busy location.

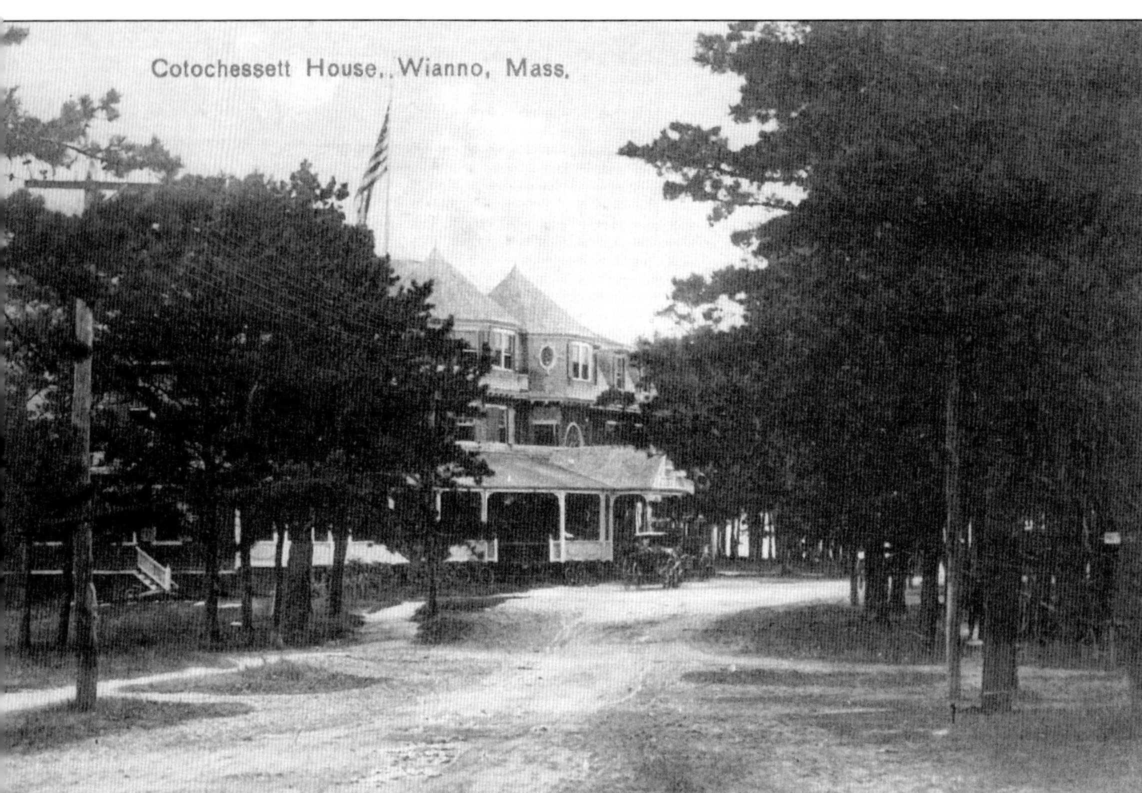

Cotochesset House, Osterville. Harvey Scudder built the Cotochesset House on Wianno Beach in about 1869. This hotel quickly became very popular with the upscale crowd from Boston. William Lloyd Garrison lived in Osterville for a time after he retired from being editor of the *Liberator*, an abolitionist newspaper based in Boston. It was believed that he was in the habit of staying at the Cotochesset House during the summer months. In 1877, the hotel was purchased by J.C. Stevens. One day in July 1887 at 6:00 a.m., members of the waitstaff discovered a fire on the third floor. Guests were quickly woken by staff and had time to retrieve their belongings before the hotel burned to the ground. The hotel was managed by Mrs. Granville Ames, who was able to get the guests out of the building without incident. The loss was estimated at $25,000, and rebuilding started almost at once.

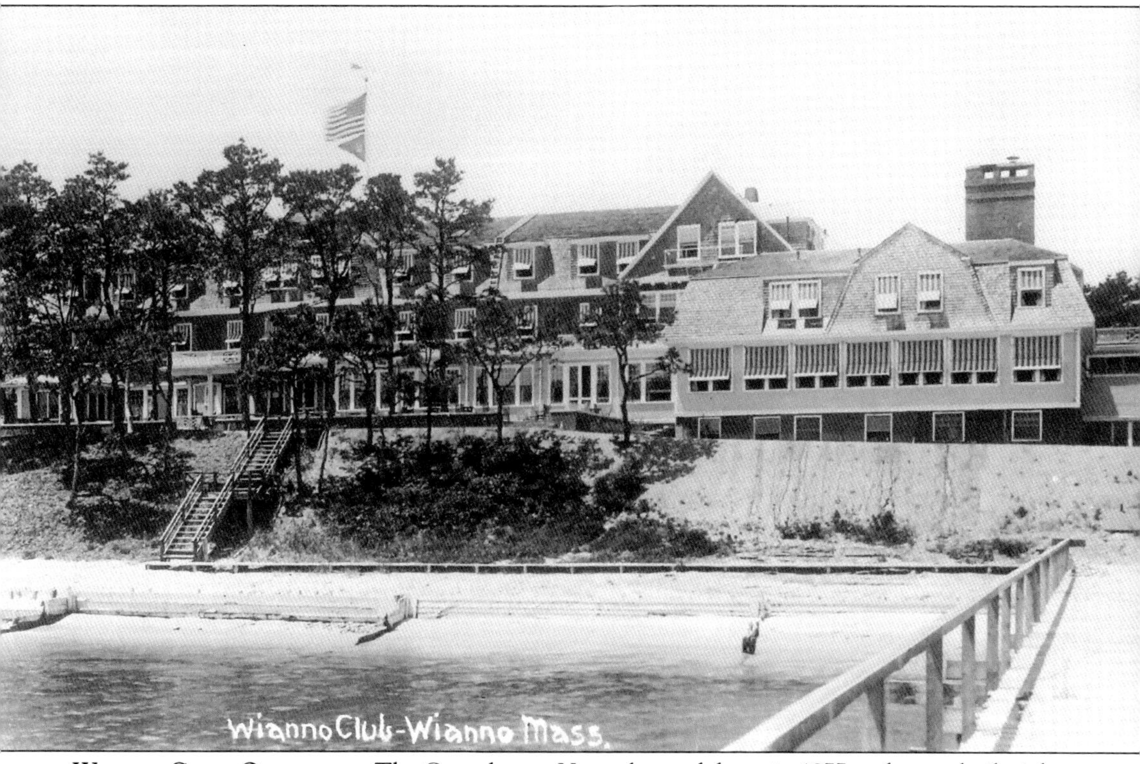

WIANNO CLUB, OSTERVILLE. The Cotochesset House burned down in 1877 and was rebuilt right away. As the house was being rebuilt, a time capsule containing letters, records, and other articles was placed in the foundation. By the summer of 1916, the Cotochesset was bought by a group of investors, some of whose families had been long-term summer visitors. They renamed it the Wianno Club. Once papers were passed on, work began at once to modernize the club. The main building was made over at a cost of $100,000. Private bathrooms were installed in the rooms, along with electricity, steam heat, and telephone service. The old dining room was turned into a function room, and a new dining room was built on the ocean side of the club. A new billiard room was added and a new pier built out on the beach. A brick terrace was added on the side of the club and a golf course was planned. Twenty new boats were also acquired. To celebrate the new club, a fireworks display was arranged for the Fourth of July.

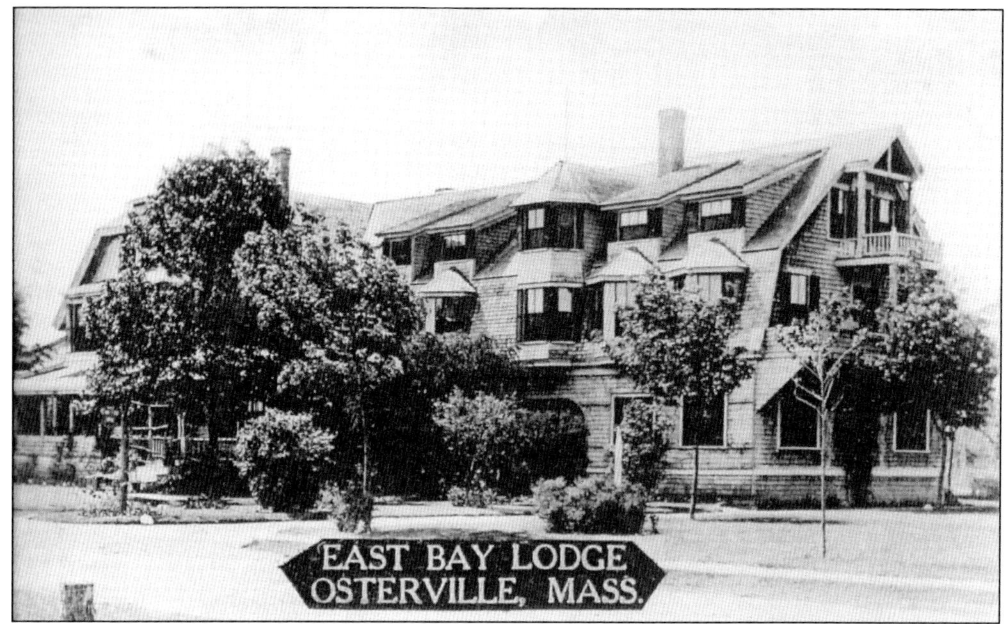

East Bay Lodge, Osterville. The East Bay Lodge, like many hotels in Barnstable, started as a sea captain's house. In this case, Capt. Nelson Bearse and his wife, Mary, turned their home into a hotel and restaurant in 1906 and ran it for 28 years. East Bay would have multiple owners over the years.

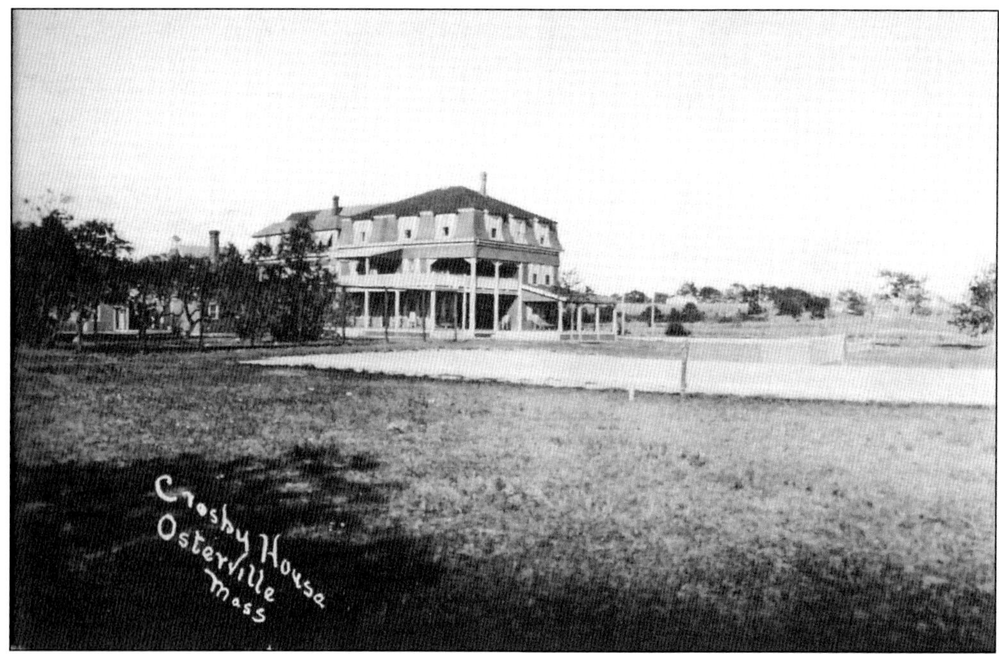

Crosby Inn, Osterville. This inn is one of many that opened up in the 1870s to take advantage of the lucrative tourist trade. Horace Crosby opened his hotel sometime around 1872. The Crosby House did not have the amenities of the Wianno Club, but people found Horace Crosby and his wife very genial hosts. Year after year, they added rooms to their establishment until they had about 50 total.

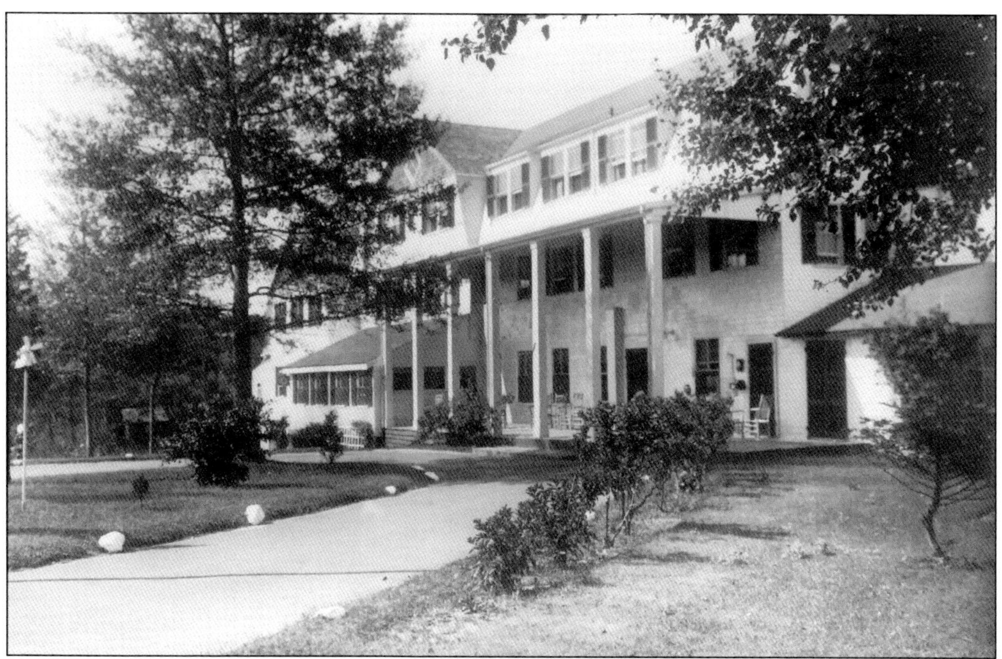

West Bay Inn, Osterville. With 65 rooms, the West Bay Inn, built in 1906 by Edward S. Crocker, had its own dedicated following. By 1935, the inn was unoccupied and was put up for sale. It caught fire and burned to the ground in a spectacular blaze. It was reported that hundreds in Osterville turned out to watch it burn.

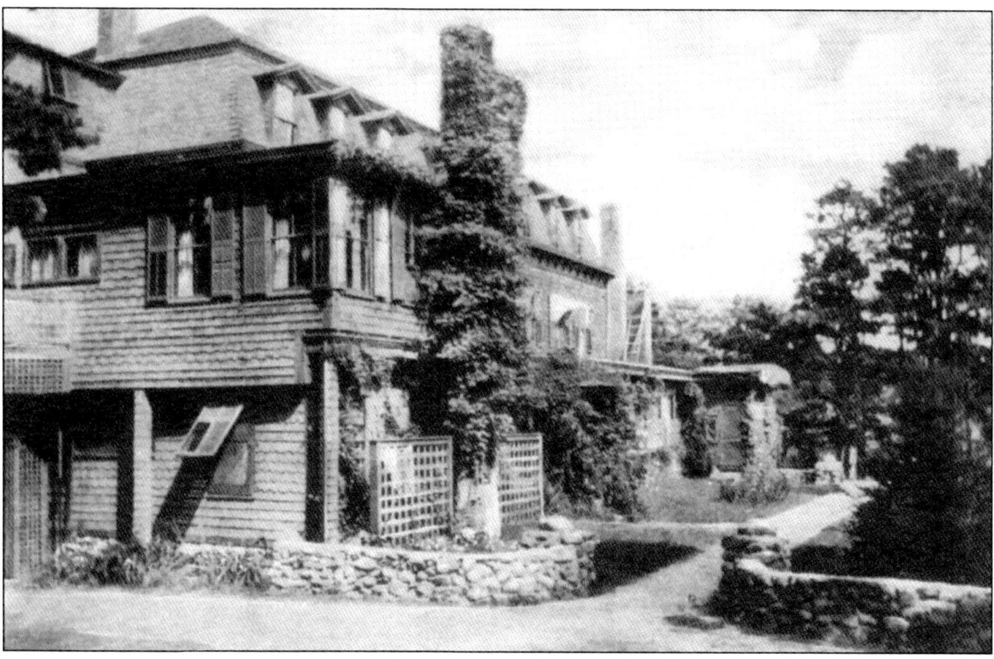

Chequaquett Inn, Centerville. The Chequaquett Inn, originally called the Sturgis House, was built by Capt. Dennis Sturgis in 1872. The three-story inn went through a number of name changes; it was briefly known as the Sabens House and the Chequaquett House. It had an outdoor dancing pavilion and tennis courts.

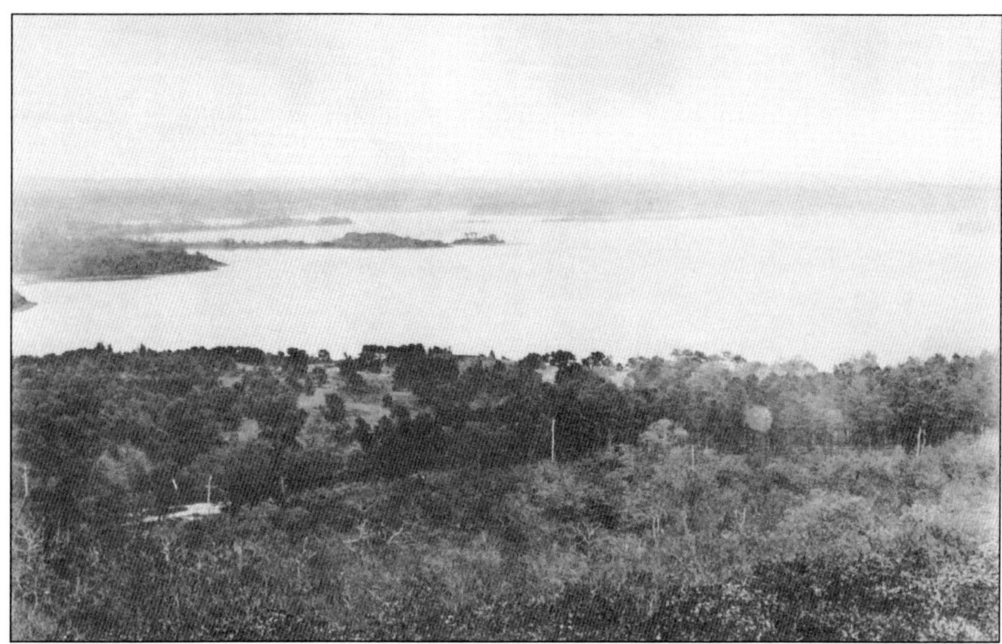

Nine Mile Pond, Centerville. Nine Mile Pond is now known as Wequaquett Lake. In the very early 1900s, the lake was a very important part of social life in Centerville. Known for its fishing, the lake also had tourist lodgings, restaurants, and Camp Opechee.

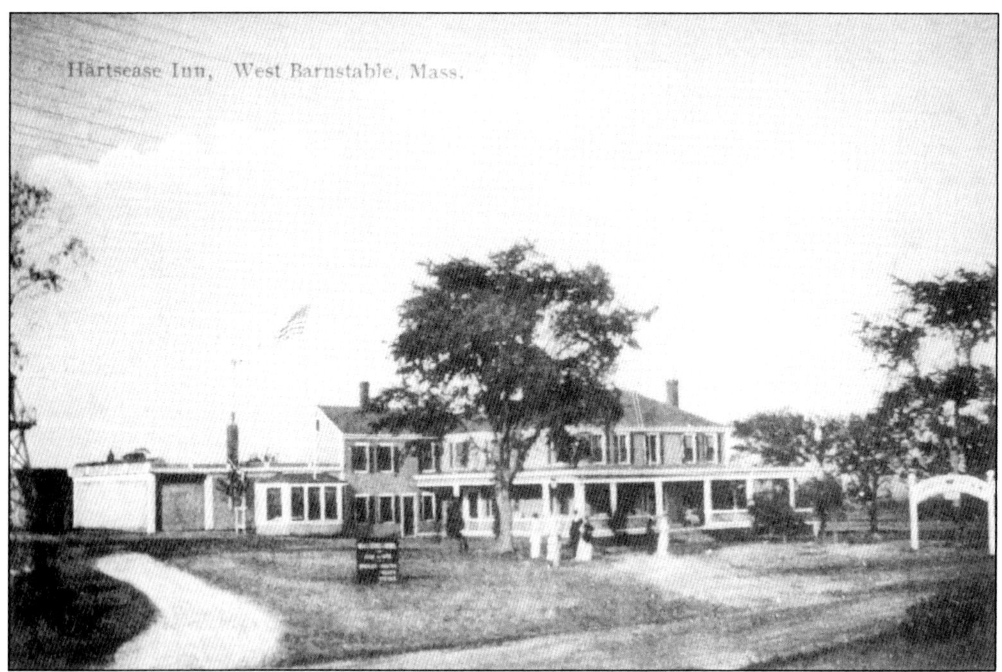

Harts Ease Inn, West Barnstable. Harts Ease Inn is the former Daniel Bursley estate that was either close to or on the land that the Otis family of West Barnstable owned. The Harts Ease Inn would later burn to the ground.

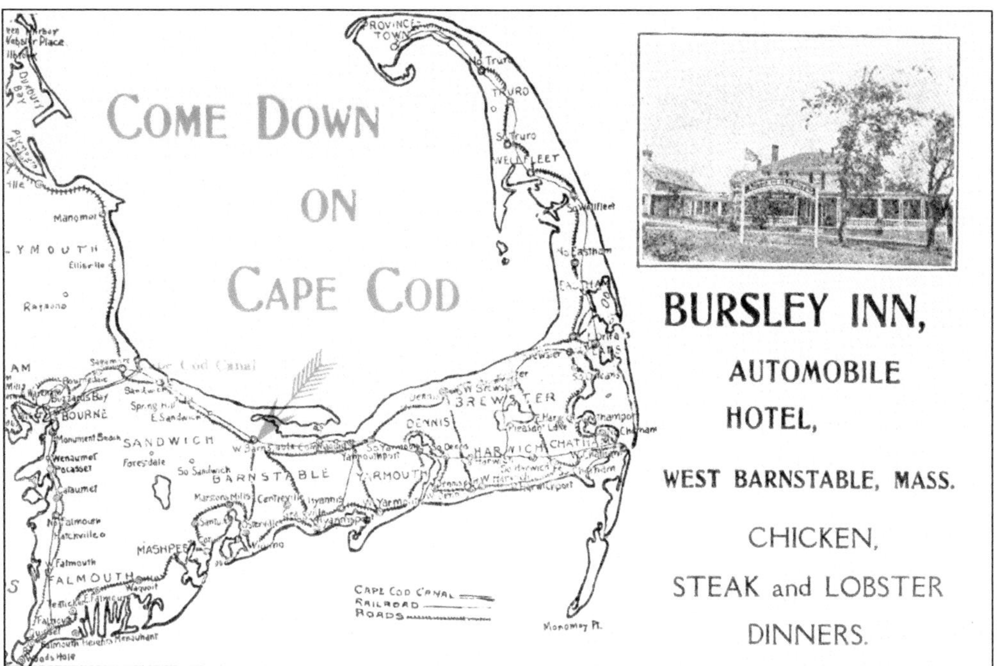

BURSELY INN, WEST BARNSTABLE. The Bursley Inn was the former home of Daniel Bursley, who operated the well-known Bursley Express stage line that ran between Osterville and the train station at West Barnstable.

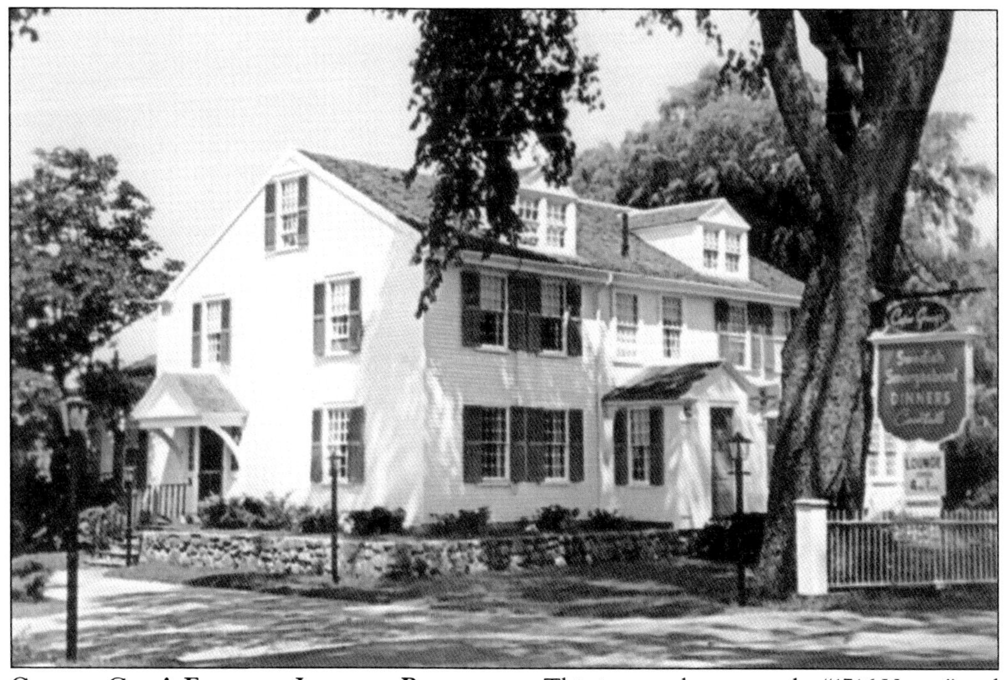

CAPTAIN GREY'S FOOD AND LODGING, BARNSTABLE. This inn was known as the "1716 House" and was thought to have been built by James Paine, the grandfather of Robert Treat Payne, a signer of the Declaration of Independence. Captain Grey haunts the building, making his presence known by slamming doors.

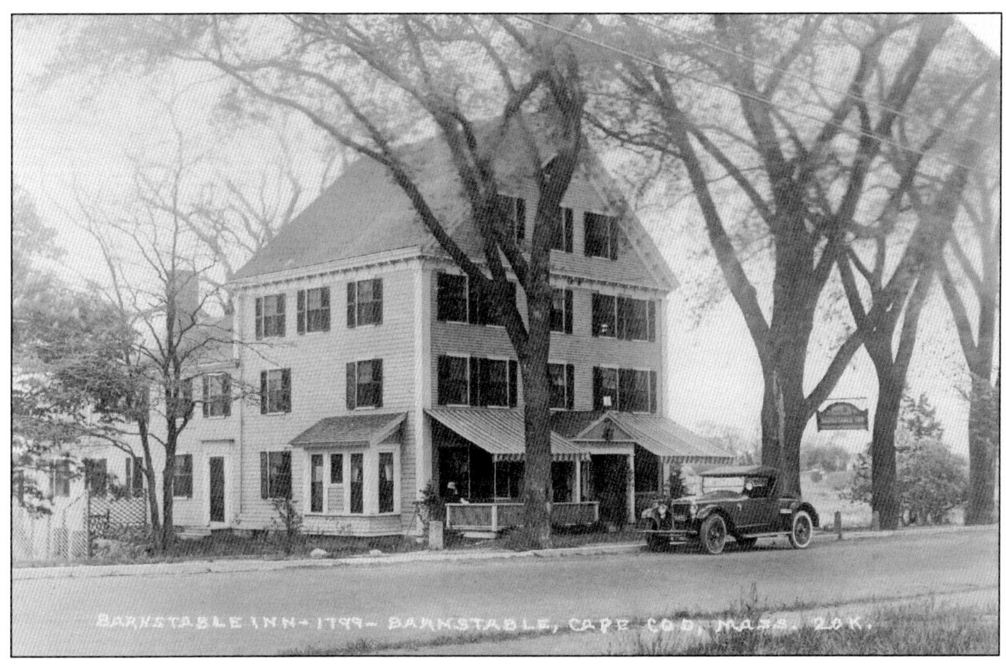

BARNSTABLE INN. The Barnstable Inn was the former Globe Hotel, owned and developed by the Eldridge family. Bought by James Turpin, it was extensively redecorated with fine furnishings while preserving its well-known exterior. Poised to take advantage of the legal trade because of its proximity to the village court buildings, it also prospered from the growing tourist trade in the 1870s.

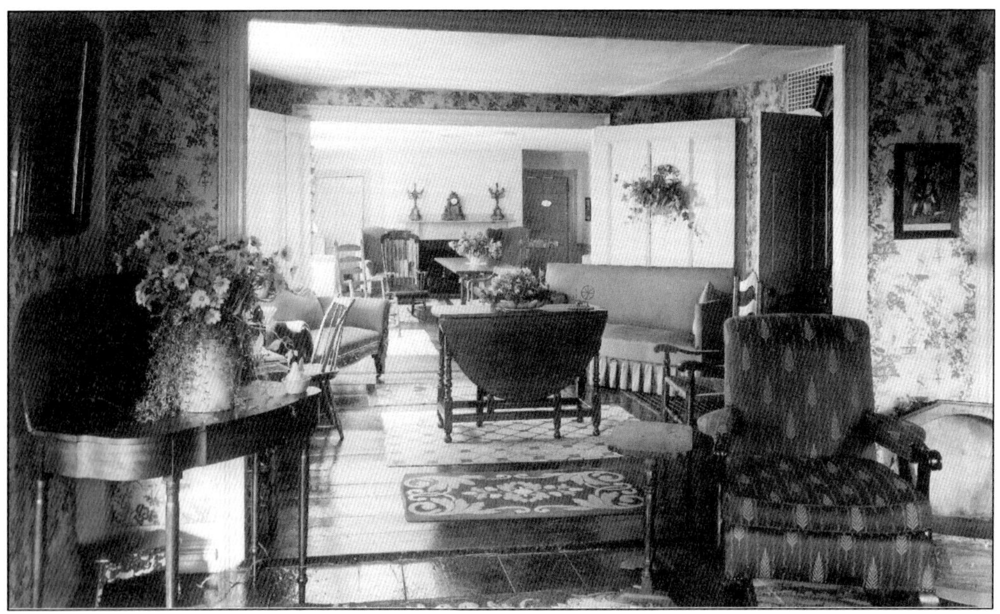

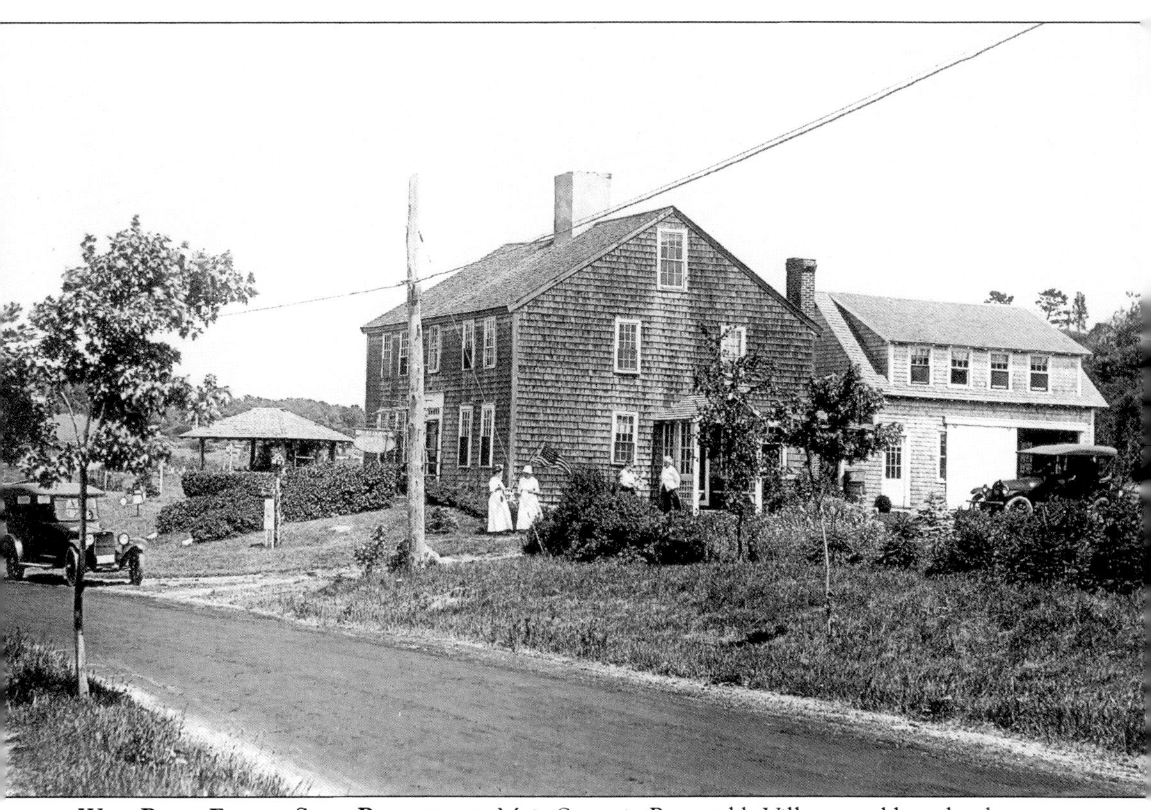

West Ridge Flower Shop, Barnstable. Main Street in Barnstable Village would see development as well, but on a smaller scale than what Hyannis experienced. Barnstable Village was also the county seat, so eventually residences and small businesses gave way to lawyer's offices. The West Ridge Flower Shop is interesting in that it was used as a commercial space and then reconverted for use as a dwelling. It was originally constructed in 1706.

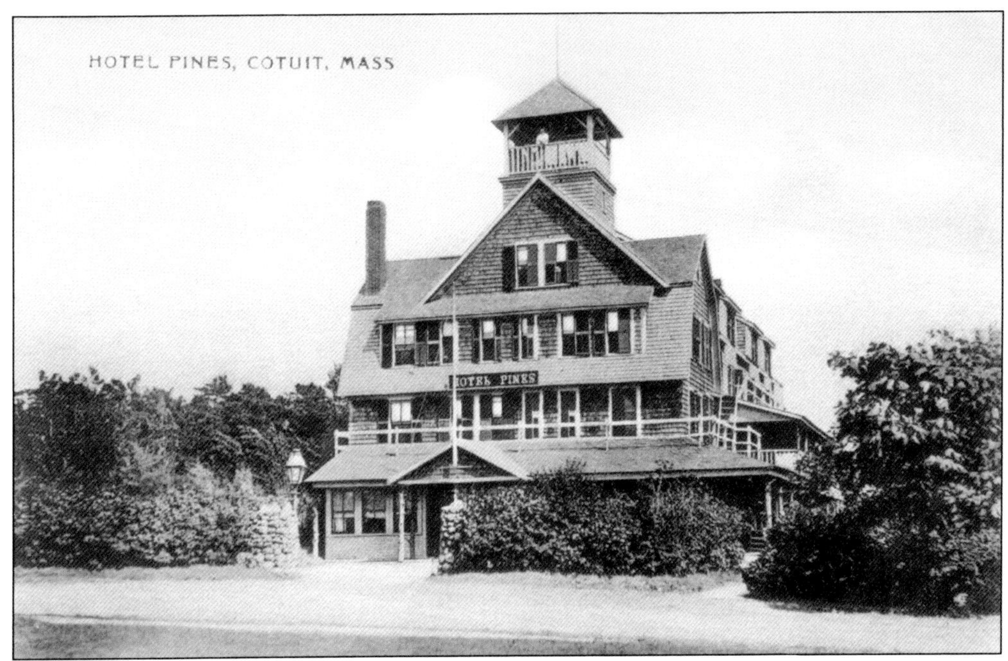

Hotel Pines, Cotuit. The Pines was started from an old sea captain's house that was first used as a boardinghouse. Managed by owners John and Elizabeth Morse, the Pines opened in 1893. Additions were built over the years, with the trademark gambrel addition constructed in early 1900.

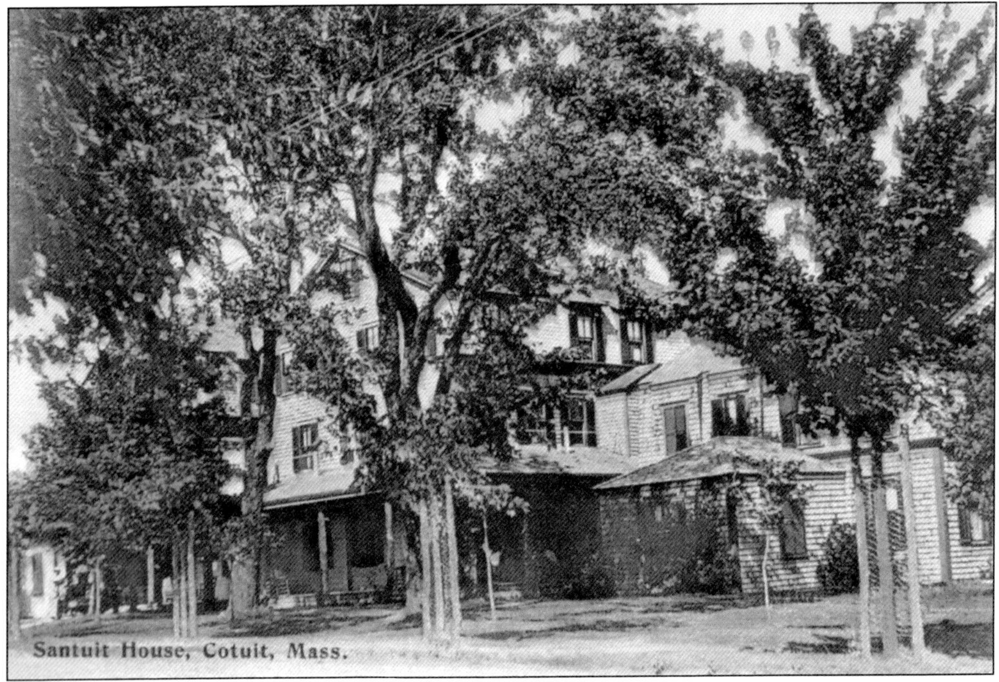

Santuit House, Cotuit. This early Barnstable hotel was based on a boardinghouse opened in 1830 by the Hezekiah Coleman family. By 1860, son Braddock had put on some major additions, including a ballroom. By the 1890s, the next generation of Coleman family owners would add an extra floor.

Four

Barnstable County Fair

The Barnstable Agricultural Society was established on May 5, 1843, and incorporated the next year with John Reed of Yarmouth as its first president. The first exhibition and fair were held at the Barnstable County Courthouse on September 4, 1844. Subsequent fairs—except for 1851 in Orleans and 1852 at Sandwich—were held in Barnstable. For several years, the fair was held at the Union Hall, which was owned by Sylvanus B. Phinney. The hall was located at the northwestern corner of Major Phinney's homestead, just east of the Customs House.

By 1858, enough land was bought and donated that the agricultural society could have a permanent fairground. Twenty acres in total, it extended from County Road (route 6A) to Maraspin Creek on the north side. During the period in which this property served as a fairground, there were additional sheds and storage buildings to the north and east of the hall, as well as a track for trotting races and a baseball diamond and grandstand, which were later removed. In addition to the usual exhibits of livestock and agricultural products, turn-of-the-century fairs had vaudeville performances, balloonists, and other entertainments.

In 1935, the property was sold to Clifford Belknap of Boston. Having been vacant for seven years, the grounds and hall were refurbished in 1938 and 1939 for use as the site of Barnstable's tercentenary fair in 1939.

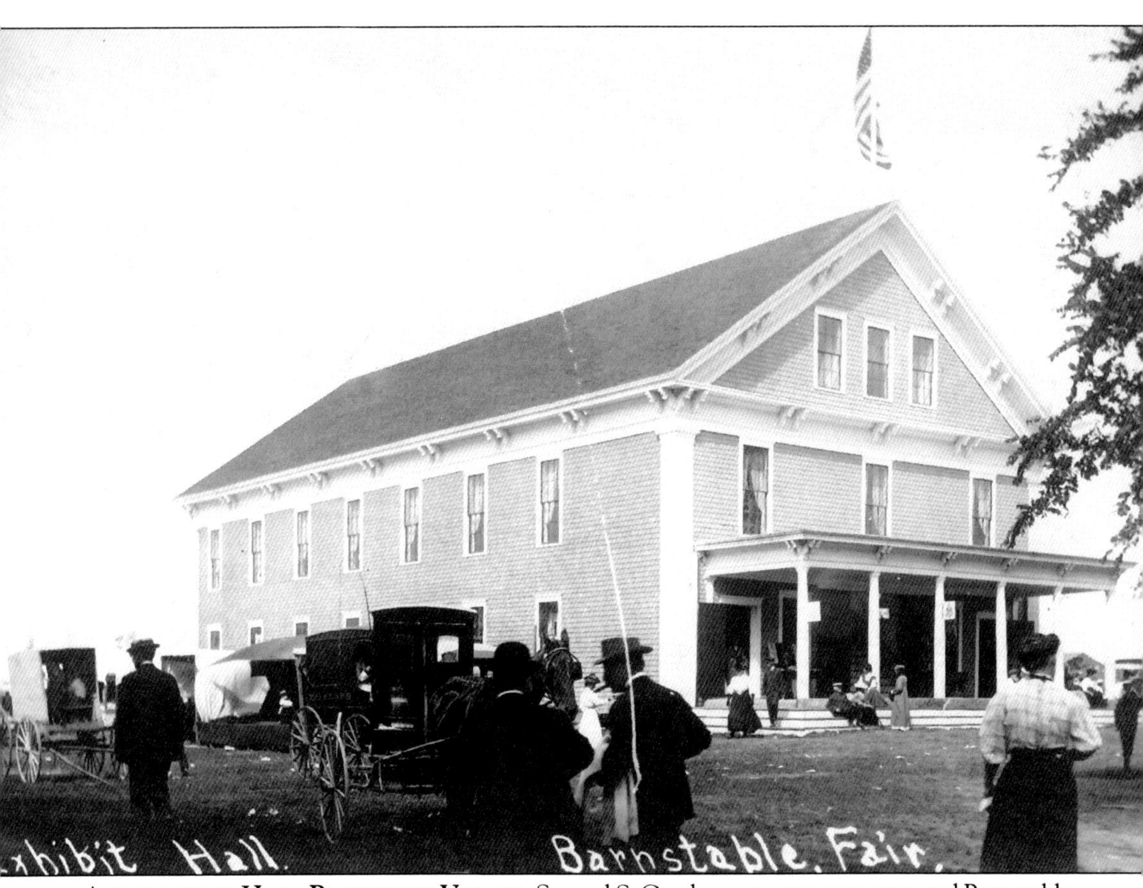

Agricultural Hall, Barnstable Village. Samuel S. Crocker, a master carpenter and Barnstable resident, constructed a building on the new fairgrounds to be used for exhibitions and public meetings. A northeast gale in 1862 demolished the fair hall by blowing the roof off and sending it a distance of about 75 feet. A second fair hall was built by October 14, 1862. Funds had been quickly raised for a new building, with William Sturgis a major donor in this effort. The new fair hall was dedicated at the fair of 1862 and served as the exhibition hall for annual fairs and the location of the agricultural ball until the fair stopped operating annually in 1931.

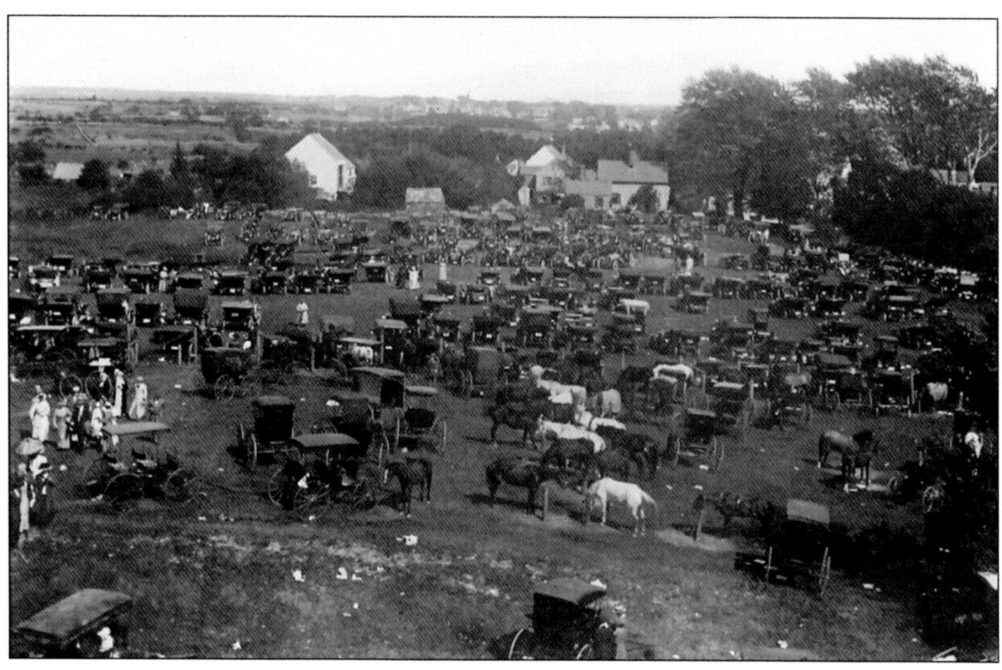

PARKING, BARNSTABLE COUNTY FAIR. The 1915 fair was the busiest to date, bringing thousands of people and about 650 automobiles. These photographs highlight the changing needs of people coming to the fair as the years progressed. Above is an area of mixed use, with horses picketed off to the side and several rows of automobiles parked adjacent to the field. However, by 1915, more and more people left their horses behind in favor of automobiles. The photograph below shows an area reserved for automobiles only.

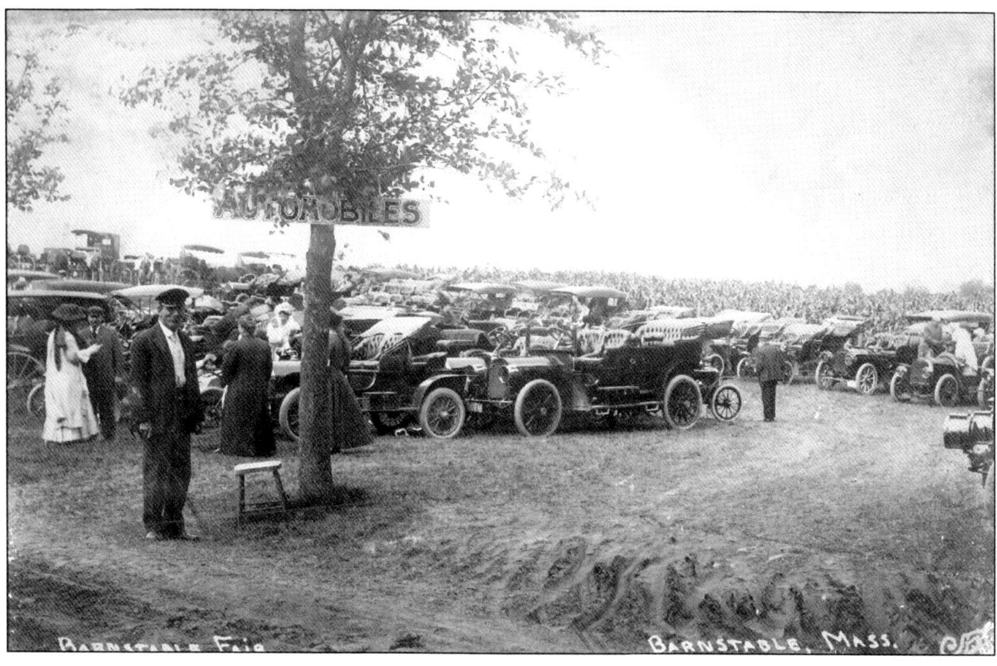

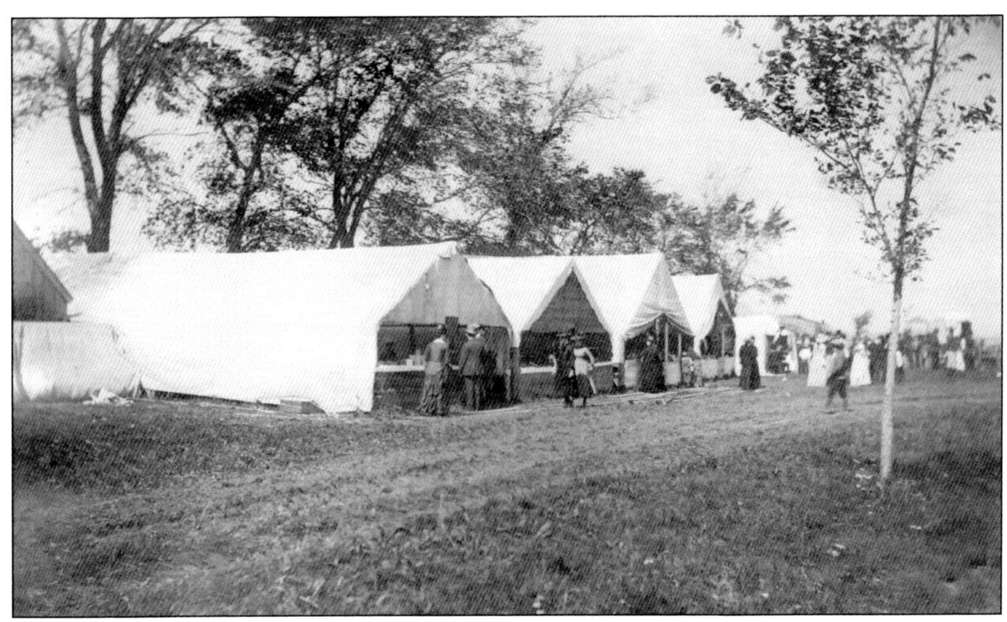

FOOD TENTS. Tents for food and various activities were arranged around the exhibit hall. There were many things to experience at the fair: exhibitions, horse racing, animal and dog judging, and of course, food. Fairgoers could purchase ice cream, candy apples, and other treats at the food tents.

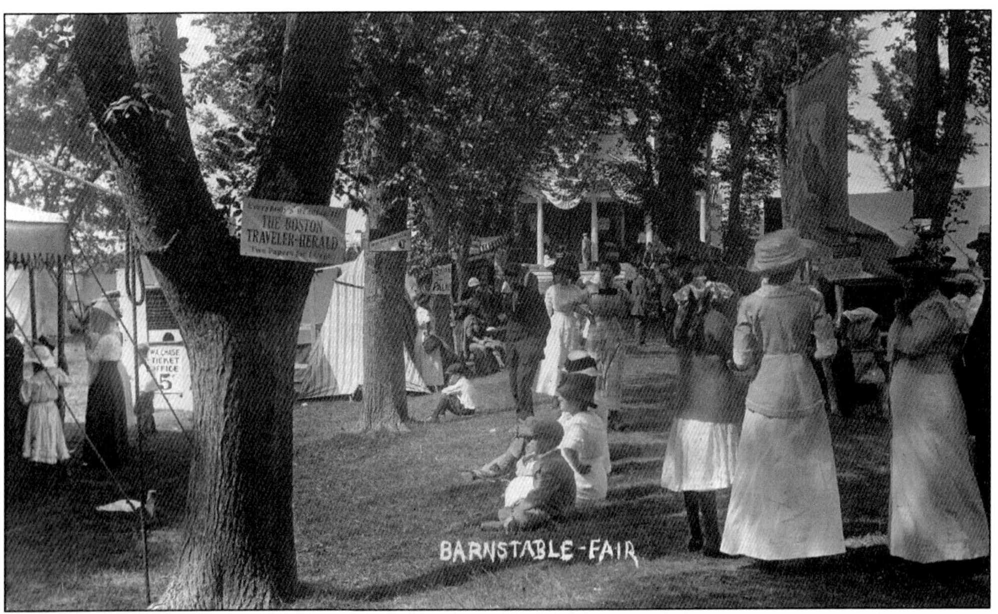

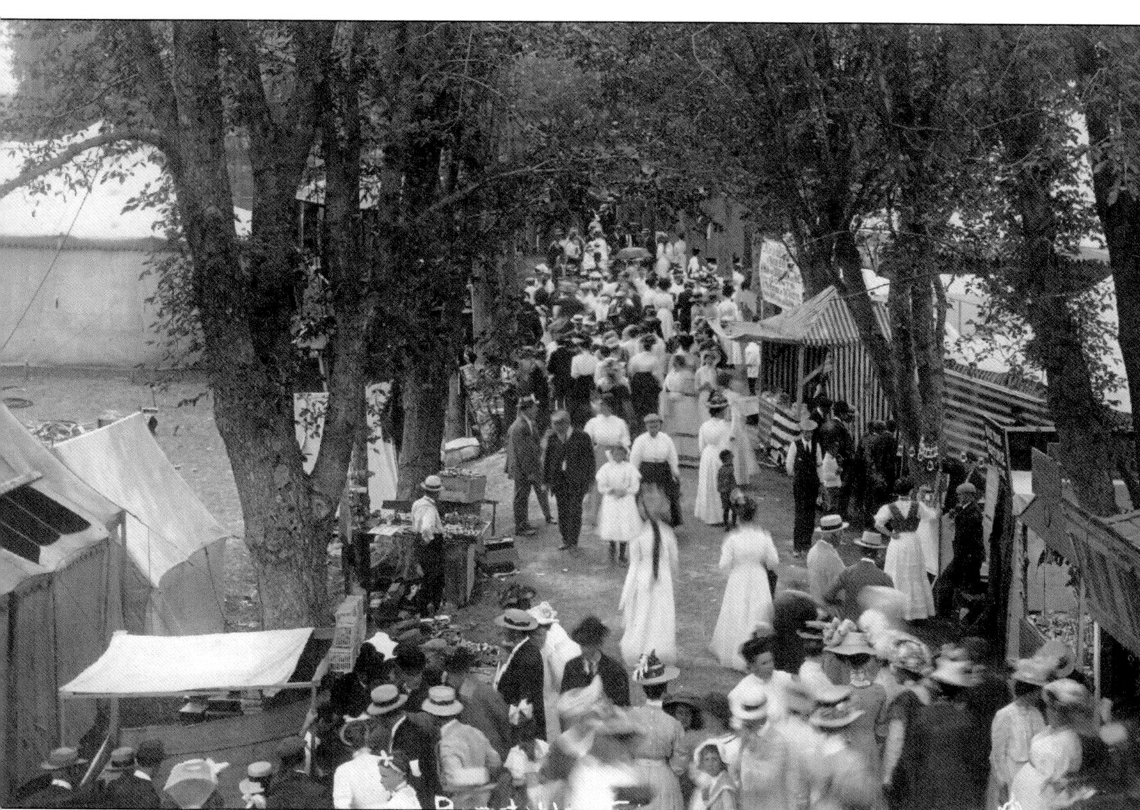

Fakir Row. Part of the entertainment at the Barnstable County Fair was Fakir Row, also known as "Faker Row," the equivalent of a modern day midway. Games, novelties, and entertainment were offered for a price. Note a number of interesting booths lining the so-called Faker Row: a barker hawking snake oil (best for rubbing onto sore joints), a booth named "Governor's Novelties," and a fortuneteller.

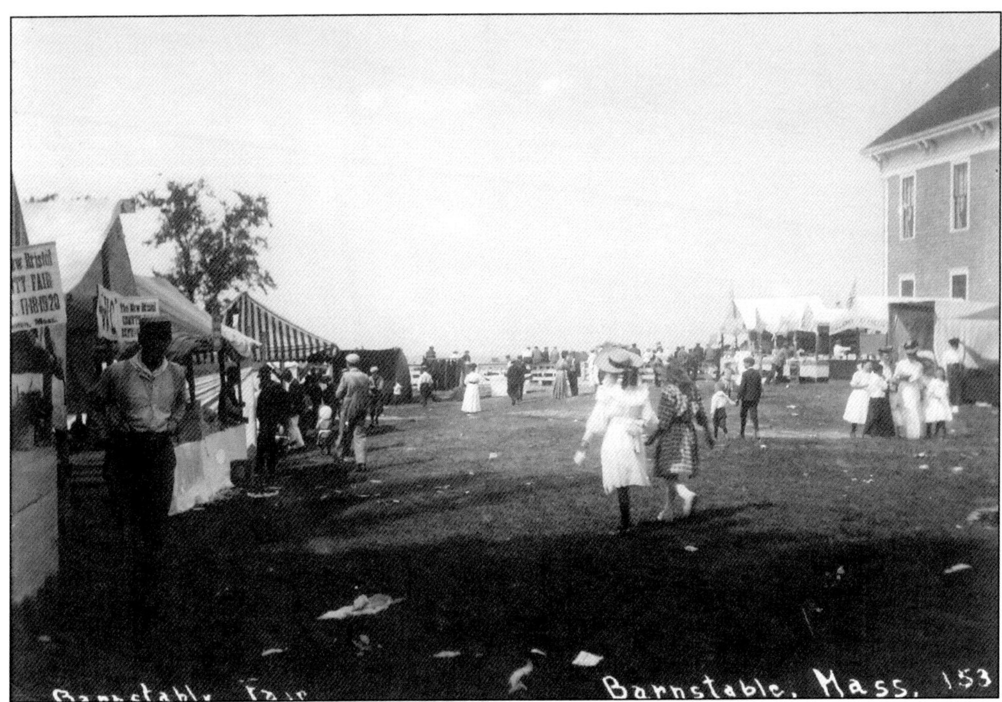

Two Girls at the Fair. These two nicely dressed girls are walking down the line of the food tent area. Just behind the corner of the hall building on the right is the ice cream tent.

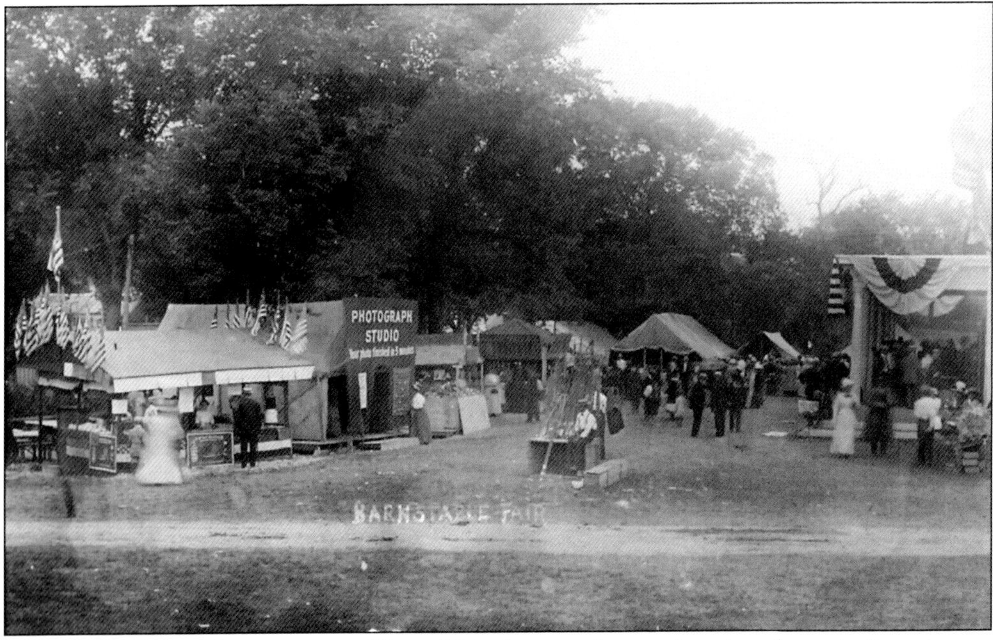

Photograph Tent, Agricultural Hall. This photograph tent advertises photos in five minutes. Right next to the photographer's tent is a beverage tent manned by the N.Y. Bottling Co.

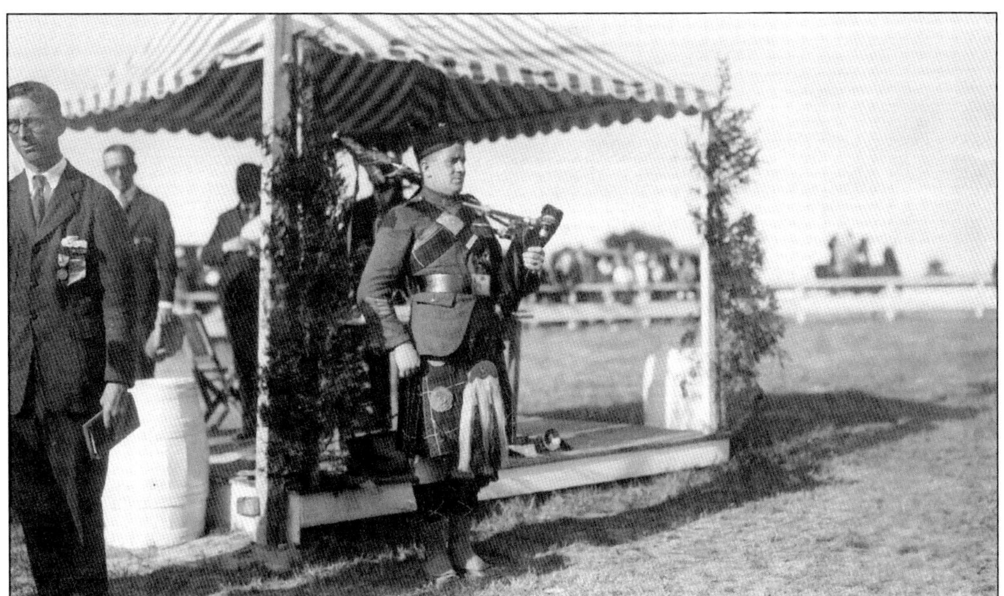

Dog Judging Tent. This curious tent is where the judges stood, or sat, for the dog competitions. Note the bagpiper dressed in highlander clothing.

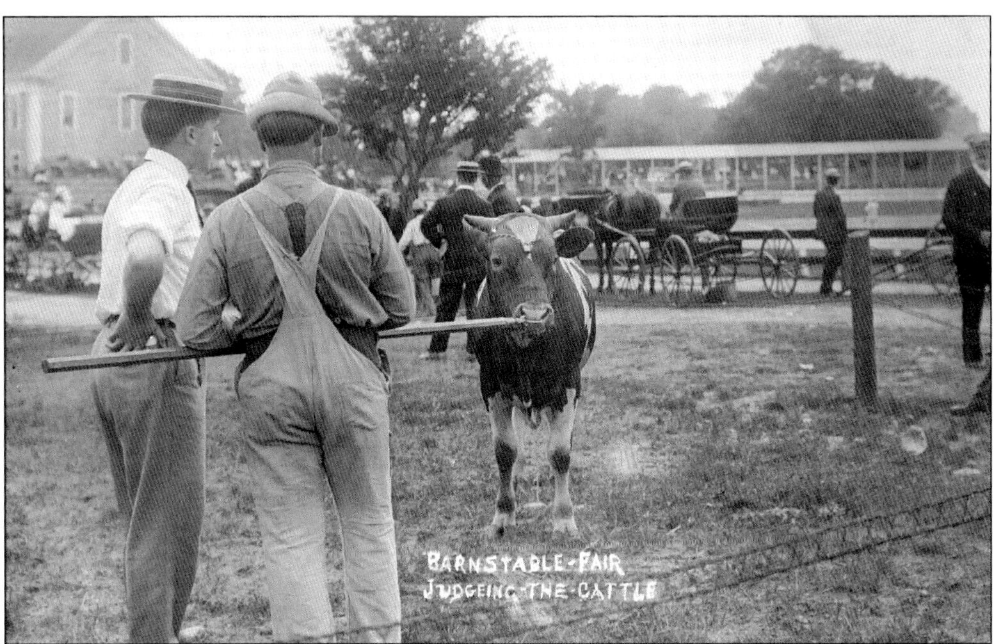

Cow Led by the Nose. Animal judging has long been an important part of any agricultural fair. Since bulls were known to be unpredictable animals, nose rings were used to help control them. This photograph shows a farmer using a bull staff to grasp the ring in the bull's nose.

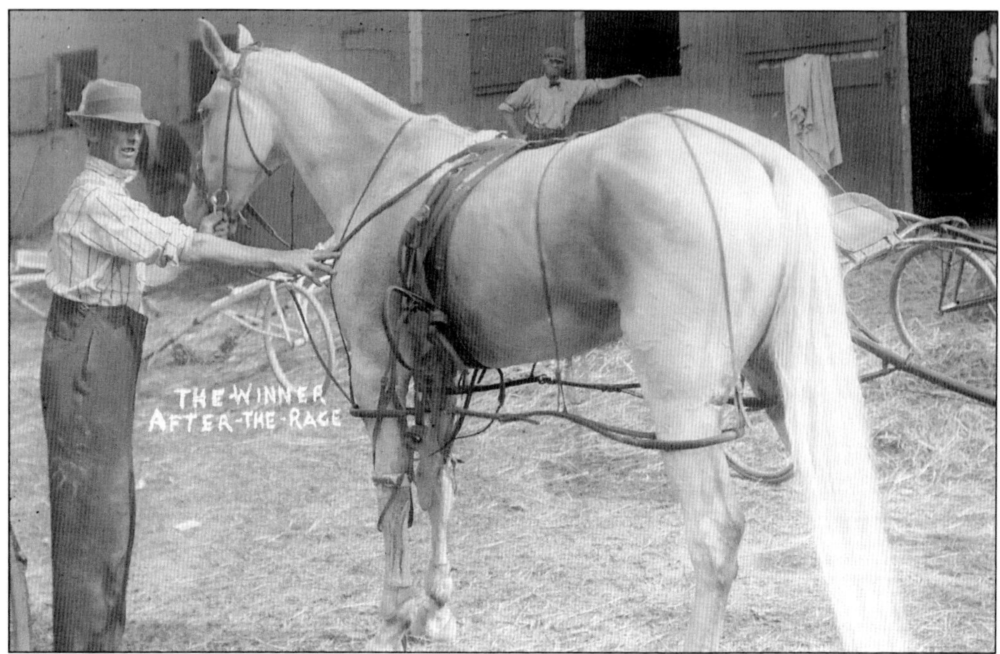

The Winning Horse. Horse racing at fairs was originally a hard sell to agricultural societies in Massachusetts. Once added, they became a mainstay of the entertainment. At the Barnstable fair, harness racing was popular. The horse was harnessed to a small, lightweight carriage known as a sulky and raced at either a trot or a pace.

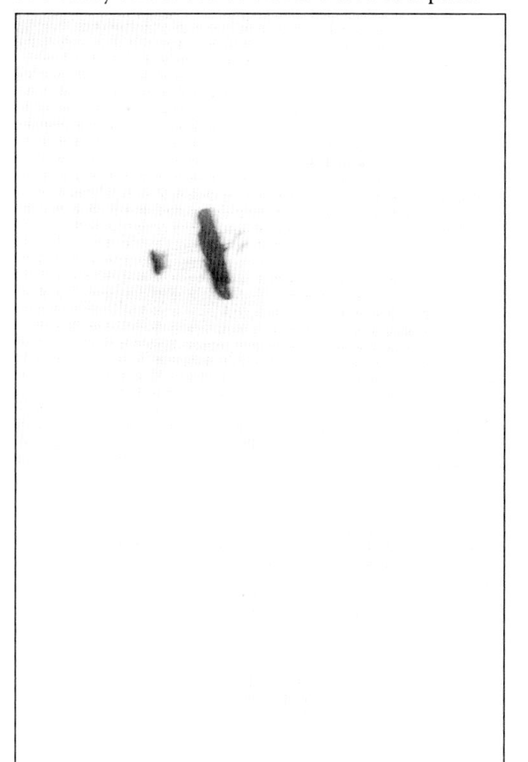

Airplane Flyover. Pictured in 1915, airplanes were just beginning to capture the imagination of the nation. After World War I, barnstorming shows became a popular attraction. Prior to that, both the Wright brothers and Glenn Curtiss entertained the crowds at agricultural fairs.

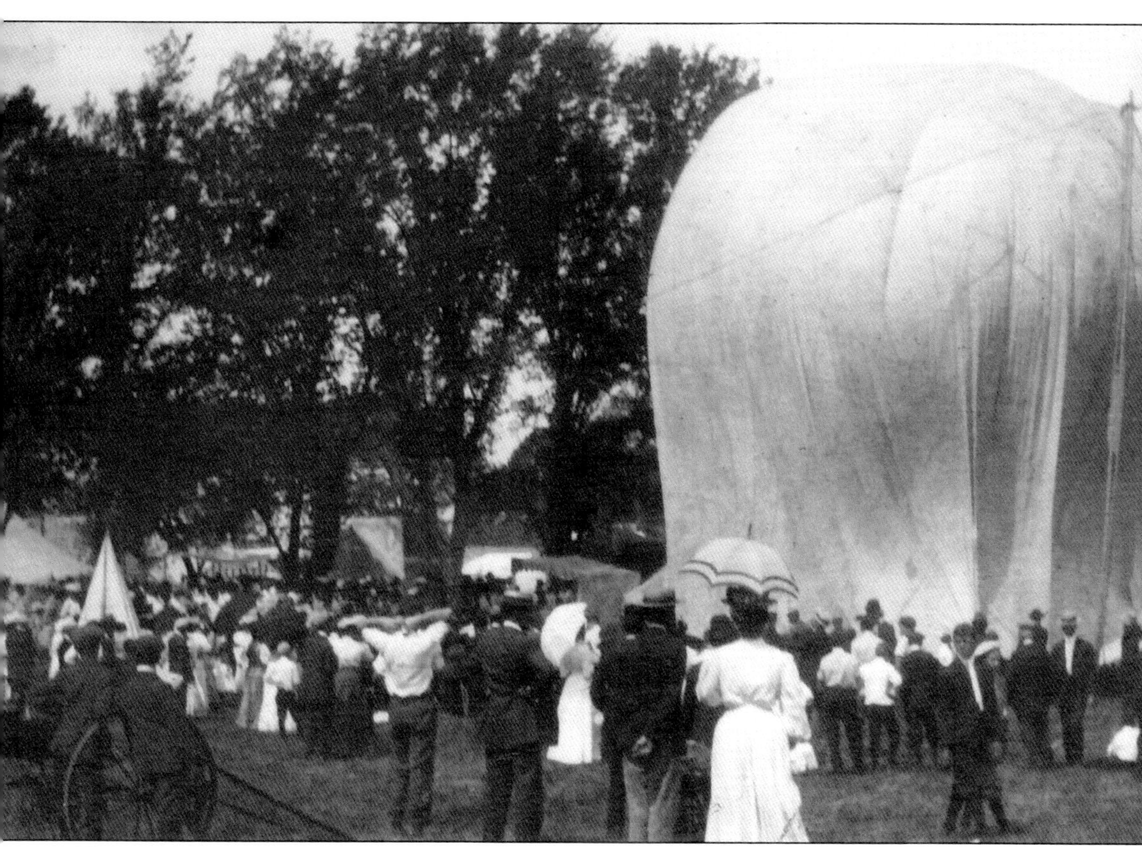

Hot Air Balloon. At the 1913 Barnstable County Fair, a hot air balloon made ascensions on Wednesday and Thursday. During the Thursday show, a parachutist jumped from the balloon and landed in a field next to the fairgrounds. The *Barnstable Patriot* provided information about the jump but didn't mention whether the balloon was tethered to the ground or not.

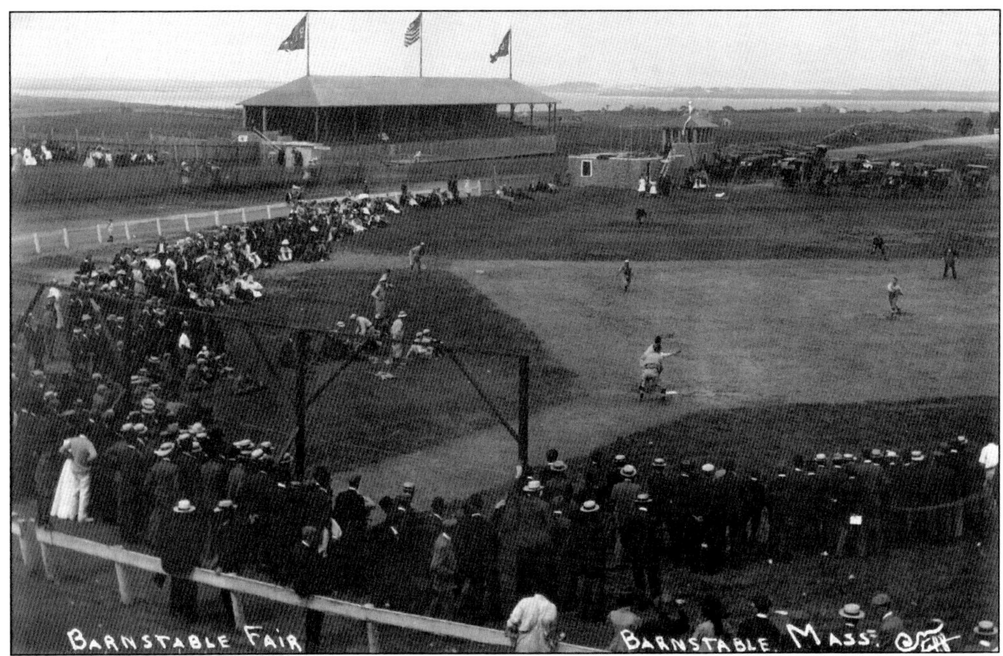

BARNSTABLE COUNTY FAIR BASEBALL. Baseball has been played as a league sport in Barnstable since 1885. Traditionally, the championship game was held at the fair. High school teams would also occasionally play there.

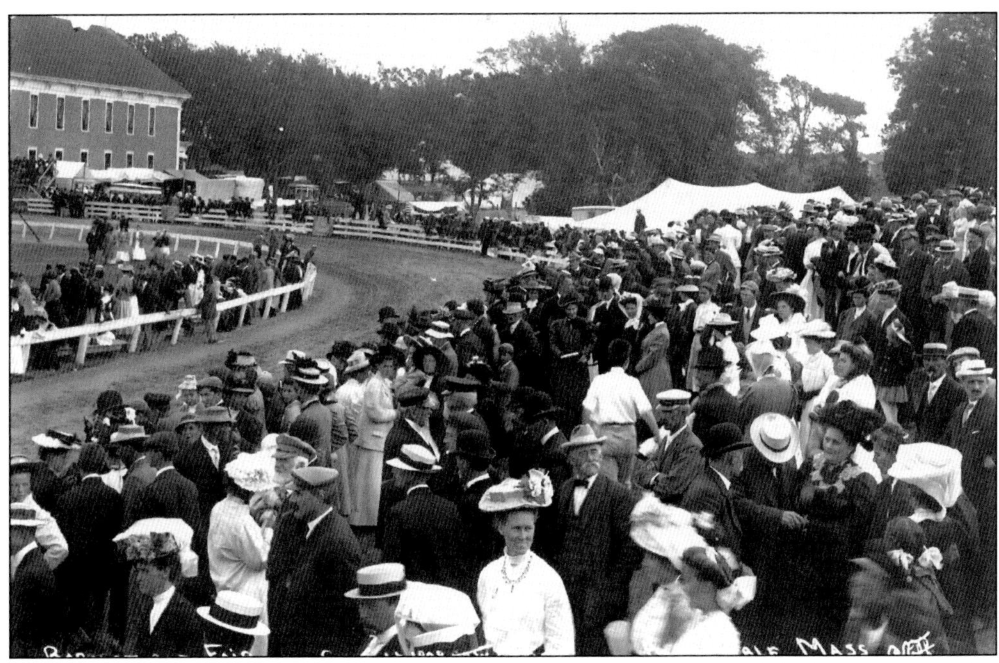

CROWD AT THE HORSERACE. This crowd is eagerly awaiting the start of the horserace. At the 1921 fair, there were 50 horses competing for 25 prizes. Many would come from far away to watch the racing.

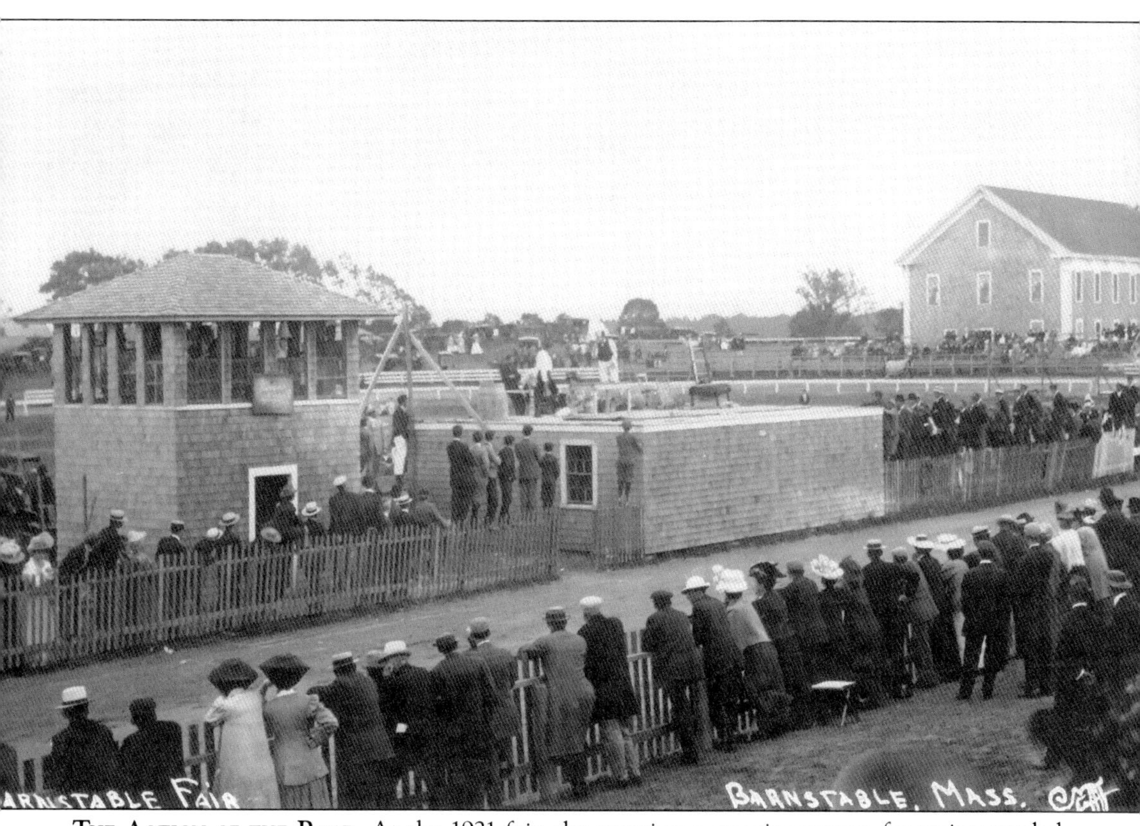

The Action of the Race. At the 1921 fair, the premiums, or prize money, for racing totaled over $600. Harness racing, rather than racing on horseback, was the popular sport for fairs. The horses would pull a sulky and the racing speed would either be at a trot or pace. About 80 percent of the races held in America were pacing races.

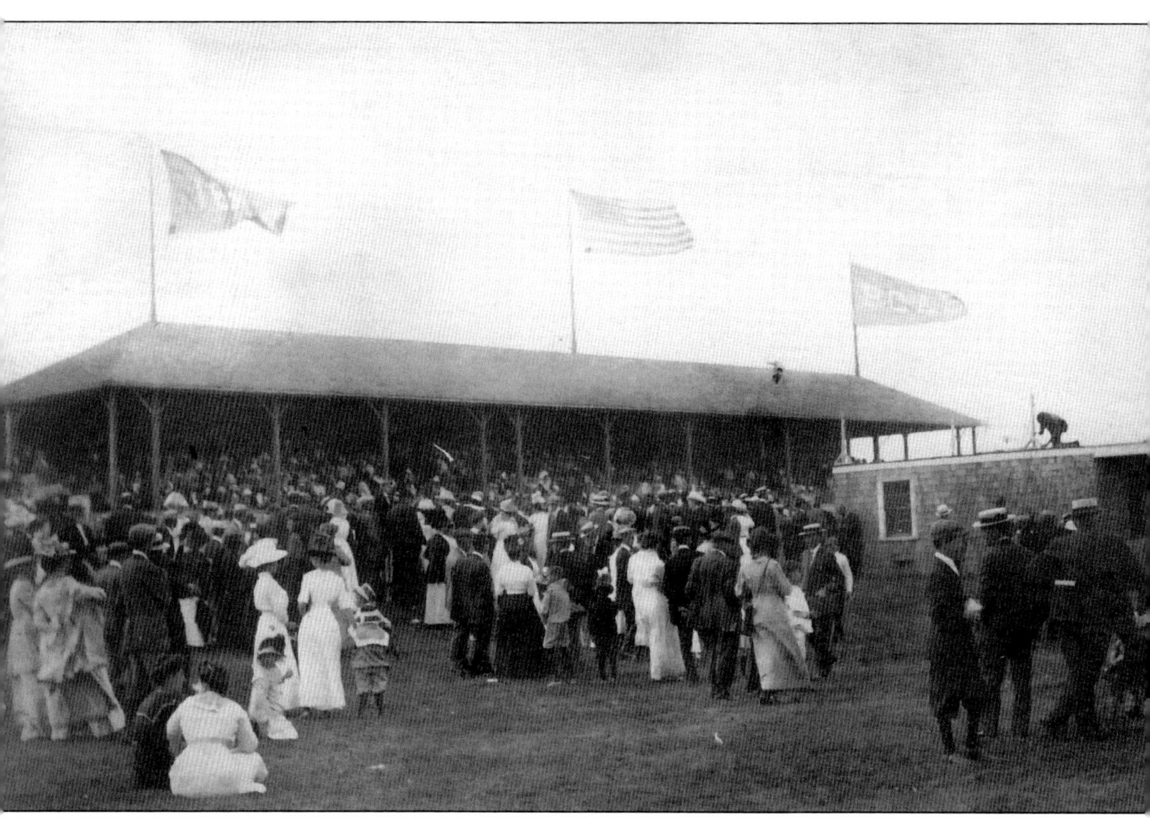

Crowd at the Bandstand. The crowd at the fair on Wednesday, also known as Governor's Day, in 1921 was estimated at 7,500 people. Local and state politicians could not pass up the opportunity to address a large crowd, and it seems that the fairgoers eagerly anticipated the governor's address. During their time in office, Gov. Eben Draper and his successor Gov. David Walsh were popular speakers at the fair. The large number of attendees in 1921 would not be topped until the fair was revived for the 1939 tercentenary celebration. The grandstand stood witness to speeches given by politicians as well as harness racing, parades, and other entertainment. However, it would not stand the test of time and had to be rebuilt for the tercentenary.

Five

Centerville

Depending on the historian, Centerville was once named either Chequaquet or Wequaquet. Amos Otis, genealogist of Barnstable, remarked on the fact that both were Native American names and discussed in great detail the etymology of both terms. The answer to these conjectures is lost in the mists of time, as no real record exists of the village's early days. Most will concur that Centerville's early history began at Phinneys Lane. At this location, the first church in the village was built in 1796.

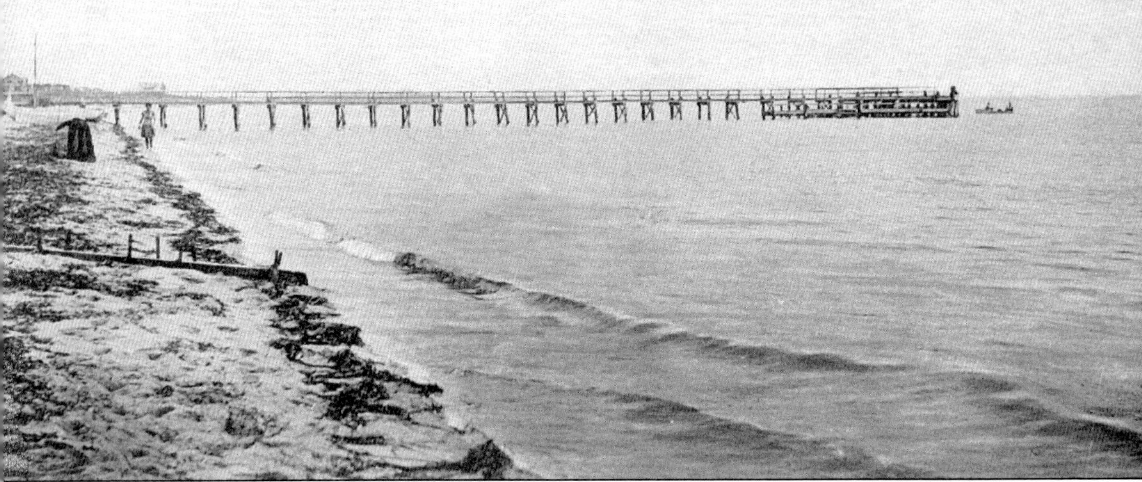

CENTERVILLE PIER, CRAIGVILLE BEACH. This pier was built around 1854 by the Centerville Wharf Company, owned by 32 stockholders. The wharf and its buildings were erected near the present location of the Barnstable municipal bathhouses at Craigville Beach. At a meeting held in 1854, it was voted to rent the shipyard on the company's premises for building vessels of 200 tons or less for $10 per vessel, including the use of the pump. The company also established a wharf tariff on items such as flour, nails, sugar, coffee, tea, cheese, apples, and coal. A charge of $2 was applied to boats tying up to the wharf for the season. In May 1879, the wharf company sold its buildings at auction for $73 to Enoch Lewis, and the land was sold to Gorham Crosby for $8.50. The records indicate that the pier was washed away in a storm sometime after 1900.

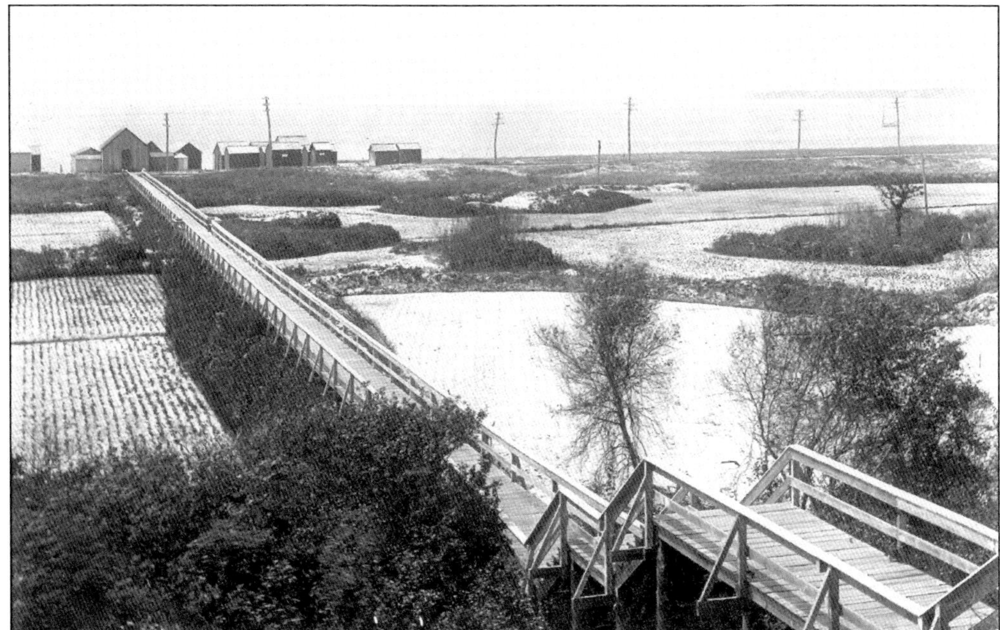

Board Walk, Craigville Beach. In 1872, the Christian Camp Meeting Association was formed after visiting ministers decided they liked the location for a religious colony. The bluff, known as Strawberry Hill, was purchased in that year, as was 800 feet of beach. A boardwalk was added to ease the walk from the bluff.

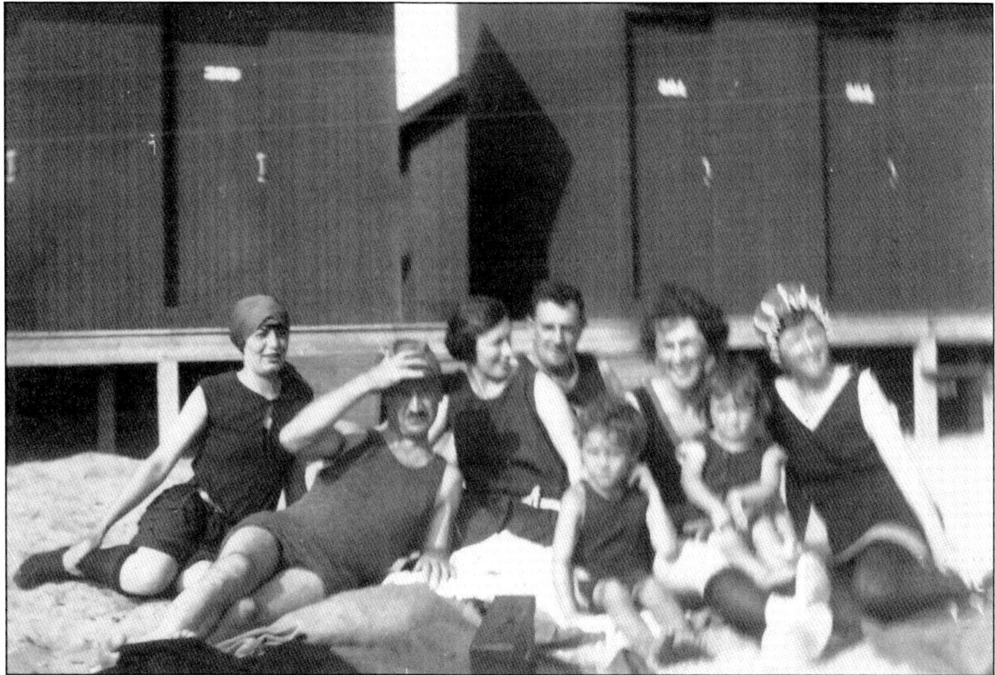

Bathers, Craigville Beach. The beach below the camp association was purchased from the Hyannis Land Company for $2,800. In 1908, the association decided to open the beach to the general public and 72 wooden bathhouses were built. In 1925, that number increased to 500.

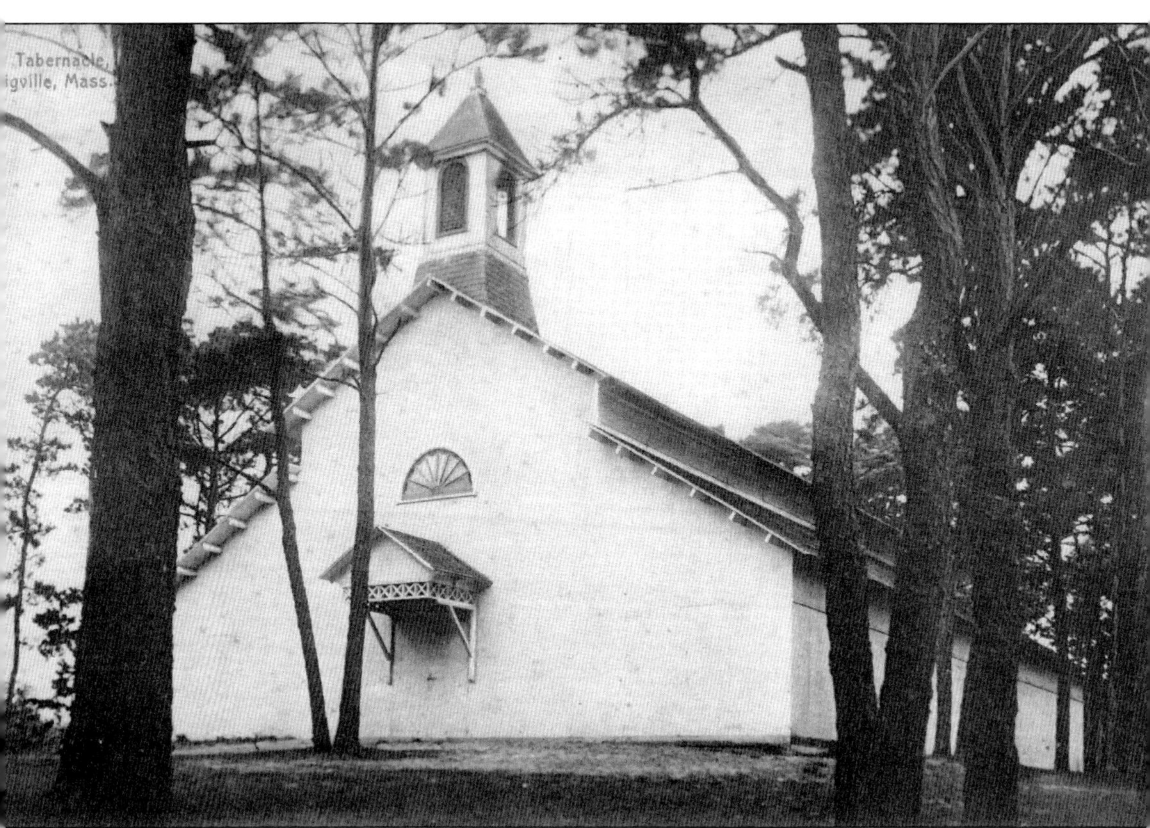

Christian Camp Meeting Association. By 1873, the CCMA was planned and laid out with 288 lots for cottages, space for a tabernacle, two hotels, a store, and two public parks. The newly constructed tabernacle had seating for 600 and cost under $1,000. It was constructed in the summer, and in it, visitors could hear sermons preached three times daily. Regular prayer meetings followed the sermons in the afternoon and evenings. Seventeen ministers were on hand that first year to assist with the services.

Civil War Monument. A committee was chosen by the Town of Barnstable in 1866 to procure and place a monument to the Civil War dead. They chose Centerville, near the store of Ferdinand G. Kelly, for the monument, which is 15 feet high and is made of granite quarried in Concord. It was dedicated July 4, 1866, with band music and an address by George Marston.

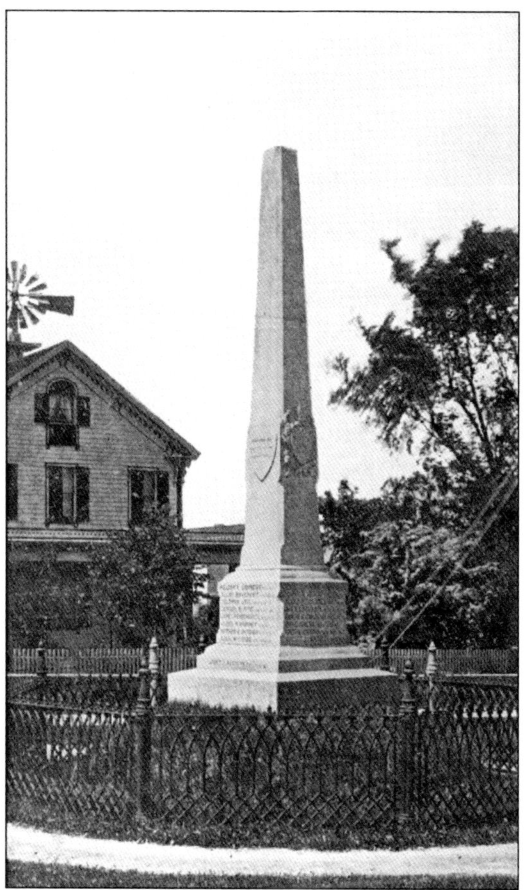

The Old School Bus. Elna Nelson recalled that local kids were once picked up by a school wagon in front of the old post office. On rainy days, the kids would crowd inside the post office, and it would get somewhat noisy. Luckily, as Elna recalled, the postmistress was quite deaf.

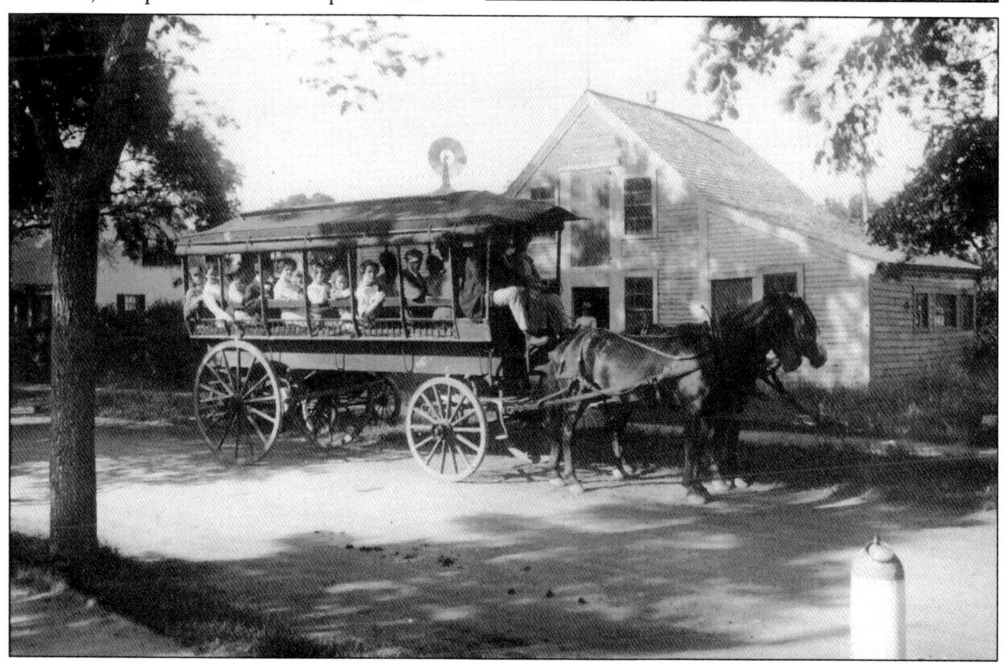

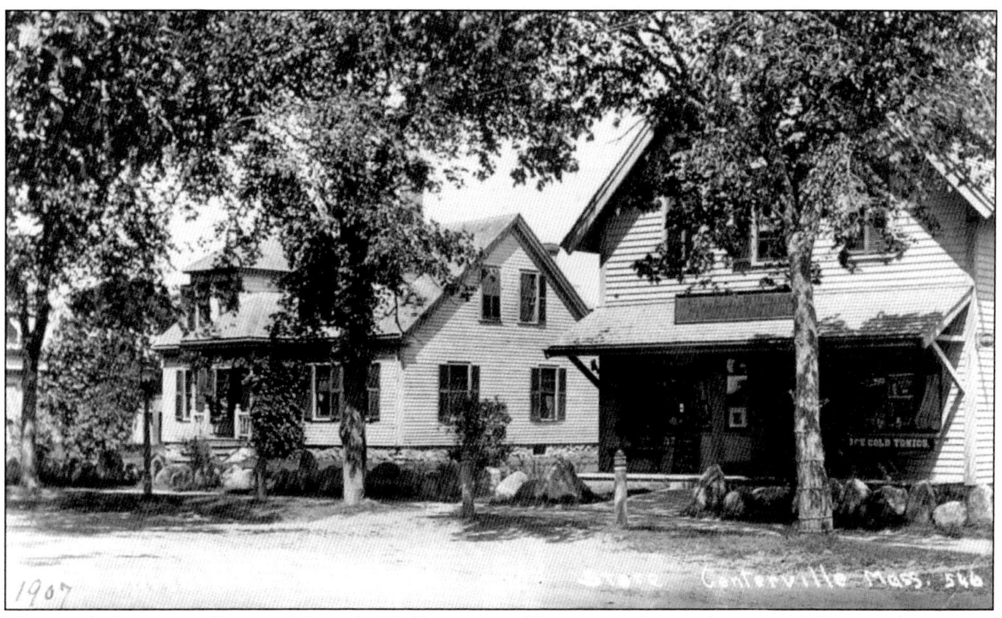

Hallet's General Store. Moses F. Hallett started his general store here in 1868, now known as the "1856 Store," He took his son on as a partner after 1874. Note that the sign on the building reads "S. Hallett."

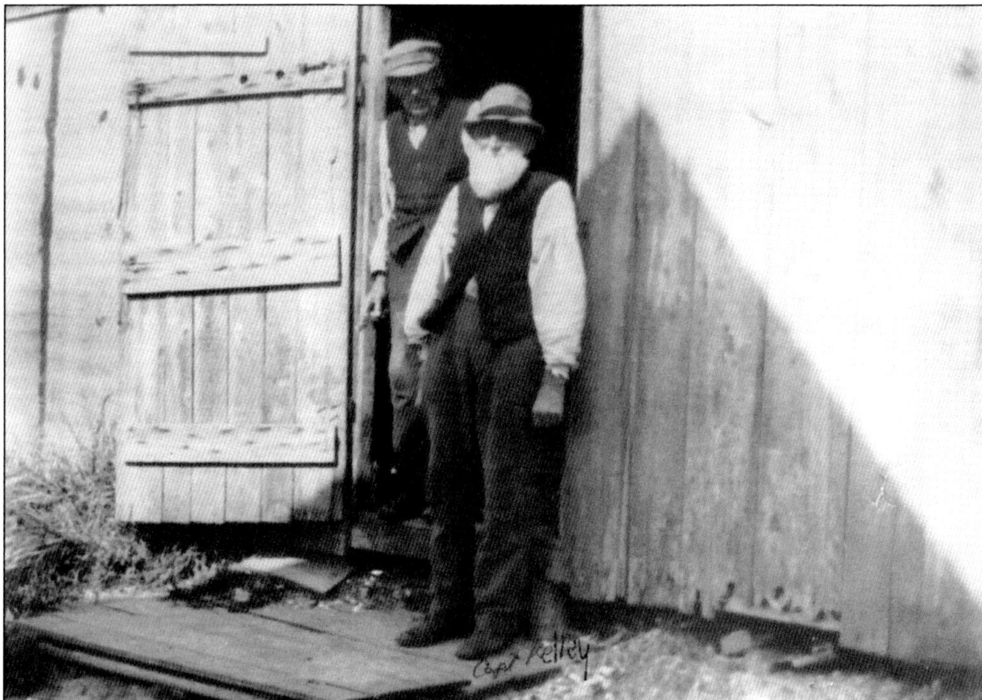

Centerville Sea Captains. Capt. Zenas Bearse (left) and Capt. James Delap Kelley are pictured here. Elna Nelson wrote that Captain Kelley was a determined old curmudgeon. He was known to village youths as the "umbrella man" because he carried an umbrella in rain or shine, winter and summer.

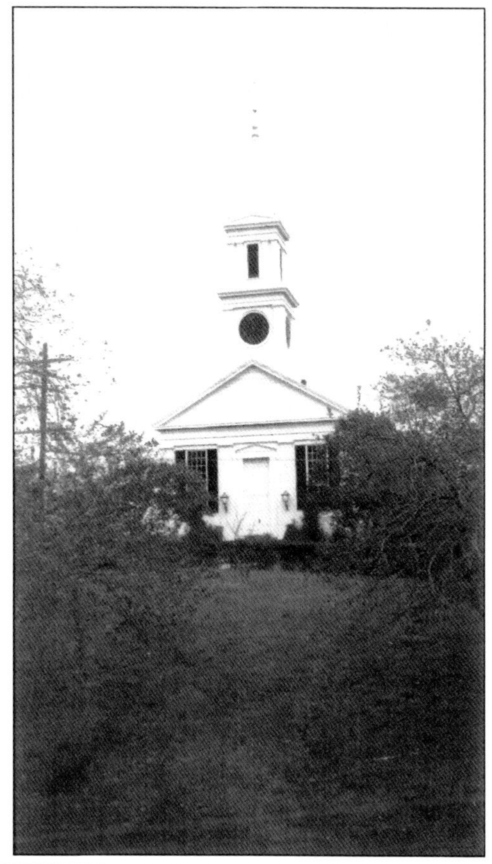

South Congregational Church. This church was originally built in 1796 in the Phinneys Lane area of Centerville. In 1828, the church was dismantled and moved by oxcart to its current location on Main Street. A steeple and bell were added in 1848.

Church Steeple, Northeast View. This is a view of Centerville from the steeple of the South Congregational Church looking northeast. The photograph shows a relatively undeveloped Main Street.

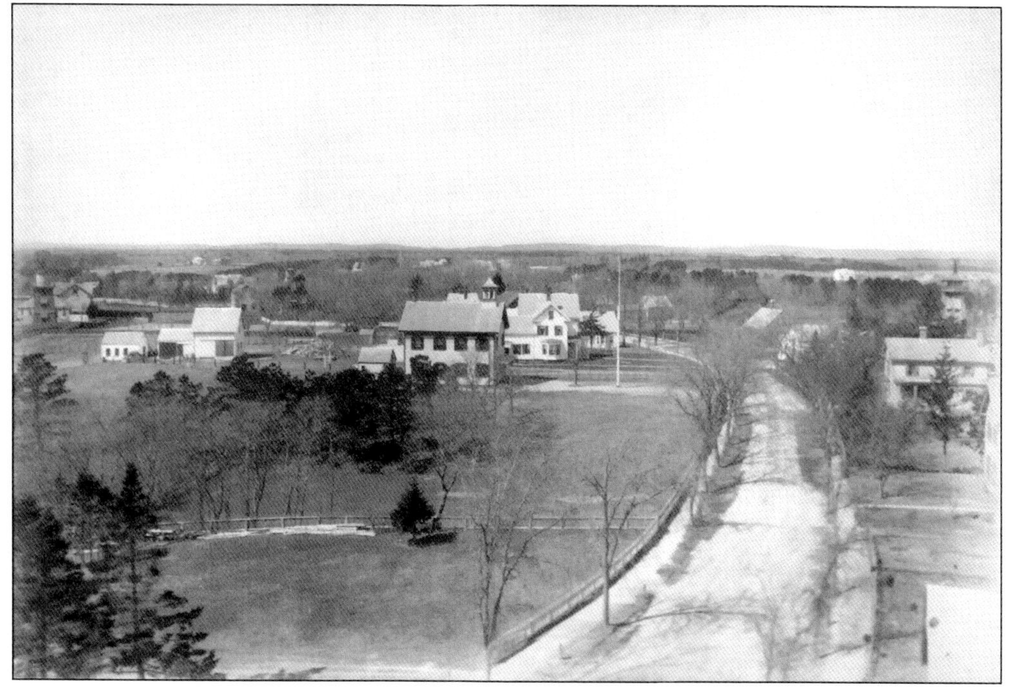

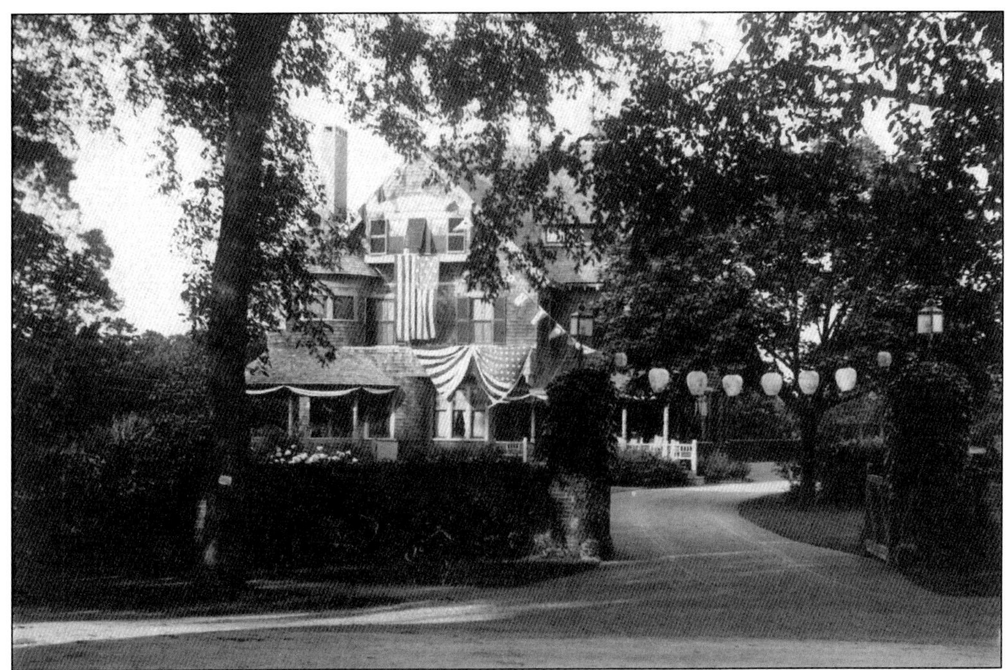

FERNBROOK, THE MARSTON HOME. This house was originally built in 1881 by Howard Marston, son of Capt. Russell Marston, founder of the Marston restaurants of Boston. It is shown here decorated for Old Home Week, which was first held in August 1904. The grounds were designed by Frederick Law Olmstead; in the early years, the Marston family would bring in children to enjoy a walk among the gardens.

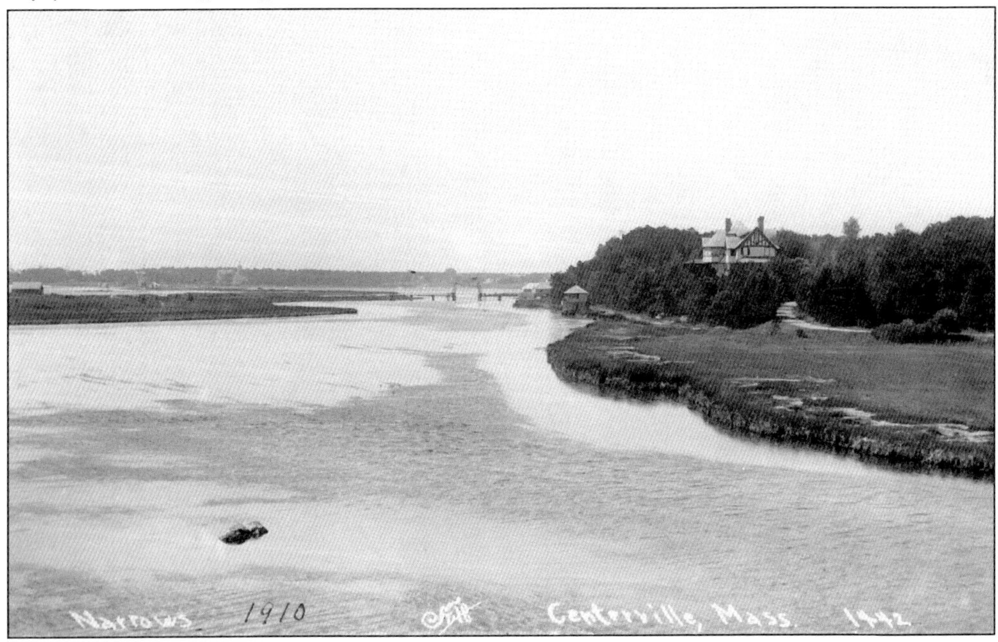

CENTERVILLE NARROWS. This is an ideal view of the Centerville River (also known as the Chequaquet River) with a bridge in place. Before the bridge was built, a ferry was operated by Prentiss Kelley. The fare was 2¢.

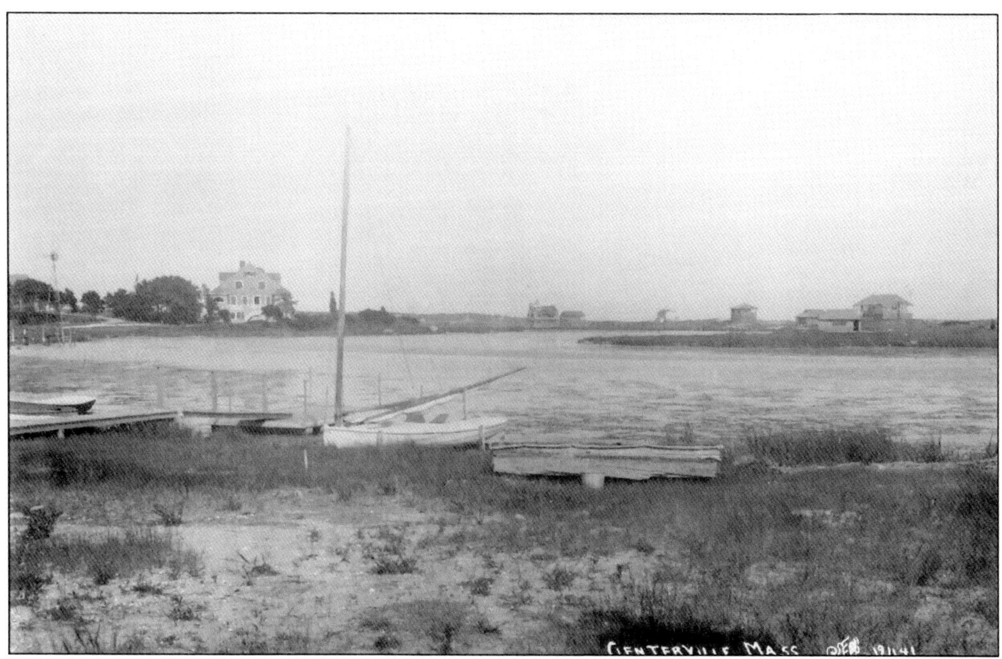

SAILBOATS, CENTERVILLE RIVER. The Christian Camp Association's new camp facility was located near this idyllic spot.

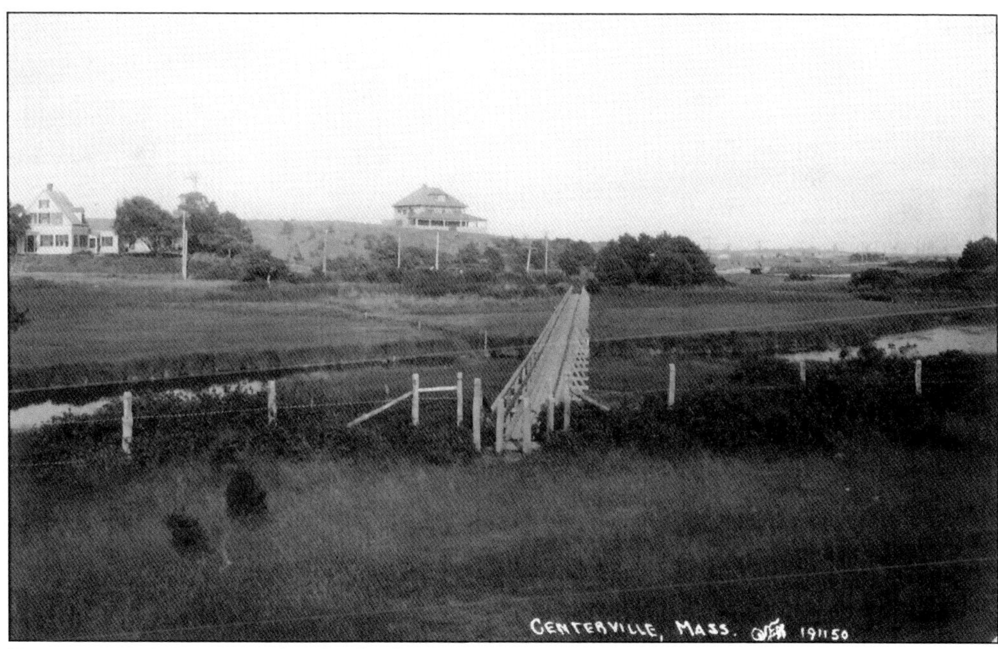

FOOTBRIDGE CROSSING. This footbridge was used to cross the marsh between Chequaquet and Oyster Island. Legend has it that a young man returning home from visiting a young lady on Oyster Island found that the bridge was gone, forcing him to walk the long way around on Bumps River Road.

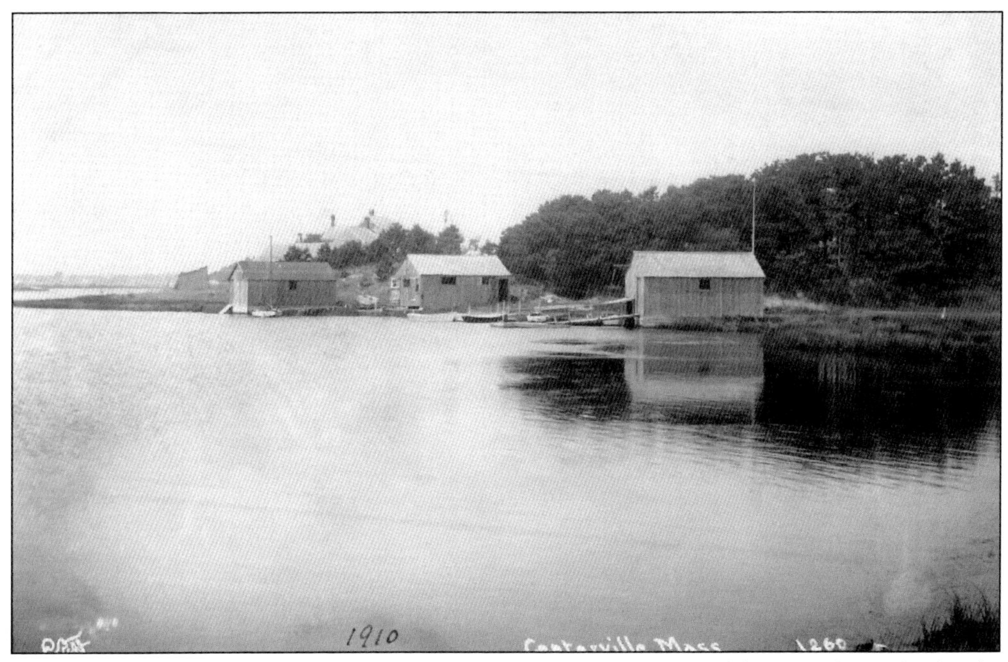

Boathouses. This picturesque scene shows boathouses on the edge of the river during high tide. The houses stored boats and gear in the off-season.

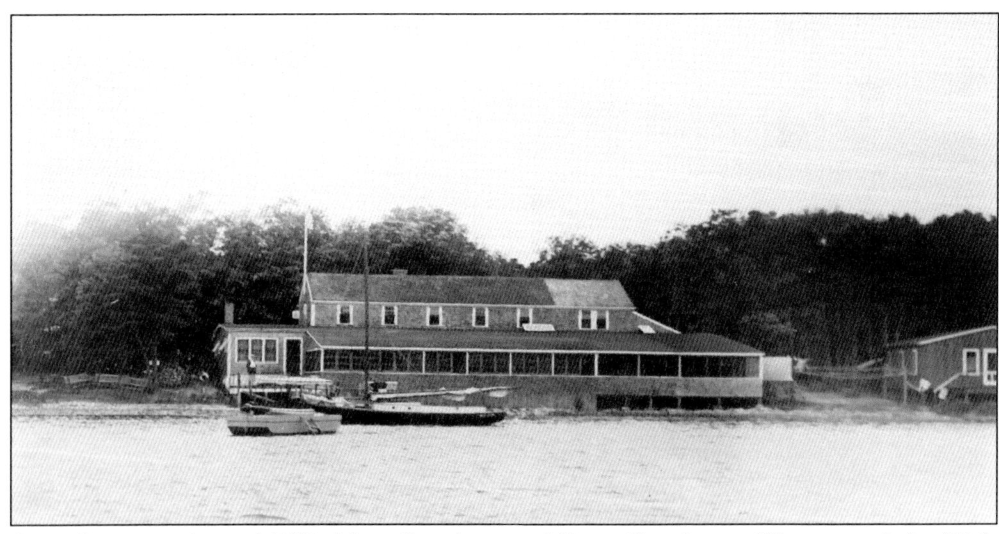

Camp Opechee. Around 1903, Albert Starck opened Camp Opechee on Wequaquet Lake. With the advent of tourism in Barnstable, by the 1870s, the lake became a prime spot for vacationing. The name was changed during an 1891 boat race from Nine Mile Pond to Wequaquet Lake sponsored by Howard Marston.

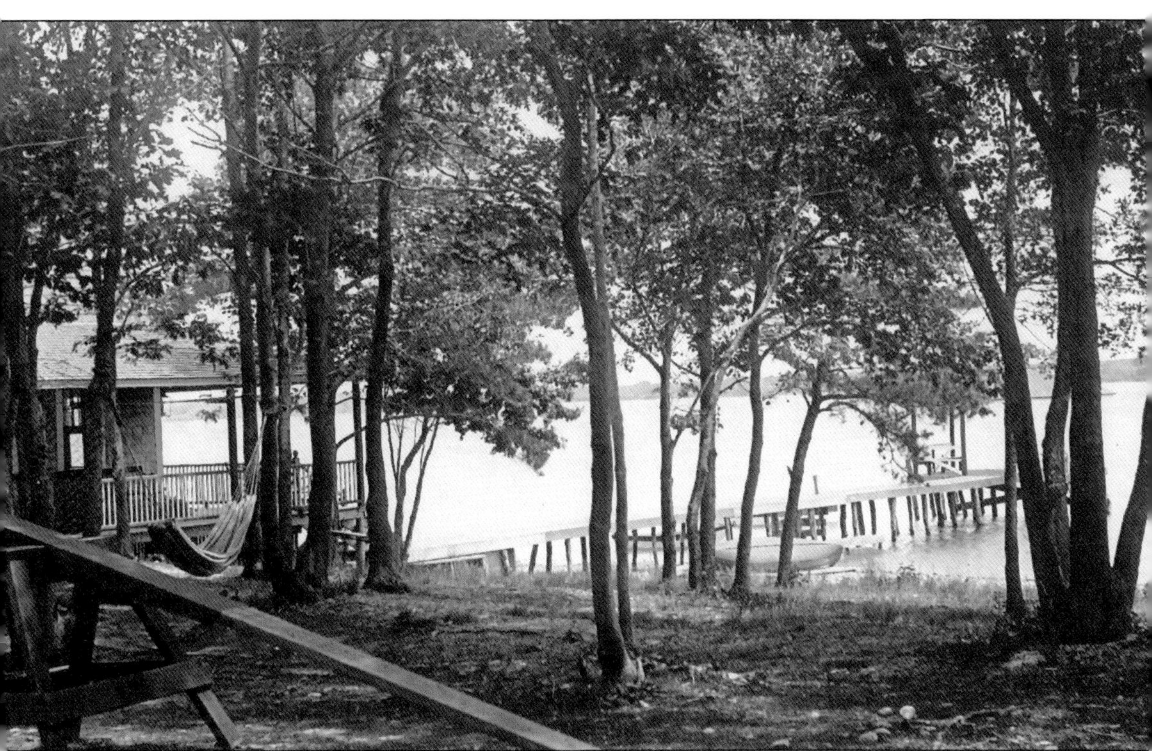

PIER AT CAMP OPECHEE. This pier was for the launching of pleasure craft for the camp at Wequaquet Lake. Boating had taken a firm hold on the town and had become a very popular activity on the lake. A small fleet of catboats navigated the waters, bringing pleasure to countless sailors. Fishing became just as popular, and in 1925, a 42-pound German carp was fished from the lake. It was estimated to be about 100 years old.

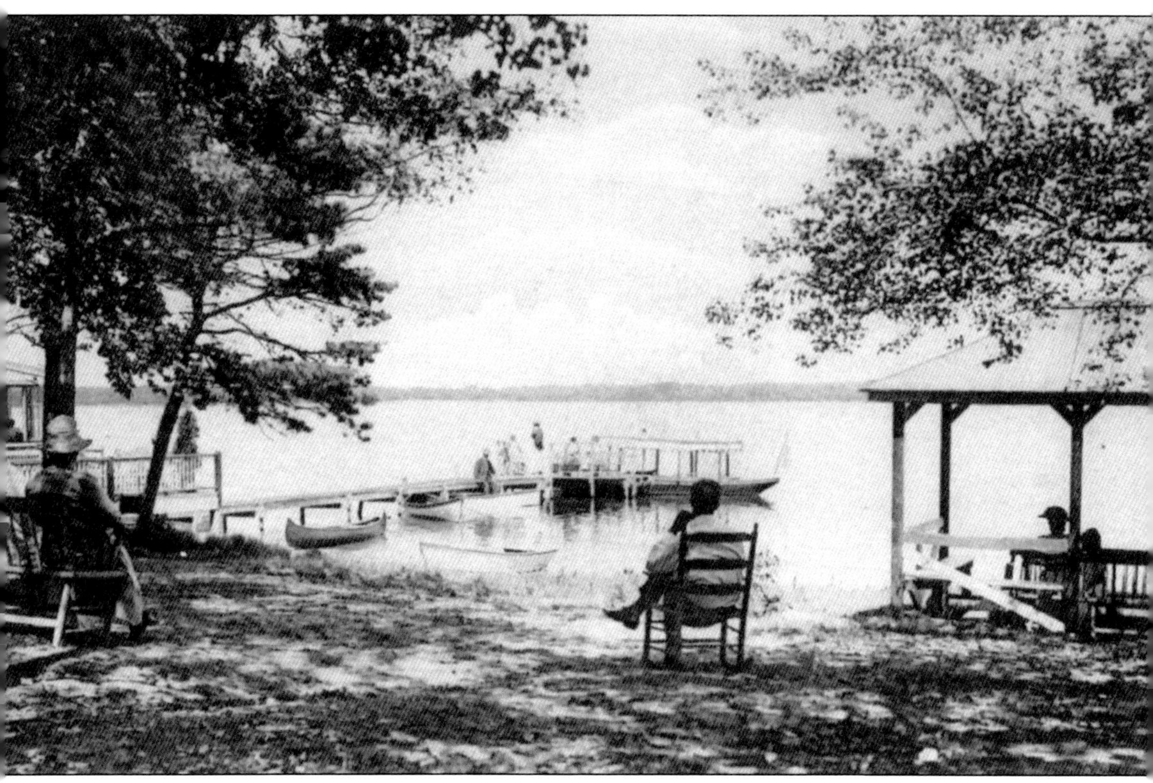

Launch at End of Pier, Camp Opechee. In addition to small catboats plying the water, there was a large steamer called the *Rambler* and smaller, gas-powered craft called naptha launches. The Rambler was used to provide tours of the lake and was a popular feature of the camp. Opechee would later become the clubhouse for the Wequaquet Yacht Club.

Six

1939 Tercentenary

At a Barnstable town meeting in 1935, the moderator was directed to appoint a committee of 10 residents to consider plans for a town-wide celebration of the tercentenary in 1939. By 1938, the plans were detailed in the town report. The general plan put forth by the committee was to arrange special church services, to put on a historical pageant that would be a celebration of the coming of the first settlers in 1639, to erect memorial tablets to honor some of the town's "worthy" men and mark important historic sites, to publish a historic volume and other materials such as a brochure, to emphasize in a series of Village Weeks the role played in the life of the town by the villages, and finally, to plan an event or series of events in which inhabitants of Barnstable, gathered together, could bring the tercentenary to a fitting close. To this end, the committee decided to revive the Barnstable County Fair. Invitations went out to many dignitaries, and to the town's delight, the mayor of Barnstaple, England, accepted an invitation, journeying across the Atlantic to join the celebration.

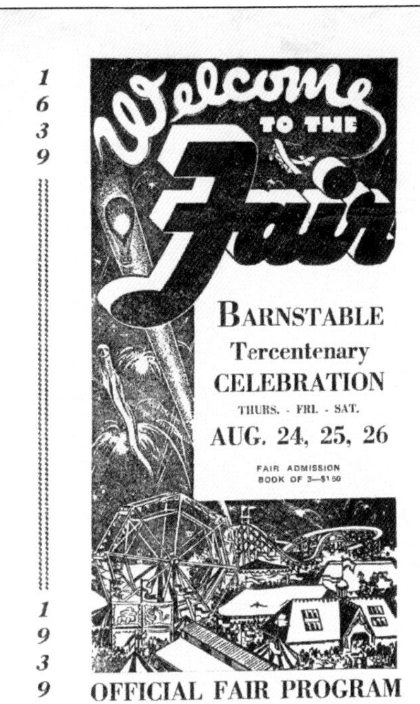

BROCHURE, TERCENTENARY FAIR. This is the brochure that was published for the revived county fair. The fair would run for three days in August and would have a full schedule of exhibits, including baseball games, trotting races, concerts, vaudeville acts, midway attractions, and a nightly display of fireworks.

TERCENTENARY COMMITTEE. The committee as appointed by the town was, from left to right, (seated) Genevieve Leonard, Evelyn Crosby, Ora A. Hinckley, Gladys Swift, and Elizabeth Jenkins; (standing) Donald Trayser, Reginald F. Boles, James F. McLaughlin, Alfred Crocker, and Thomas Otis.

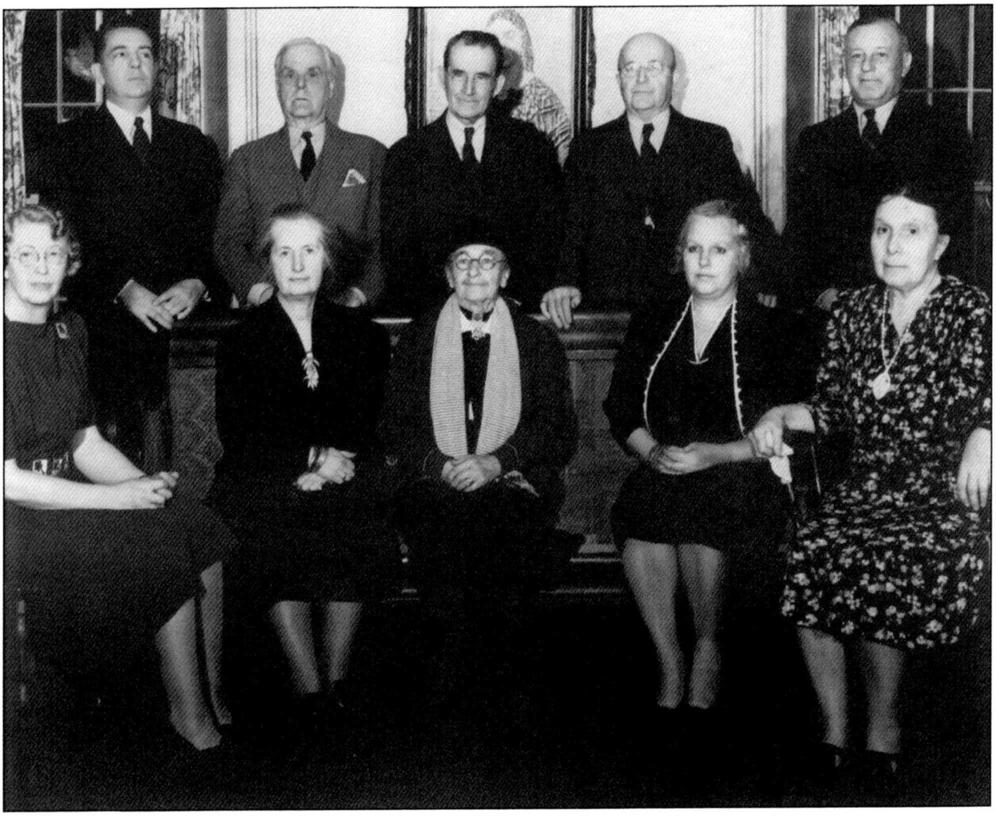

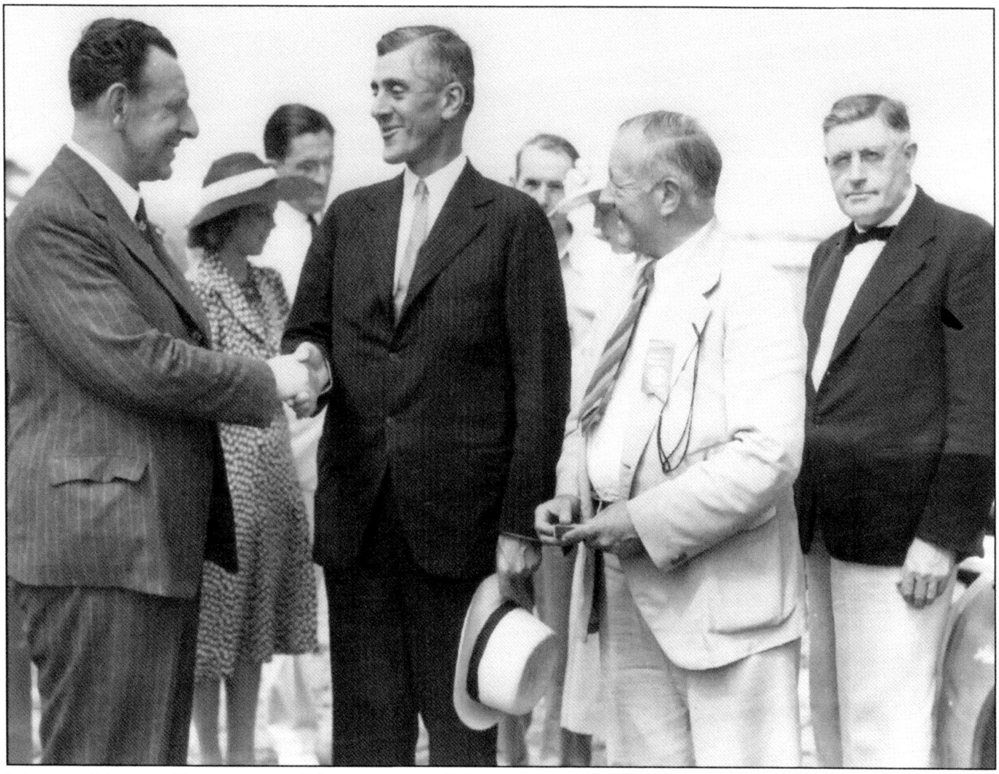

MAYOR MEETS GOVERNOR. The mayor of Barnstaple, England, Charles F. Dart (left) and his wife sailed on the *Laconia* on July 21 and arrived in New York City on July 31. Spending a week in New York, they traveled to Boston and met Gov. Leverett Saltonstall at the statehouse. The mayor and his wife then traveled to Barnstable on August 12 and were taken to the Oyster Harbor Club, where they would stay for the rest of their trip.

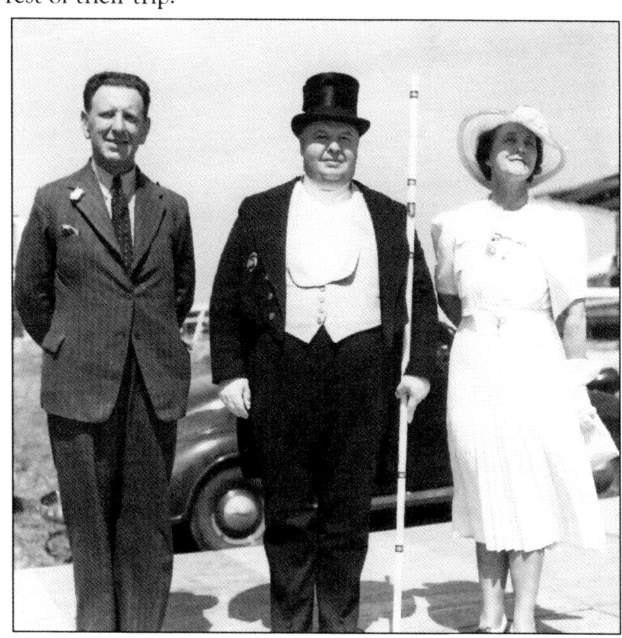

MAYOR MEETS SHERIFF. Mayor Dart (left) and his wife pose with Barnstable County sheriff Lauchlan M. Crocker. The sheriff was dressed in the ceremonial garb of his office, including a staff that he used on special court occasions.

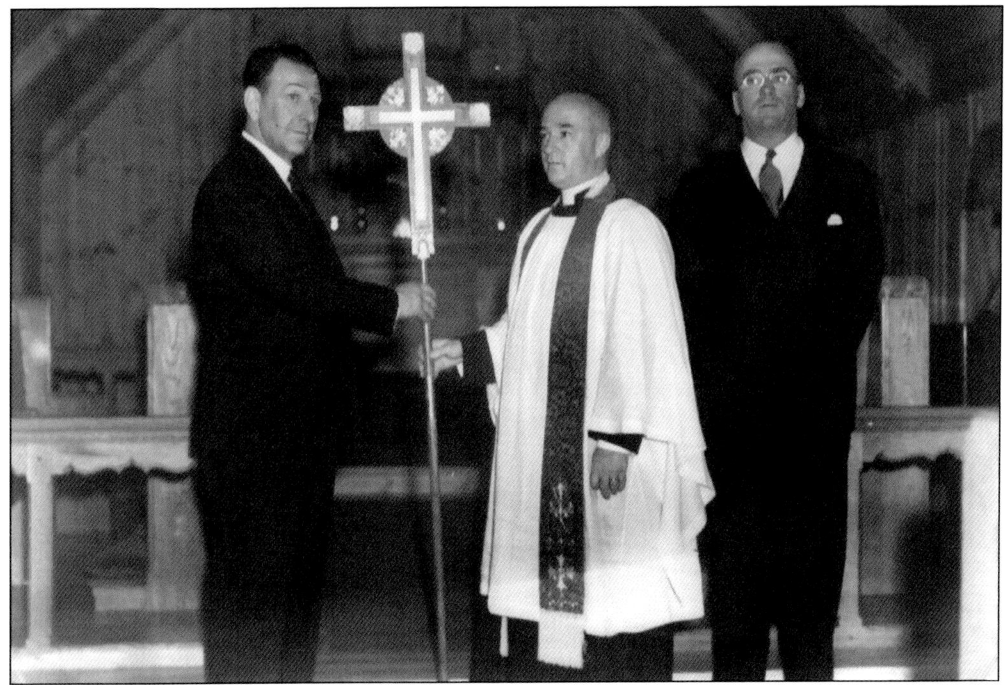

ST. MARY'S EPISCOPAL CHURCH. Mayor Dart is pictured at the presentation of the processional cross to St. Mary's Church on August 20, 1939.

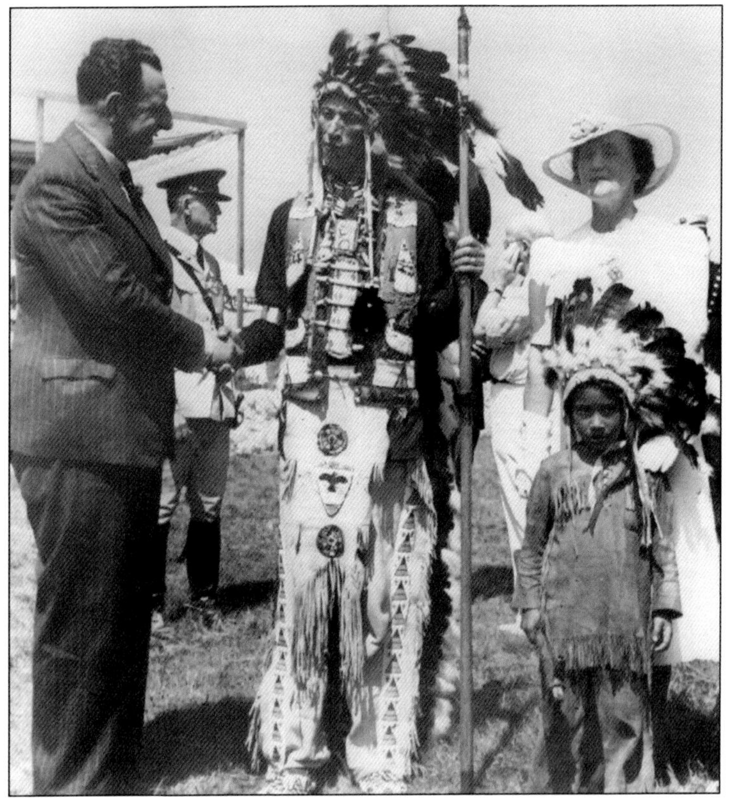

CHIEF BLACKHAWK. On the opening day of the fair, this Native American was introduced to Mayor Dart and his wife as Chief Blackhawk of the Powhatten Federation. Standing next to Mrs. Dart is Chief Blackhawk's youngest son, Wa-Te-Cee, or "Sun Eagle."

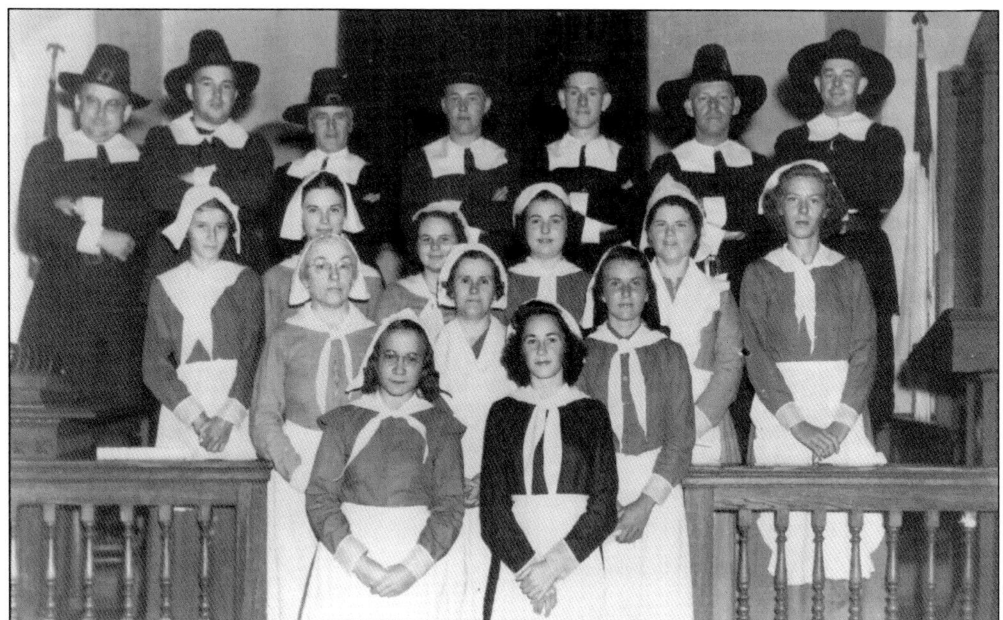

COMMUNITY SERVICE OF PILGRIM PRAISE. The Hyannis Baptist and the Federated Church in Hyannis put on a service that was reminiscent of church services during Colonial times. Both the clergy and the choir were dressed in Colonial costumes, and the address was given by Hyannis historian Clara Jane Hallett.

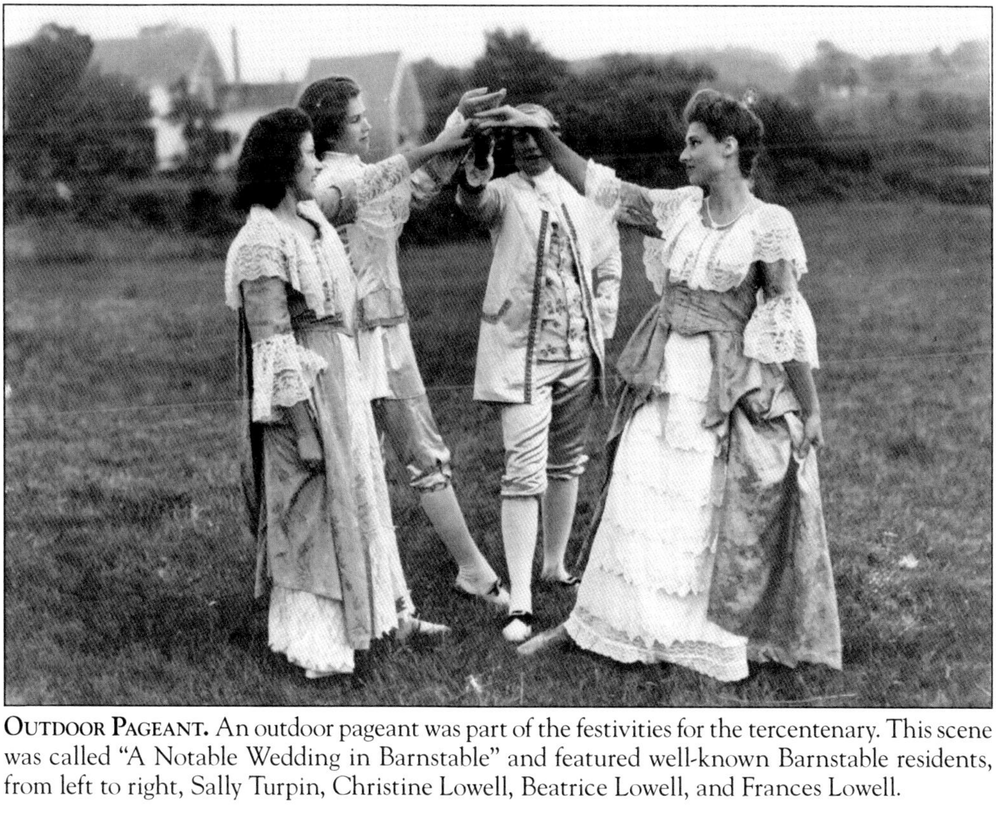

OUTDOOR PAGEANT. An outdoor pageant was part of the festivities for the tercentenary. This scene was called "A Notable Wedding in Barnstable" and featured well-known Barnstable residents, from left to right, Sally Turpin, Christine Lowell, Beatrice Lowell, and Frances Lowell.

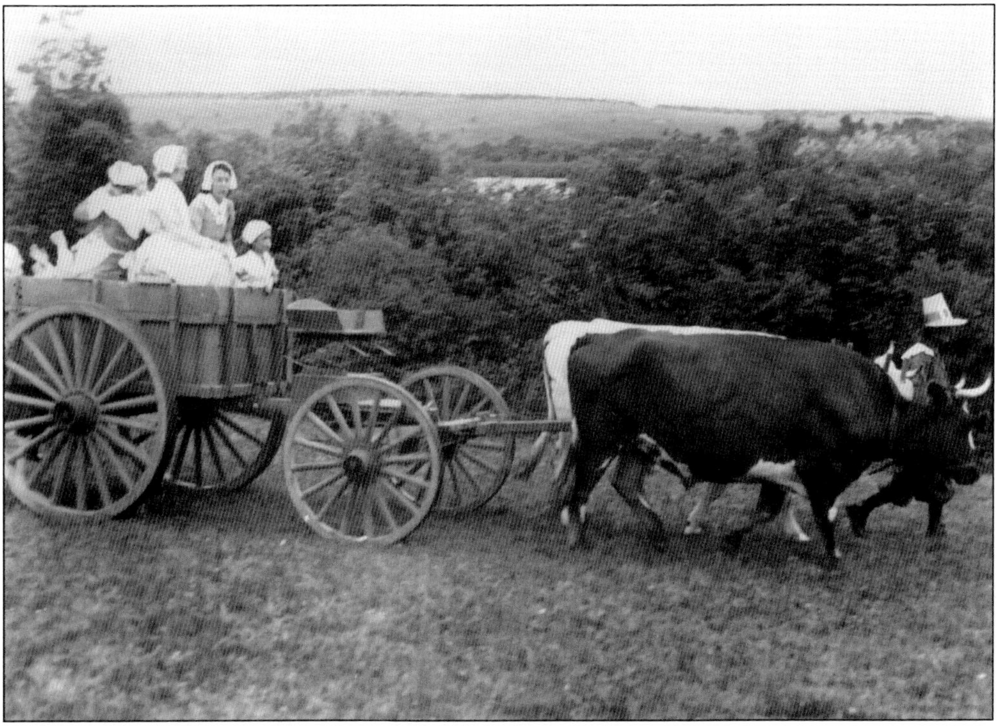

PILGRIM PAGEANT. This is probably part of the pageant "The Coming of John Lothrop, 1639." It featured men, women, and children dressed in Colonial costume pulled by two bulls.

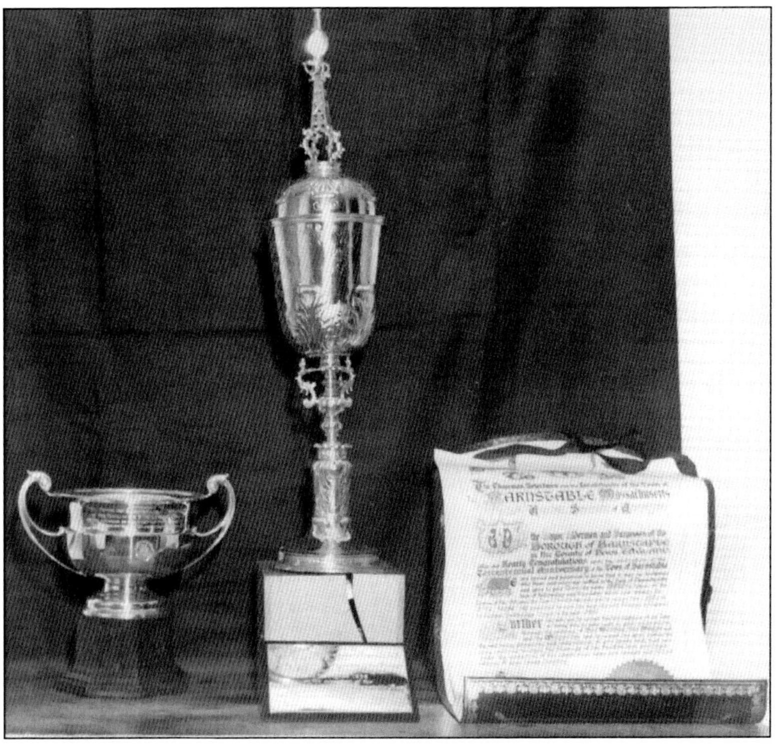

GIFTS FROM BARNSTAPLE. Mayor Dart brought three gifts from Barnstaple to the people of Barnstable. From left to right are a silver bowl from the Association of Barumites in London, a replica of the 15th-century Dodderidge Steeple Cup, and an illuminated scroll conveying municipal greetings from Barnstaple.

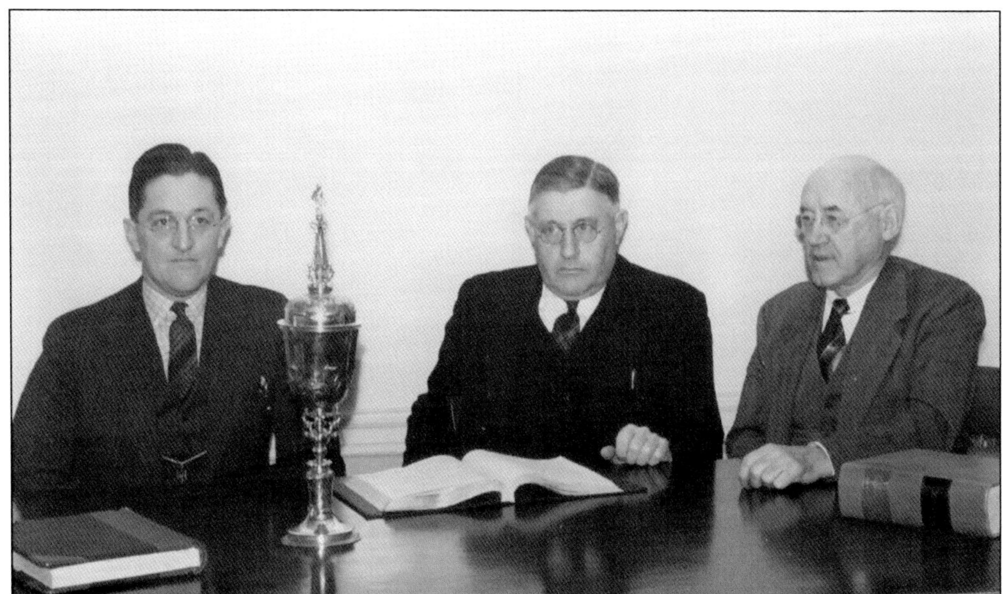

SELECTMEN OF BARNSTABLE. From left to right are selectmen Victor F. Adams, Chester A. Crocker, and James F. Kenney. The selectmen were very pleased that the celebration was considered a success. Along with this photograph, a letter of thanks was sent to the tercentenary committee.

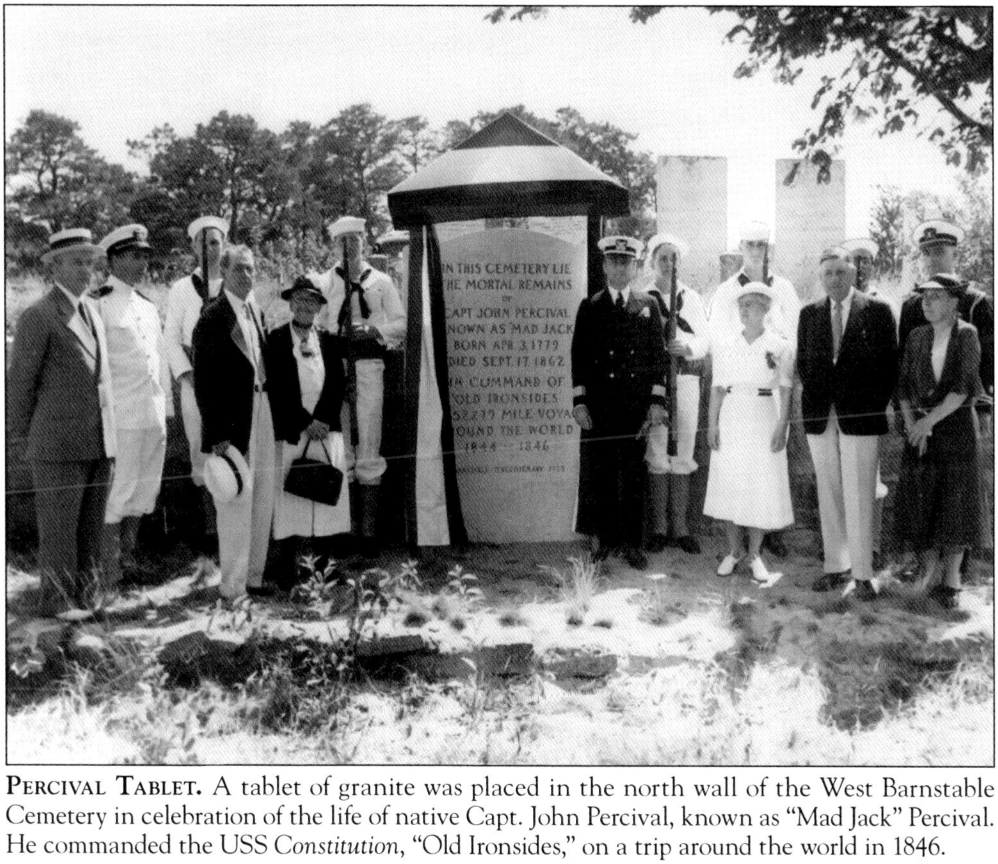

PERCIVAL TABLET. A tablet of granite was placed in the north wall of the West Barnstable Cemetery in celebration of the life of native Capt. John Percival, known as "Mad Jack" Percival. He commanded the USS *Constitution*, "Old Ironsides," on a trip around the world in 1846.

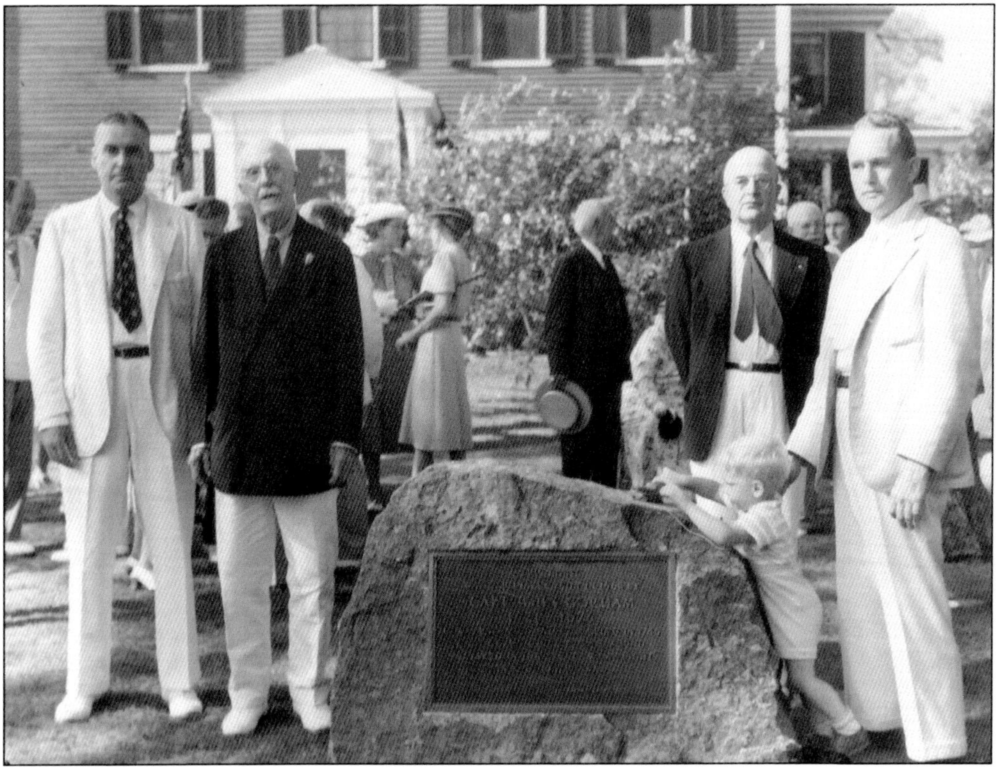

GORHAM TABLET. This tablet is dedicated to Capt. John Gorham, who lost his life in 1676 as a result of wounds suffered in the Great Swamp Fight during King Philips War against the Narraganset Tribe. From left to right are Henry C. Kittredge, Dr. Gorham Baker, Alfred Crocker, Gorham Bacon Harper, and Gorham Bacon Harper Jr.

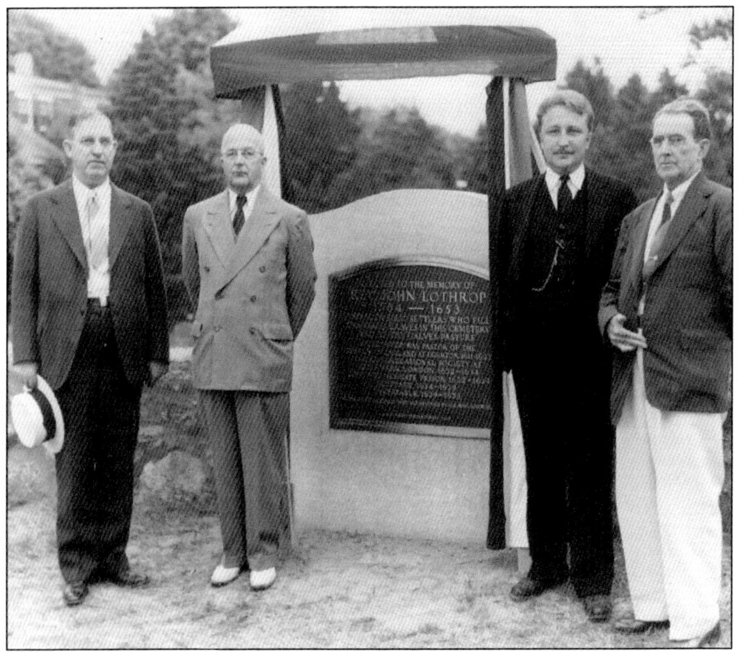

LOTHROP TABLET. This tablet was erected in memory of John Lothrop and the first settlers of Barnstable. From left to right are Representative William F. Jones, Alfred Crocker, Rev. Donald Lothrop, and James McLaughlin.

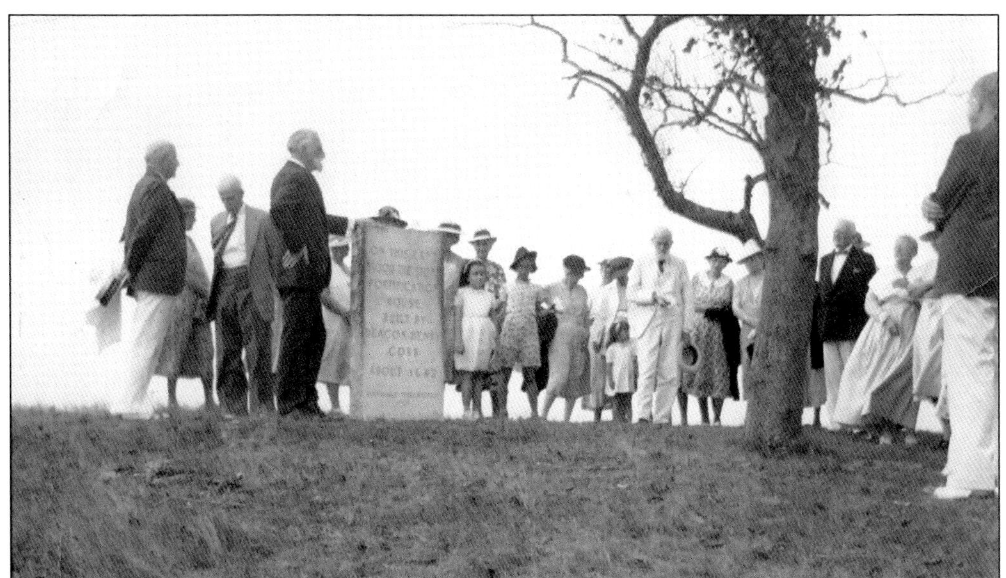

Elder Cobb Tablet. Early settler Henry Cobb was charged with building a fortification house in order to protect settlers from Native Americans. Among those pictured here are George Lyman Kittredge, Richard Cobb, Dorothy Anne Woodward, and James F. McLaughlin.

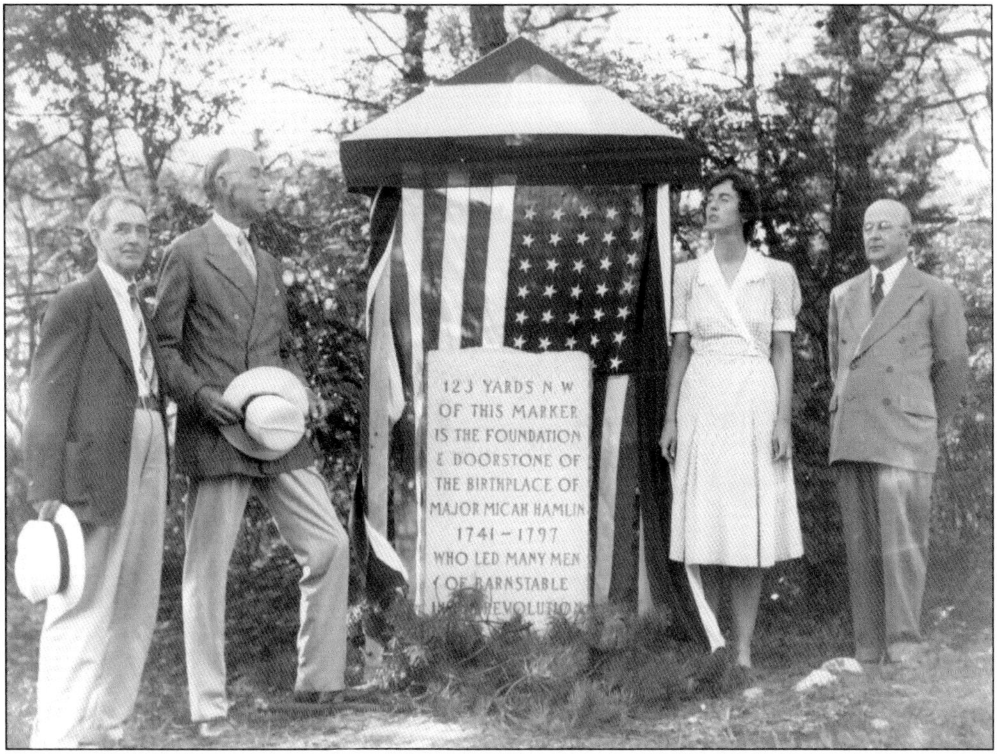

Hamlin Tablet. This tablet is dedicated to Major Mica Hamlin (also spelled Hamblin, Hamblen, and Hamlen), a veteran of the Revolutionary War. He served in several different volunteer Massachusetts regiments during the American Revolution, including the Continental Army. Jane Hamlin is to the right of the tablet.

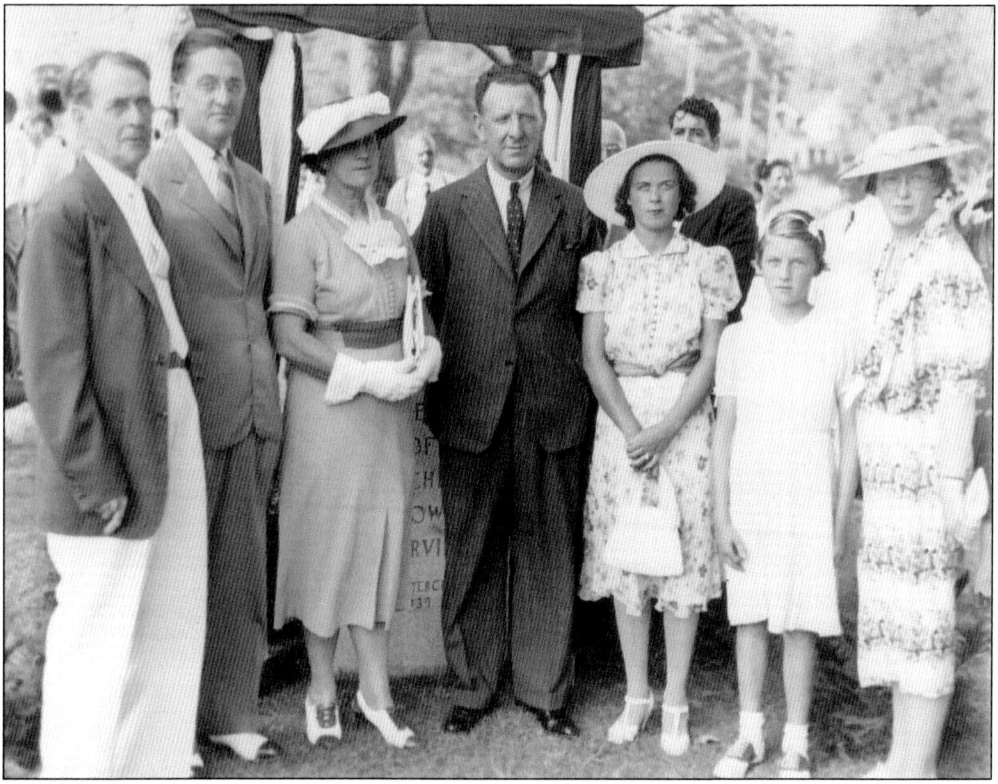

Osterville Tablet. This tablet honors the early settlers of Cotachesset. From left to right are James F. McLaughlin, selectman Victor F. Adams, Mrs. Dart, Mayor Dart, Anne Goodspeed, Genieve Leonard, and Mrs. Victor F. Adams.

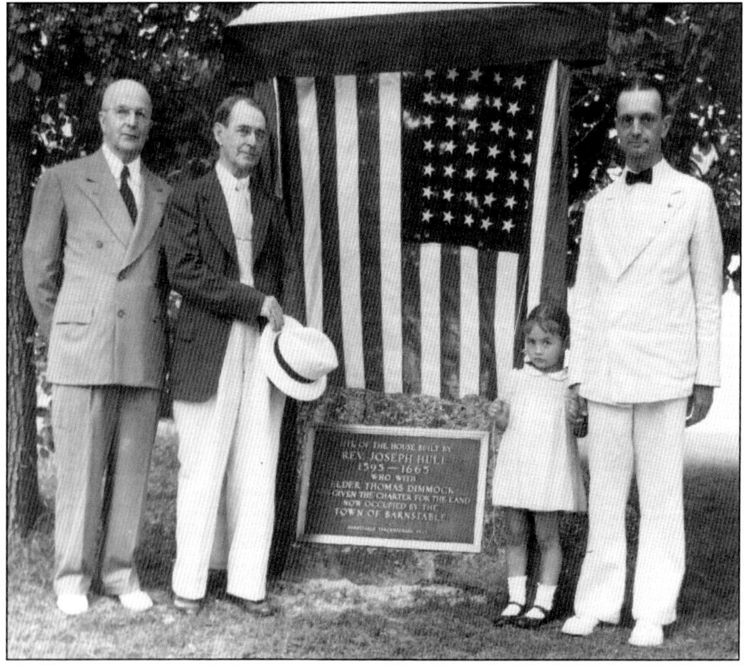

Hull Tablet. This tablet is dedicated to Joseph Hull, who, tradition has it, preached the first sermon in Barnstable before John Lothrop arrived. From left to right are Alfred Crocker, James F. McLaughlin, Anne Howland Maraspin, and Davis G. Maraspin.

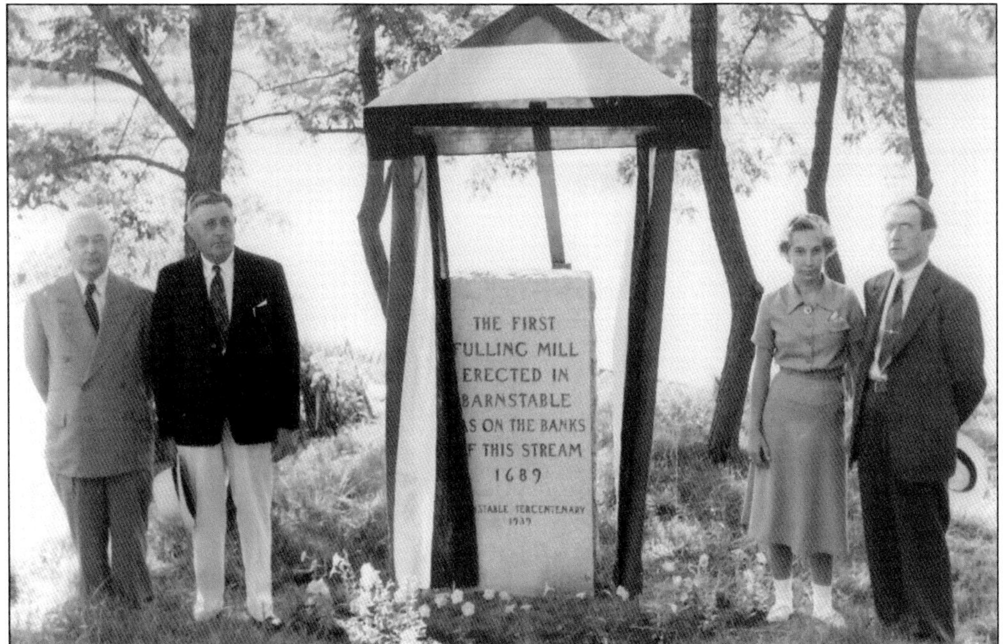

Marstons Mills Tablet. This tablet is dedicated to the first Barnstable fulling mill, erected on Marstons Mills River in 1689. From left to right are Alfred Crocker, Chester A. Crocker, Lena F. Jones, and James F. McLaughlin.

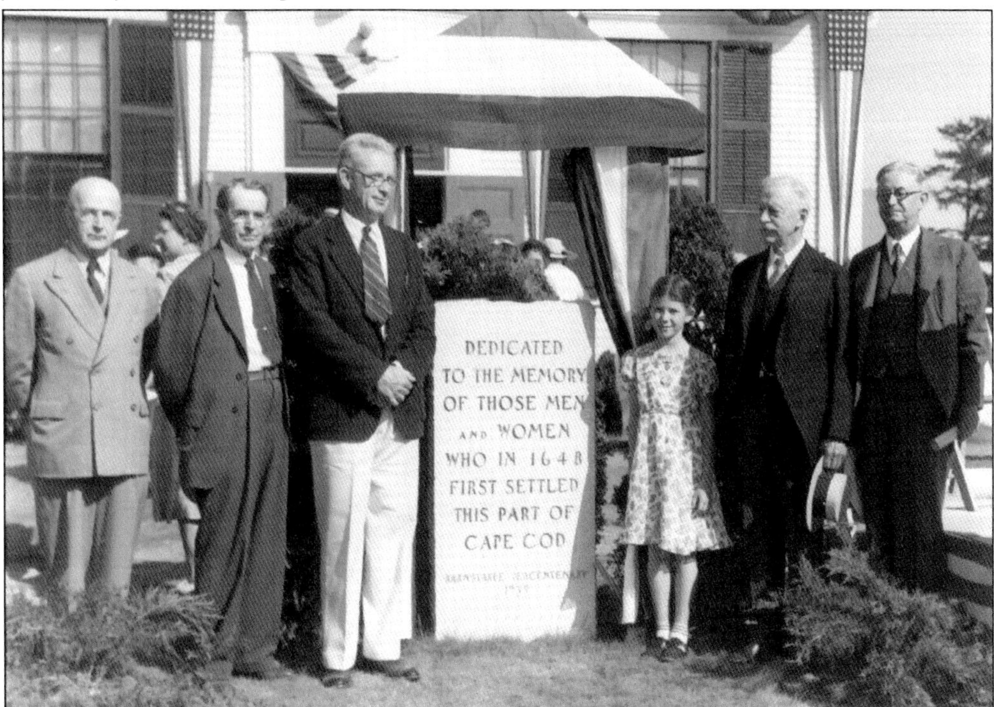

Cotuit Tablet. The Cotuit Tablet is dedicated to the memory of the 1648 pioneer settlers of Cotuit. From left to right are Alfred Crocker, James F. McLaughlin, Calvin D. Crawford, Marion Dottridge, Dr. A. Lawrence Lowell, and Congressman Charles F. Gifford.

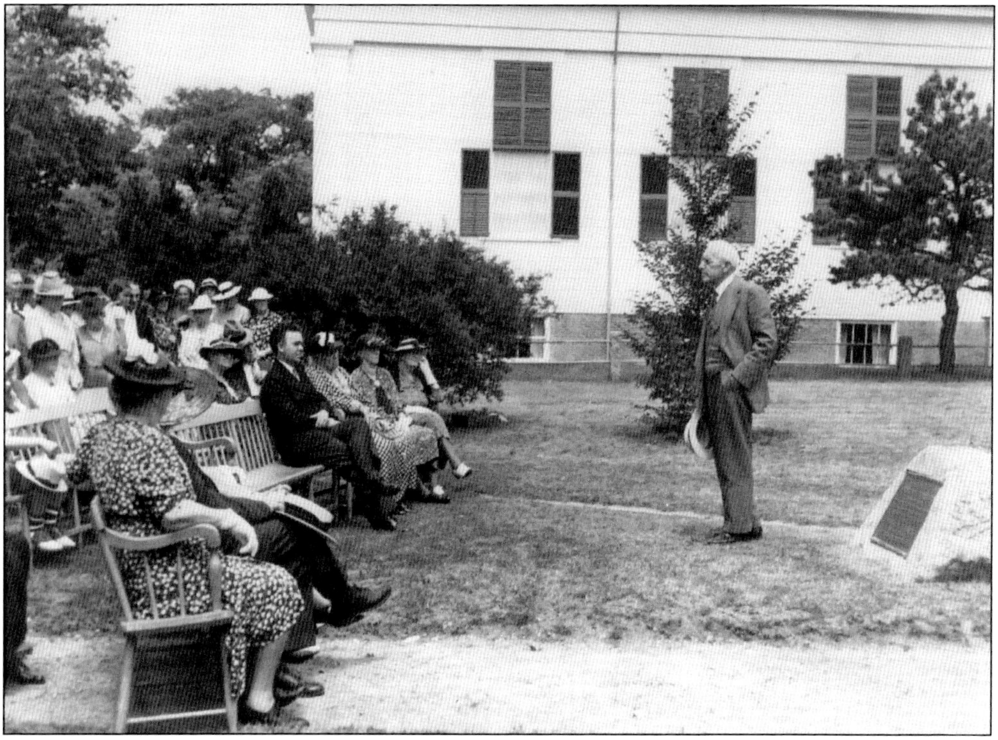

CENTERVILLE TABLET. This tablet was installed in memory of the first residents of the village of Chequaquet, now known as Centerville. Elisha B. Worrell, resident of Centerville and Boston, delivered the address before a large crowd.

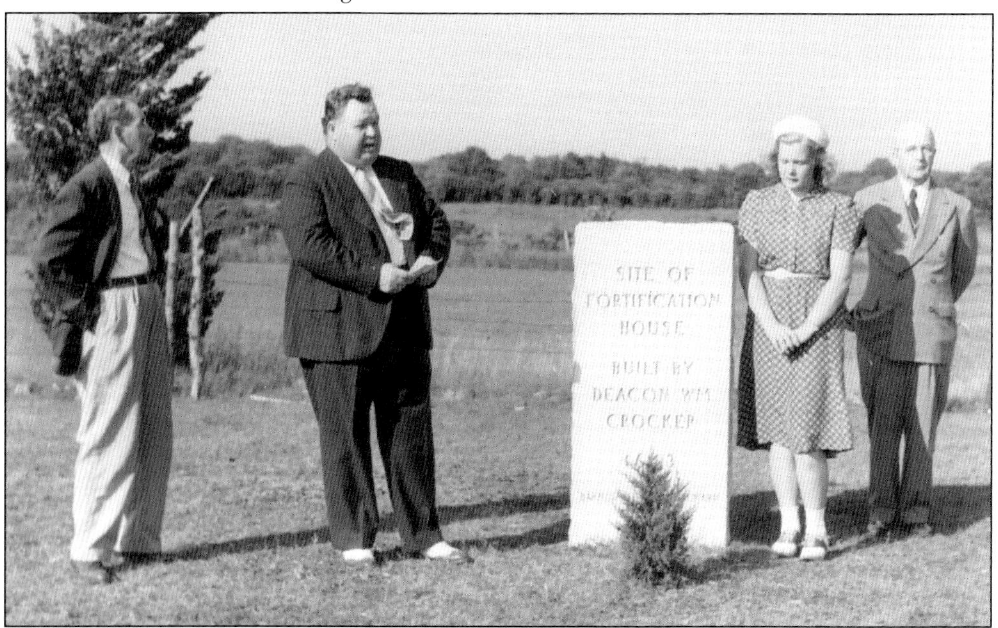

DEACON CROCKER TABLET. This tablet marked the site of the West Barnstable Deacon Crocker fortification, constructed in 1643 as protection against Native American attack. From left to right are James F. McLaughlin, Sheriff Lauchlan M. Crocker, Doris V. Crocker, and Alfred Crocker.

Seven

Osterville, Cotuit, Marstons Mills, West Barnstable, and Sandy Neck

Osterville, Cotuit, Marstons Mills, West Barnstable, and Sandy Neck are compressed into one chapter for several reasons. Marstons Mills was by and large unaffected by the surge of tourism. It would briefly be part of economic development when a group of businessmen attempted to open a commercial airport in the Mystic Lake area in the early 1920s, but they were outdone by the Hyannis airport, which was more successful in promoting commercial air traffic in Hyannis. Cotuit and Osterville hosted visitors in the summer early on, but did not see the dramatic changes that came to Hyannis. West Barnstable was also largely unaffected by 1870s tourism. Even though a rail station and brick factory were built in West Barnstable, the village was primarily a transit point for travelers headed to other destinations within the town of Barnstable.

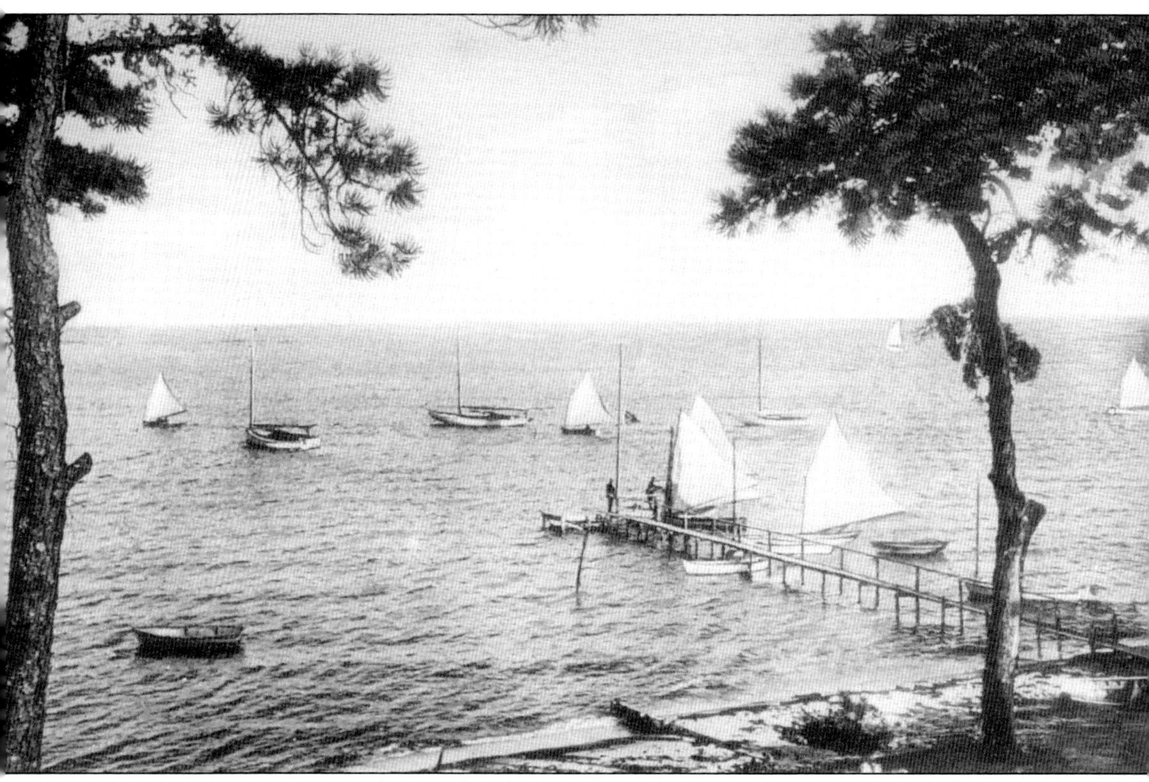

COTUIT LOWER HARBOR. The people of Cotuit have, since the village's beginning, enjoyed its access to the sea. Sailing was a favorite activity, and this photograph shows plenty of sailboats in the harbor. Throughout the 19th century, Cotuit, more than the other villages, retained its maritime trade. A small coasting fleet of 25, of no more than 300 tons, hailed from Cotuit in 1866, increasing to 32 by 1883. By 1890, the number had declined to 10.

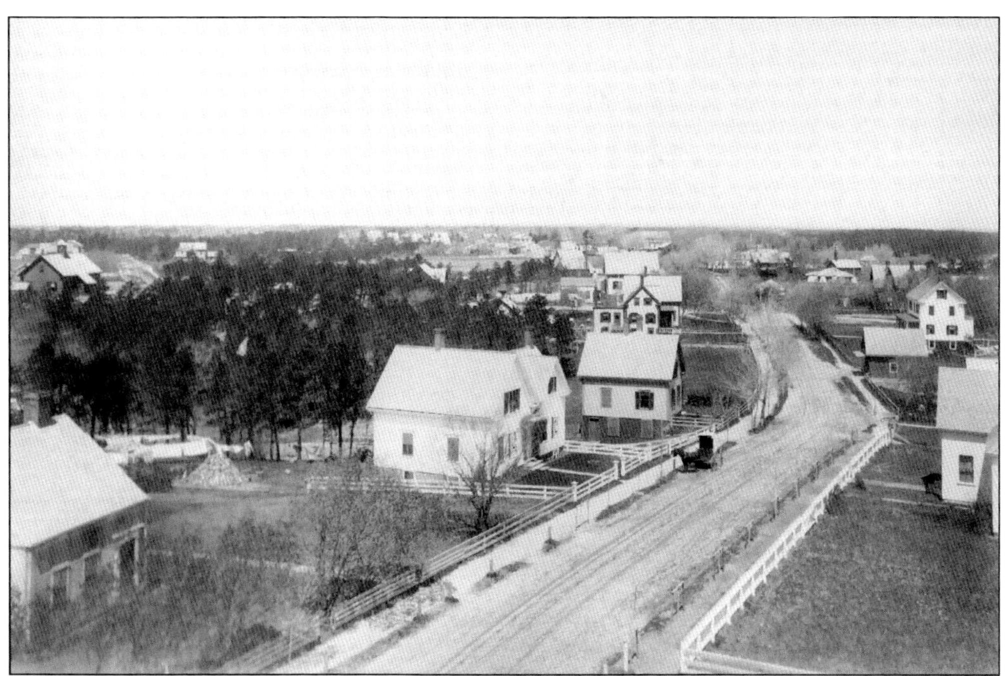

MAIN STREET, COTUIT. *Cotuit* is a Native American term for "long fields" or "planting fields." On behalf of Barnstable, John Alden and Capt. Josiah Winslow handled the purchase of the Cotuit area from Native American Sachem Paupunnuck in 1658.

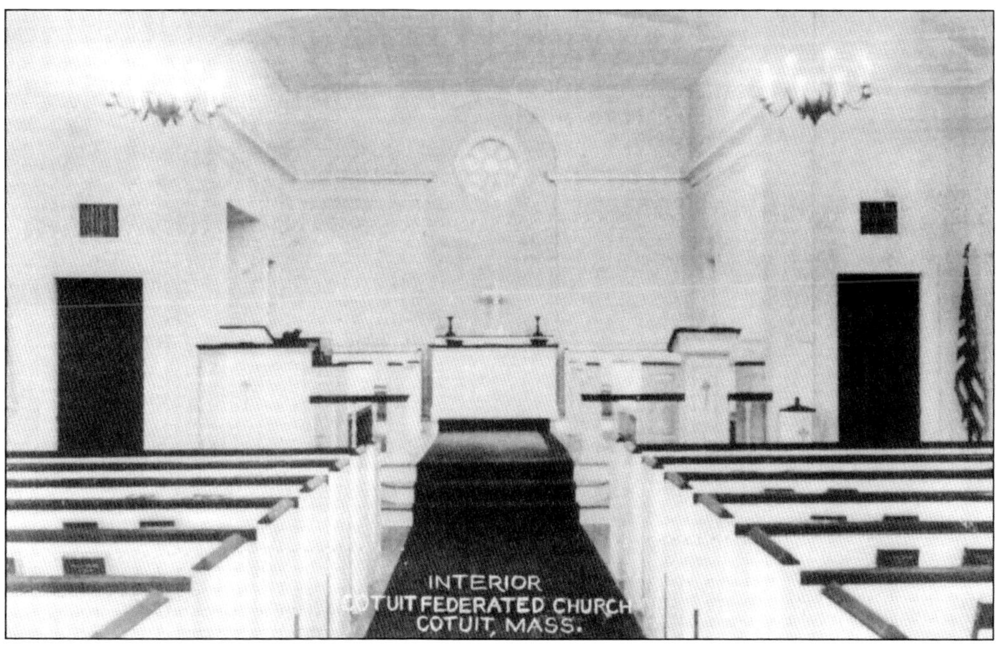

FEDERATED CHURCH, COTUIT. In 1846, a combination of Methodists, Baptists, and Congregationalists formed the Union Religious Society of Cotuit. The Federated Church was built around 1846 and was known as "The Little White Church."

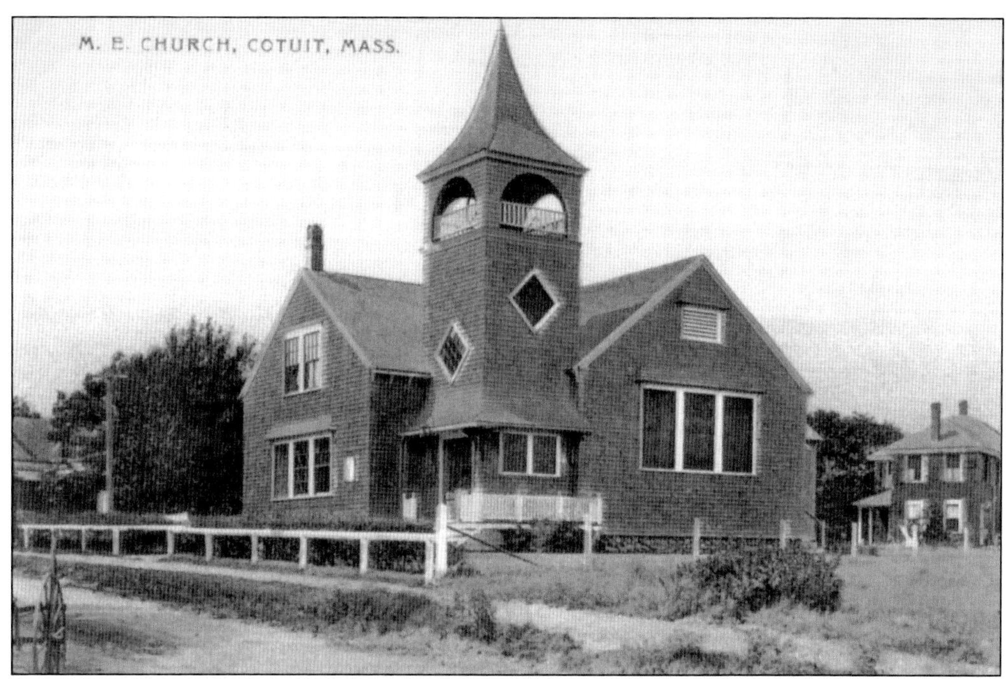

METHODIST CHURCH, COTUIT. Methodists shared The Little White Church until they withdrew in 1900 and organized a separate congregation. Rejoining with the Federated Church around 1923, The Little White Church was sold and a newer building constructed for worship.

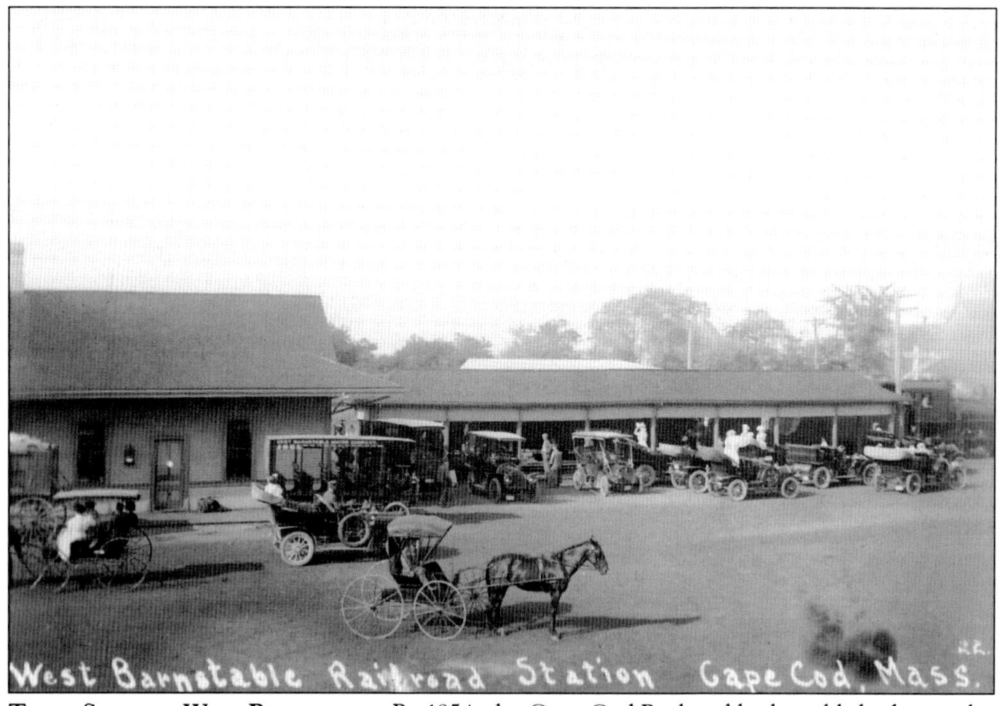

TRAIN STATION, WEST BARNSTABLE. By 1854, the Cape Cod Railroad had established a regular route to West Barnstable. It took approximately six years of wrangling to plan out the route from the town of Sandwich to the town of Barnstable.

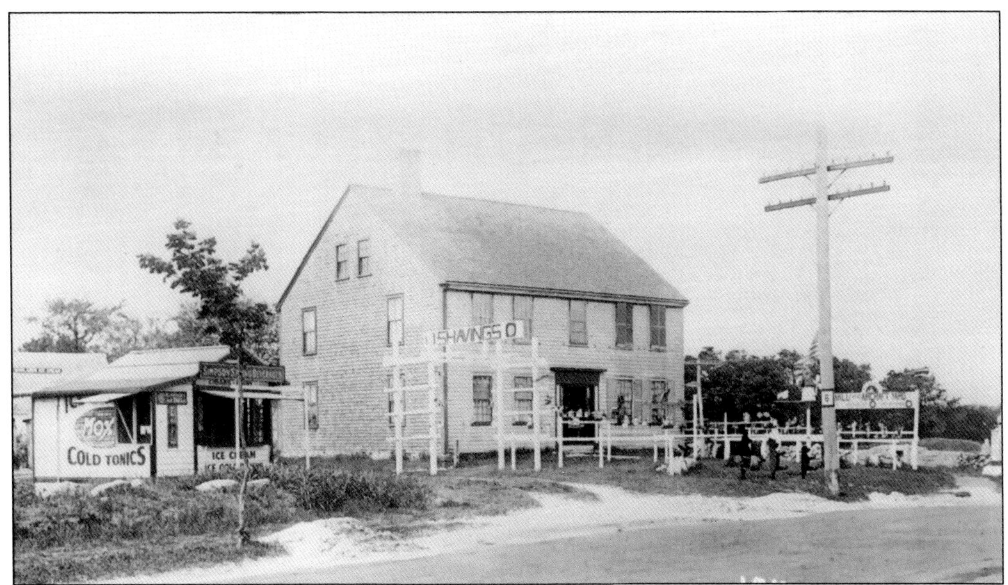

Shavings, West Barnstable. In 1918, local author Joseph Lincoln published *Shavings*, based on a windmill and whirl-a-gig maker and the cast of characters who hung about his shop. The business pictured here was the only one to get permission to use the title of the book, the publication of which sparked a new interest in this kind of lawn decoration.

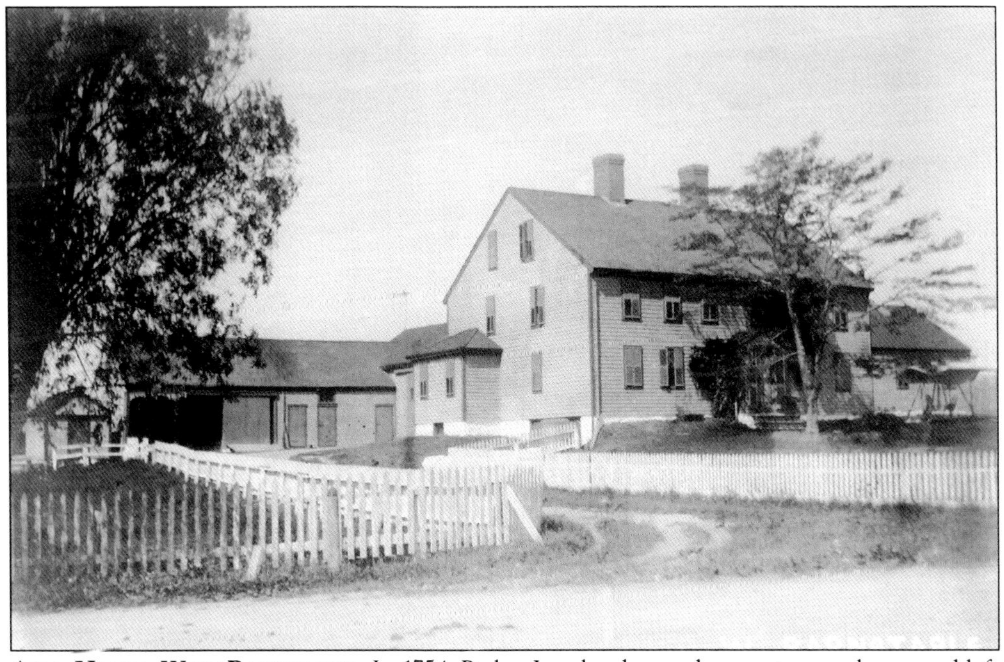

Alms House, West Barnstable. In 1754, Parker Lombard passed away at an early age and left his farm of 50 acres to the town of Barnstable for the use and benefit of the town's poor. A new house was erected on the property, which was at the center of West Barnstable. Those judged insane were locked in cells in a barn on the property.

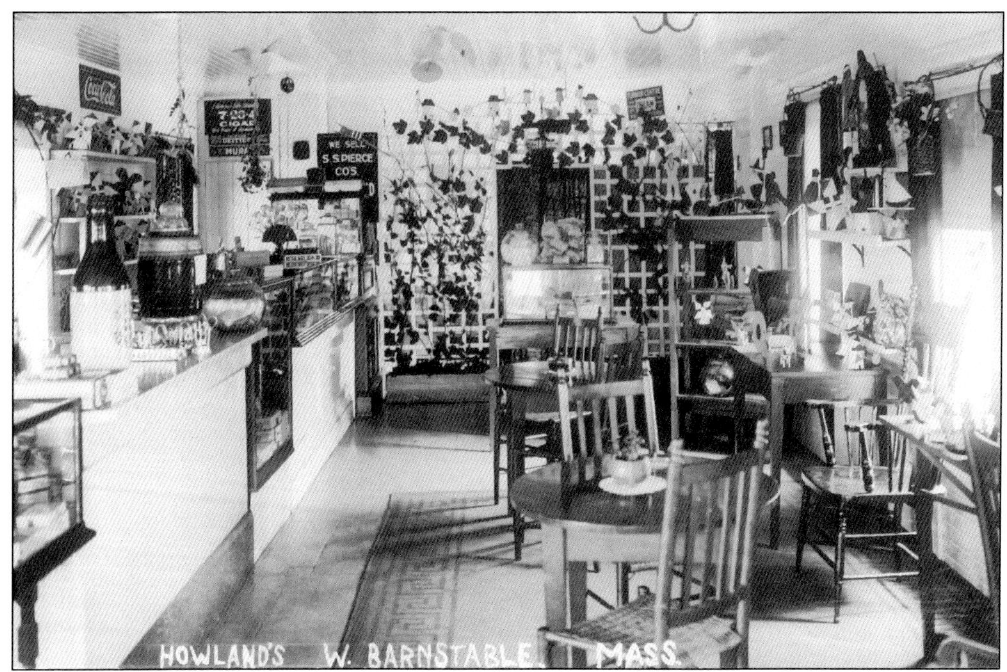

Howland's, West Barnstable. Howland's was operated by Jabez Howland, the first stationmaster and postmaster for West Barnstable. His store was opened in a small house built in his orchard that also saw use as the post office.

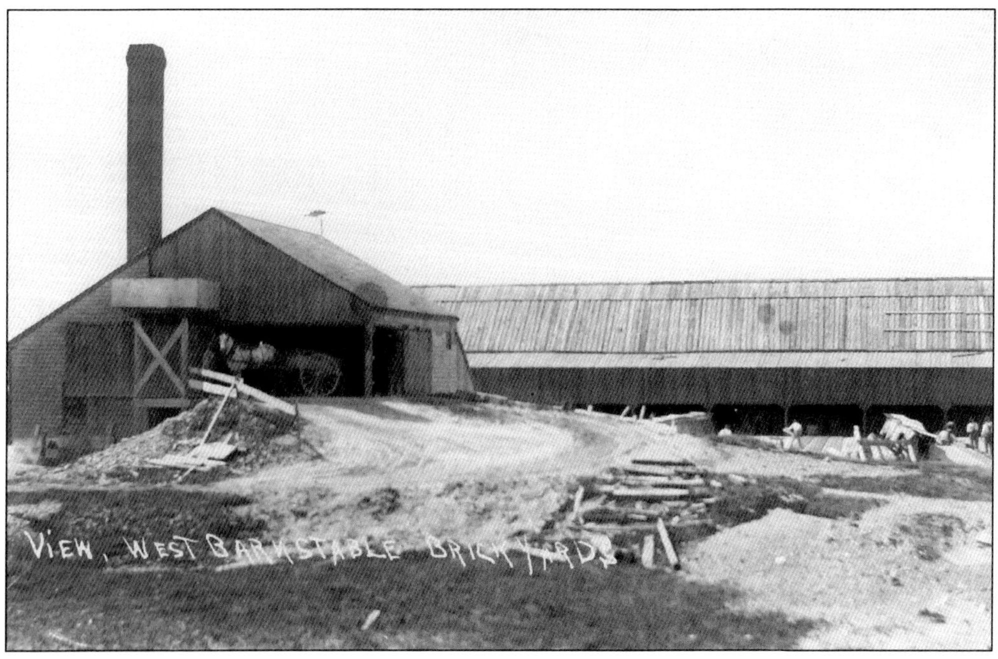

Brick Factory, West Barnstable. Although West Barnstable was, by and large, not affected by the tourist trade, a brick factory opened in 1878 and operated until 1929. Bricks from this old factory are now highly-prized collector's items.

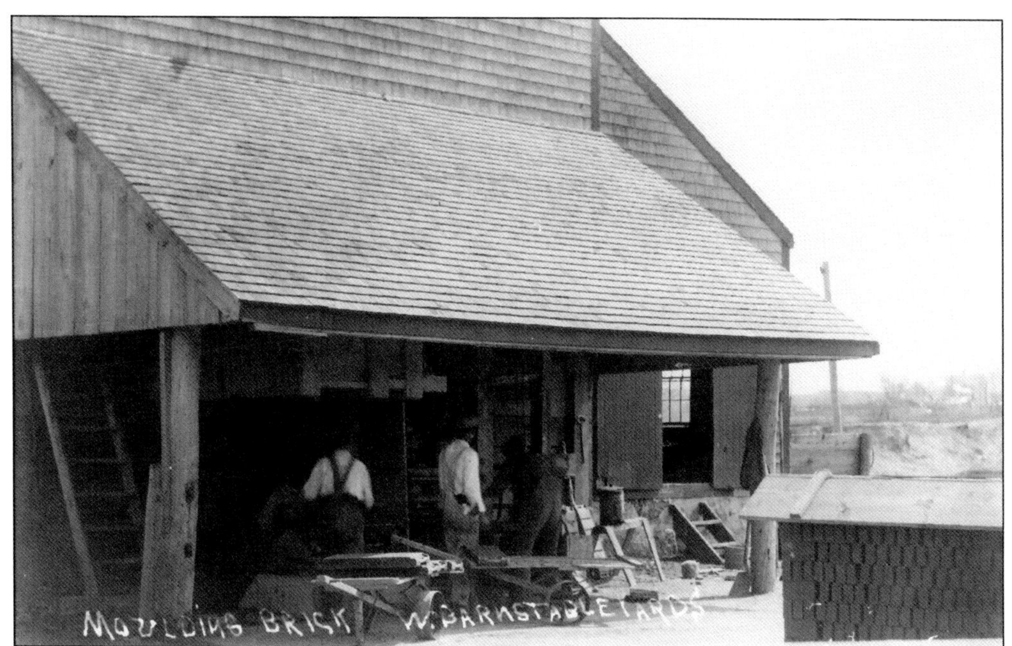

BRICK DRYING, WEST BARNSTABLE. Except for wood, the factory was largely self-sufficient due to the natural deposits of clay found in the soil. Originally opened by Levi Goodspeed, Noah Bradford, and Charles Crocker, the factory was purchased by A.D. Makepeace, owner of many acres of cranberry bogs.

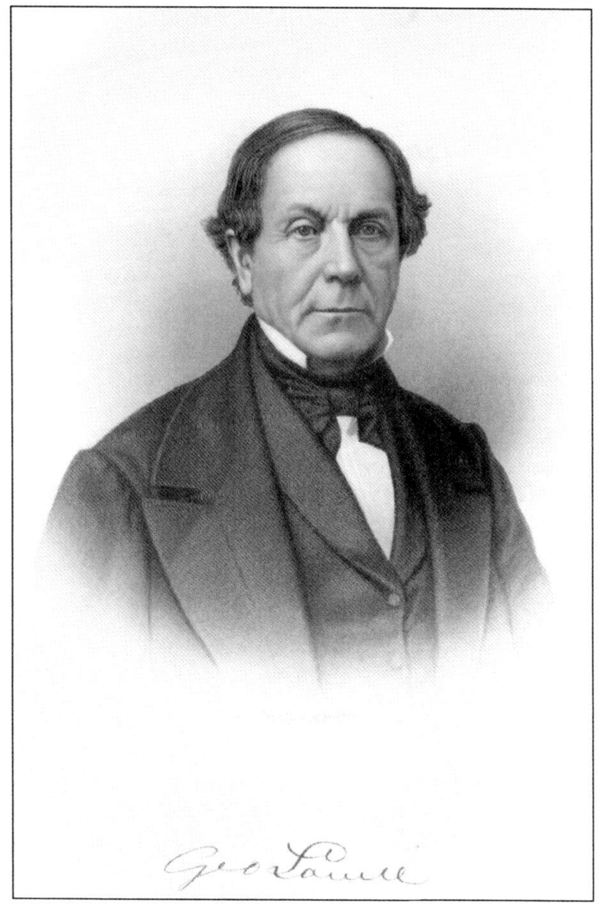

GEORGE LOVELL, OSTERVILLE. In the early years of Osterville, so many Lovells settled here that the area was called "Lovell's Neighborhood." The name "Osterville" came into use in 1815 at a celebration of the signing of a peace treaty with Great Britain, ending the War of 1812. George Lovell was a leading citizen of the village in the mid-1800s.

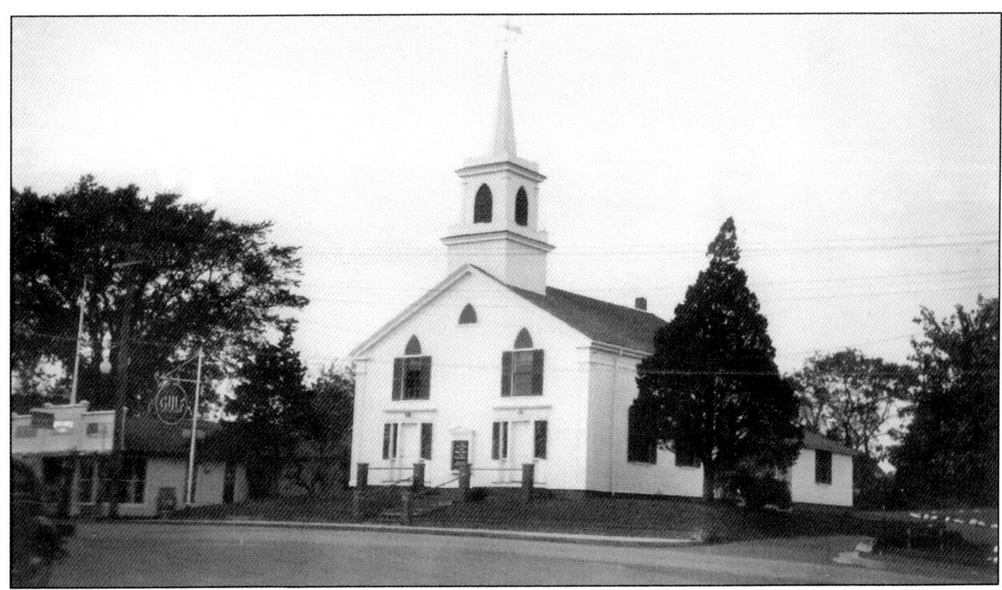

Baptist Church, Osterville. Built in 1838, this church was founded by members of the Baptist Church in Hyannis. The people who donated to the building fund were all old Barnstable families with names such as Lovell, Hallet, Blount, Jones, Robbins, and Hinckley.

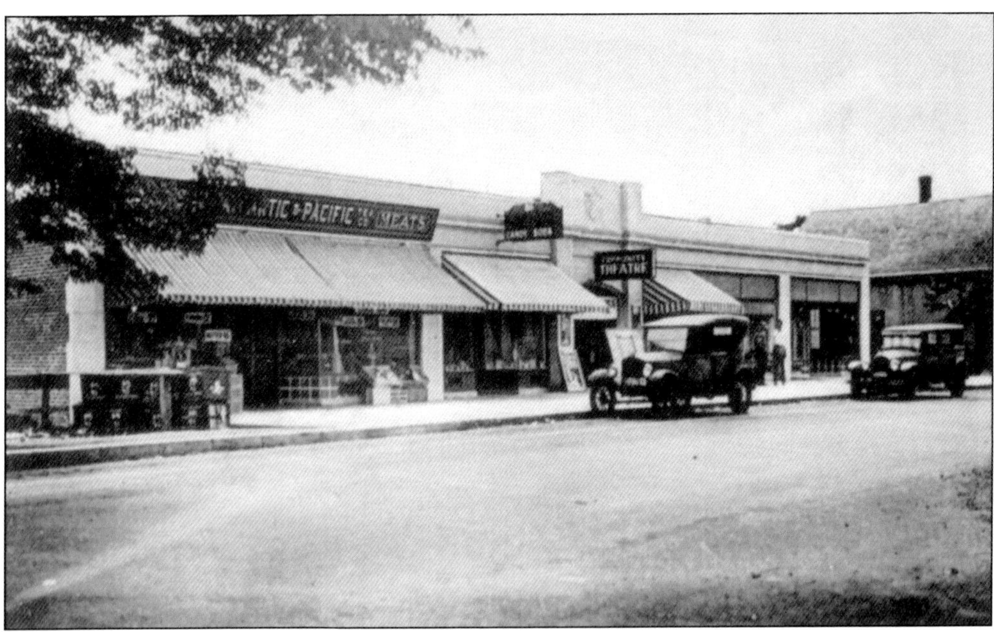

Main Street, Osterville. This early 1900s photograph shows Main Street in Osterville. It shows a branch of the Atlantic and Pacific Tea Company, a candy store to the right, and the old Osterville movie house, then named the Community Theater. The movie theater would remain in operation until it was renovated into retail space.

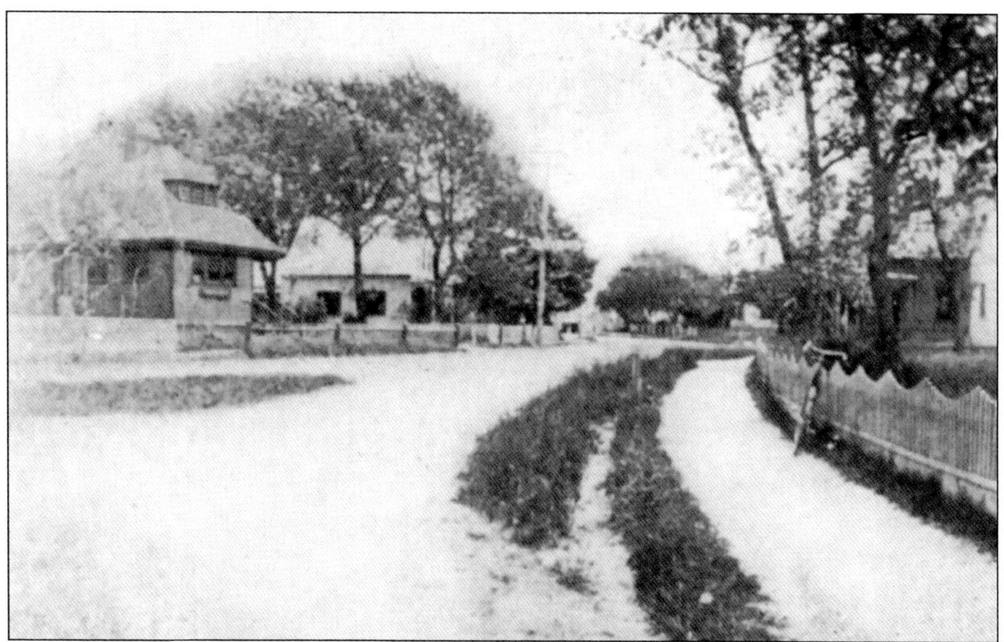

Osterville Free Library. The Osterville Free Library opened in 1882 with a collection of 1,209 books. An annual fair was held for the benefit of the library, which has since become a yearly event. There were several renovations over the years, and eventually, a new 20,000-square-foot building was built in 2012.

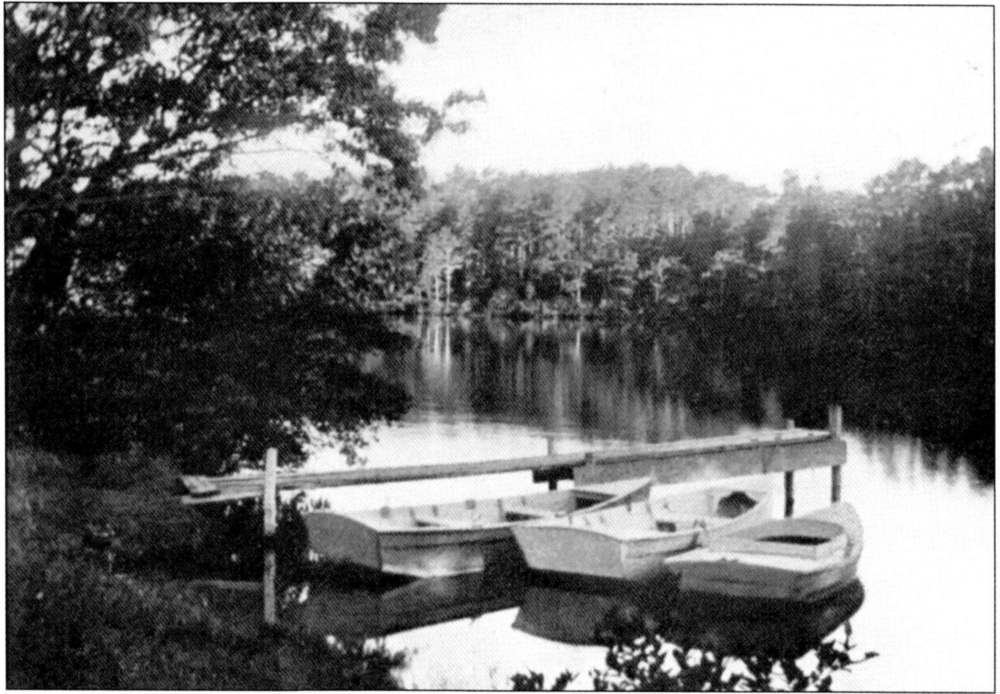

Crystal Lake, Osterville. Crystal Lake was located in the Wianno section of Osterville, making it part of the reason a summer colony was so successful there. The lake is adjacent to the Osterville Episcopal Church, which was formed in 1903 for the benefit of summer visitors.

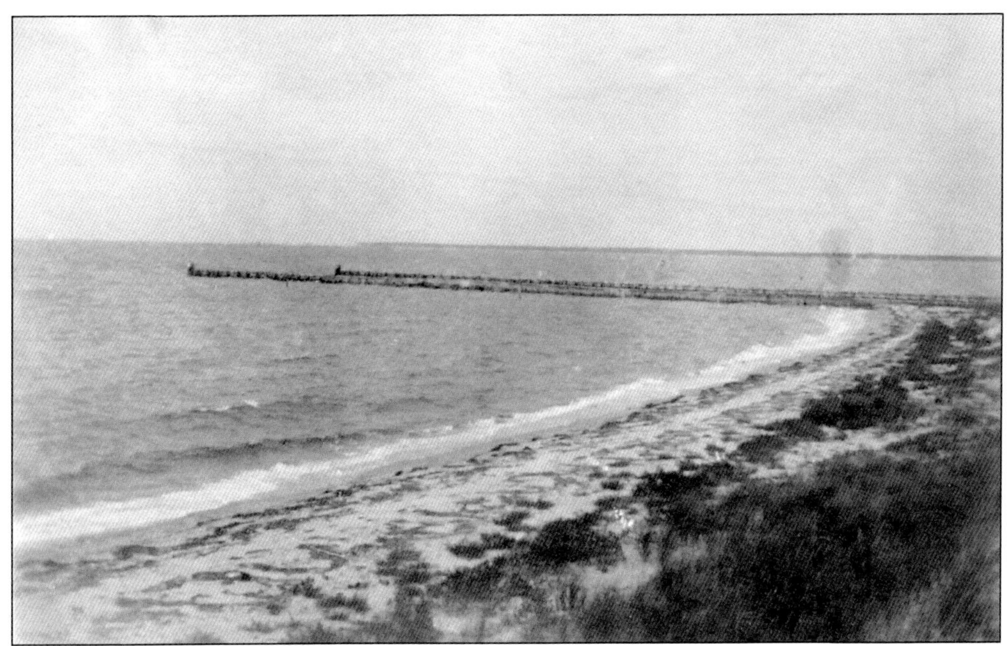

Dead Neck Beach, Osterville. Dead Neck Beach stretched from Eel River to Sampson's Island. Osterville residents desired better access to the Nantucket Sound and eventually built a cut through Dead Neck to the West Bay in 1899. A breakwater protects the cut in this photograph.

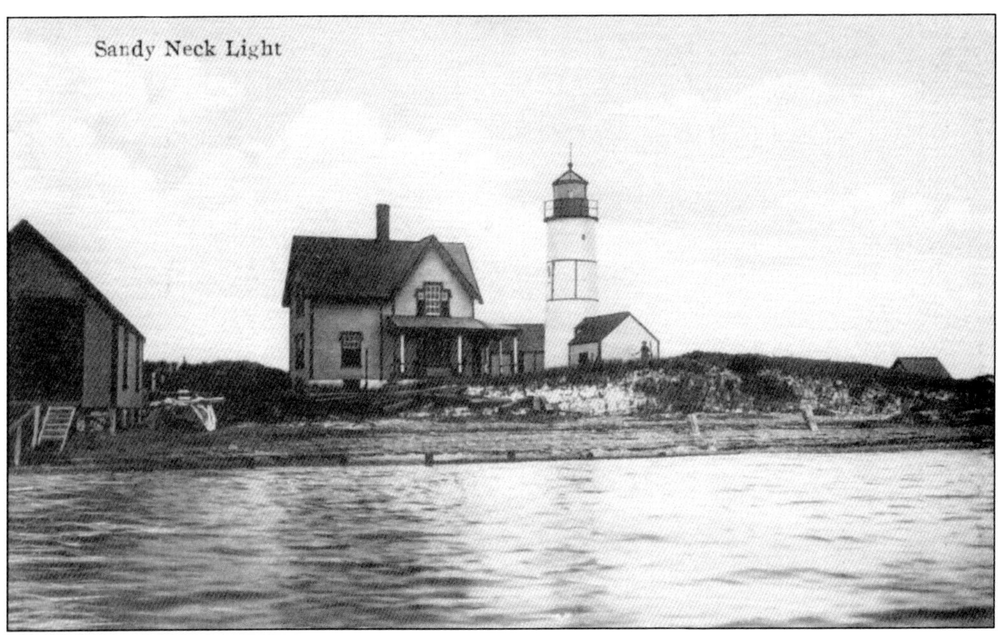

Lighthouse, Sandy Neck. In 1825, the US government acquired a site for a lighthouse on Sandy Neck. Built by 1836, the light later fell out of use and was replaced by an automatic light in 1931. When the lighthouse was active, its light could be seen for 13 miles.

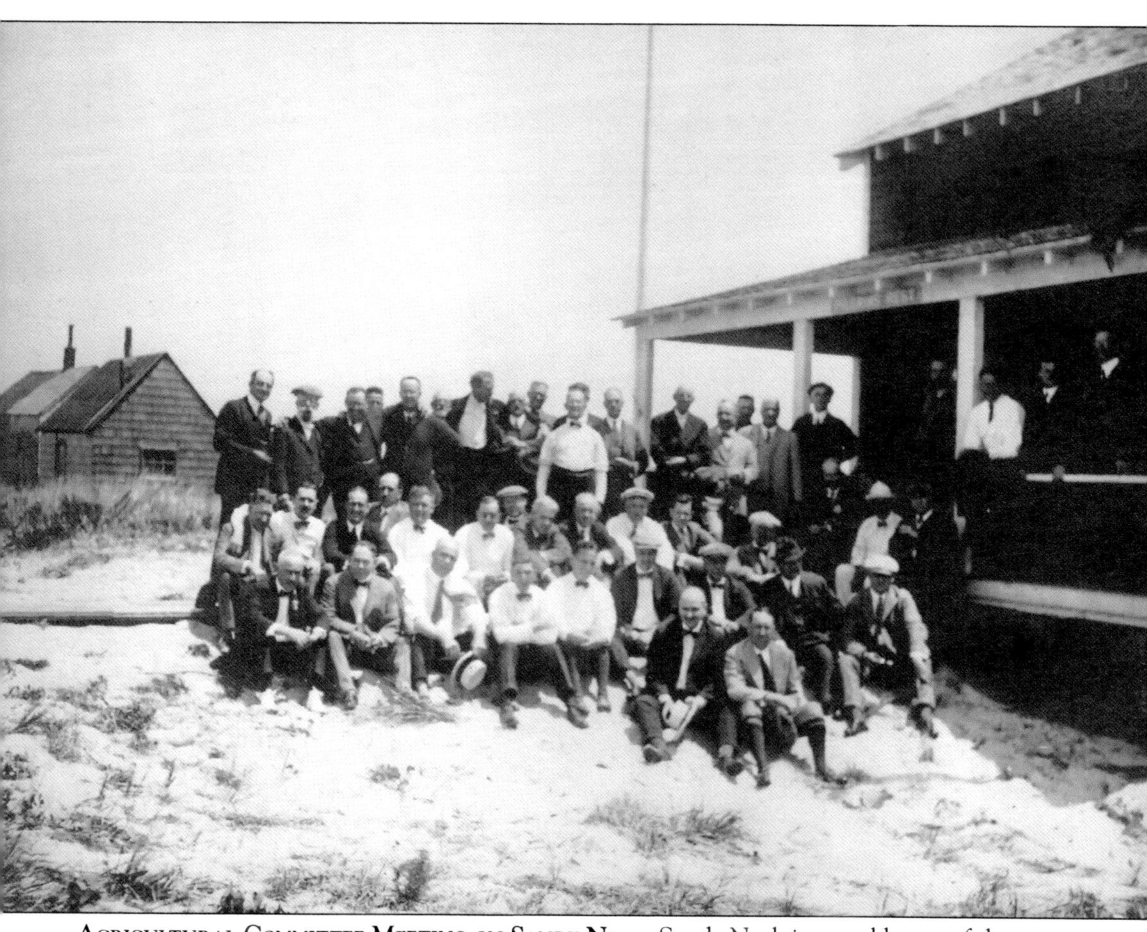

Agricultural Committee Meeting on Sandy Neck. Sandy Neck is arguably one of the most interesting natural formations in Barnstable. It pushes out into the Cape Cod Bay from West Barnstable and Sandwich and runs parallel with the coastline for a distance of about 10 miles. Sandy Neck hosted a small community of summer dwellers that over time included a summer camp and a restaurant that served boaters.

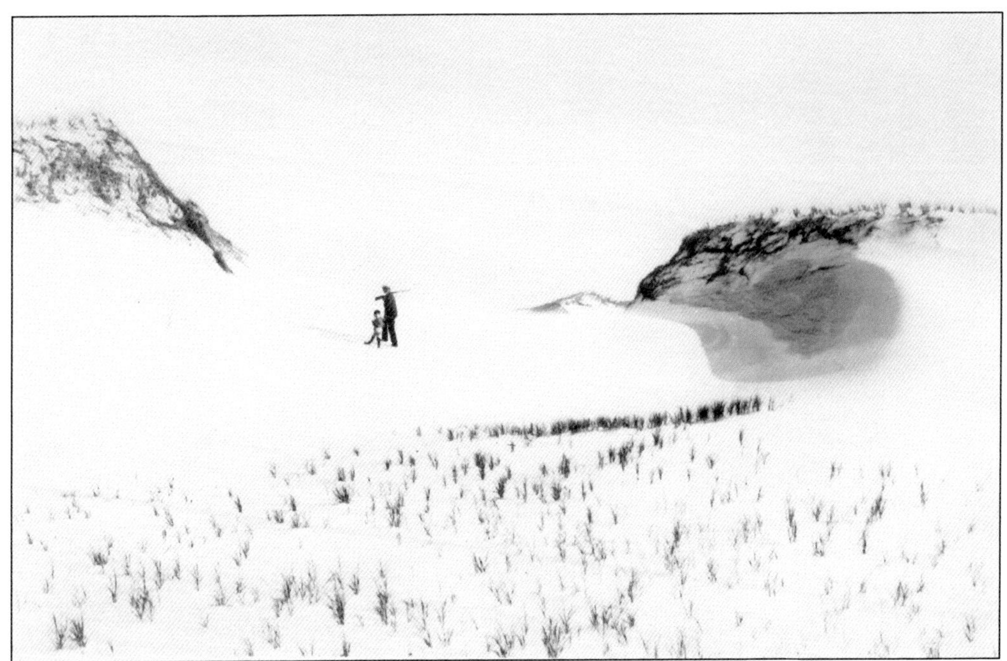

HUNTING, SANDY NECK. Hunting and fishing were favored activities on Sandy Neck. But the area was first used for whaling in Barnstable, and several tryworks for blubber rendering were established in the early 1700s.

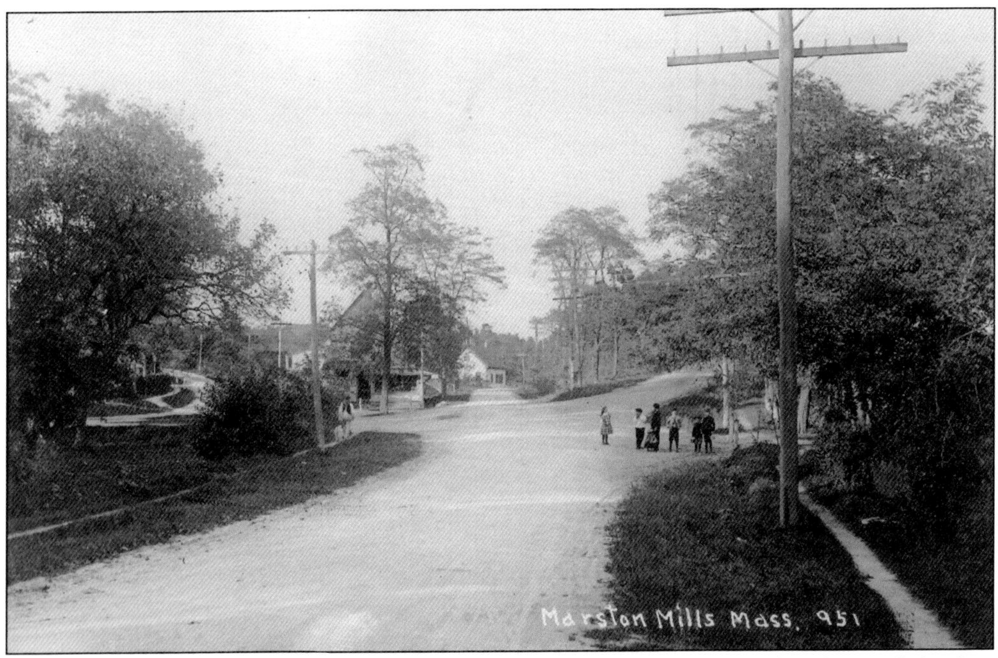

VILLAGE SQUARE, MARSTONS MILLS. Roger Godspeed is generally considered one of the first settlers (or the first settler) in Marstons Mills, building his house in 1653 on River Road. This photograph shows the village square with the Cash Market at center rear and the post office next to where the children are standing.

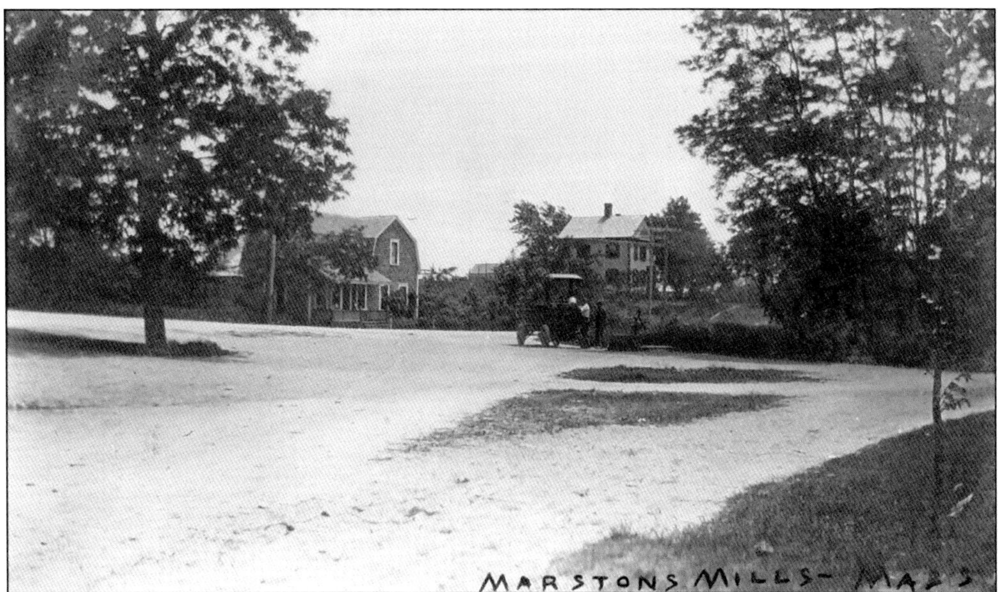

Village Square, Marstons Mills. This view of the square shows the old tree that stood in front of the Cash Market. The tree stood until the 1990s, when old age and disease were cause for it to be cut down.

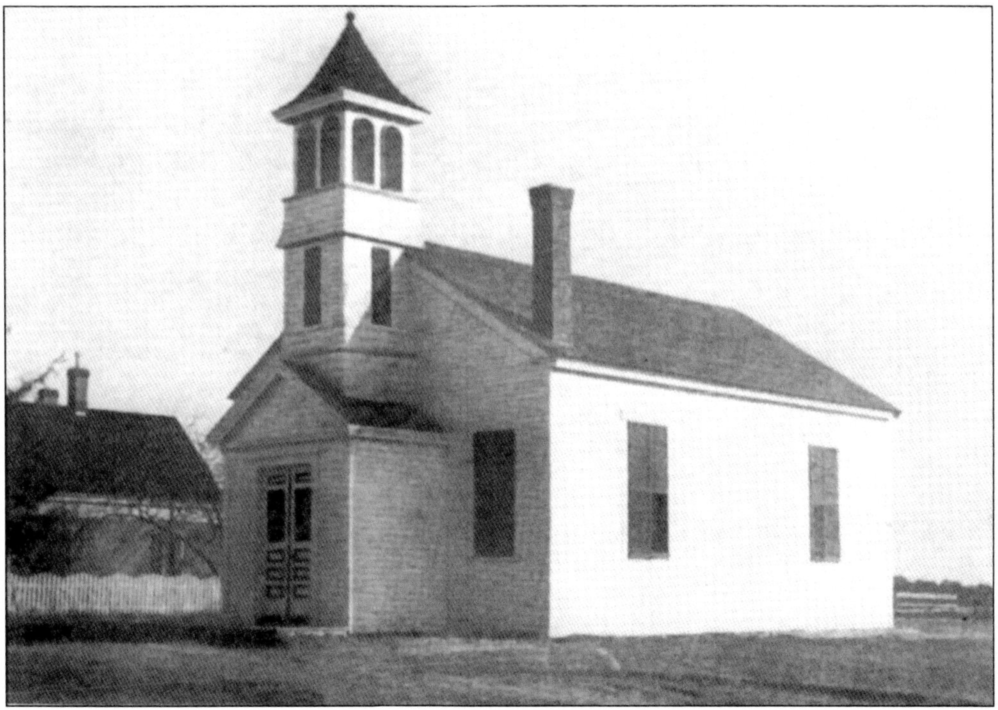

Methodist Episcopalian Church, Marstons Mills. The Marstons Mills Episcopalian Society was formed prior to 1830, when the society purchased a church building. The church, originally erected in Yarmouth, was moved to Marstons Mills and is now known as the Marstons Mills Community Church.

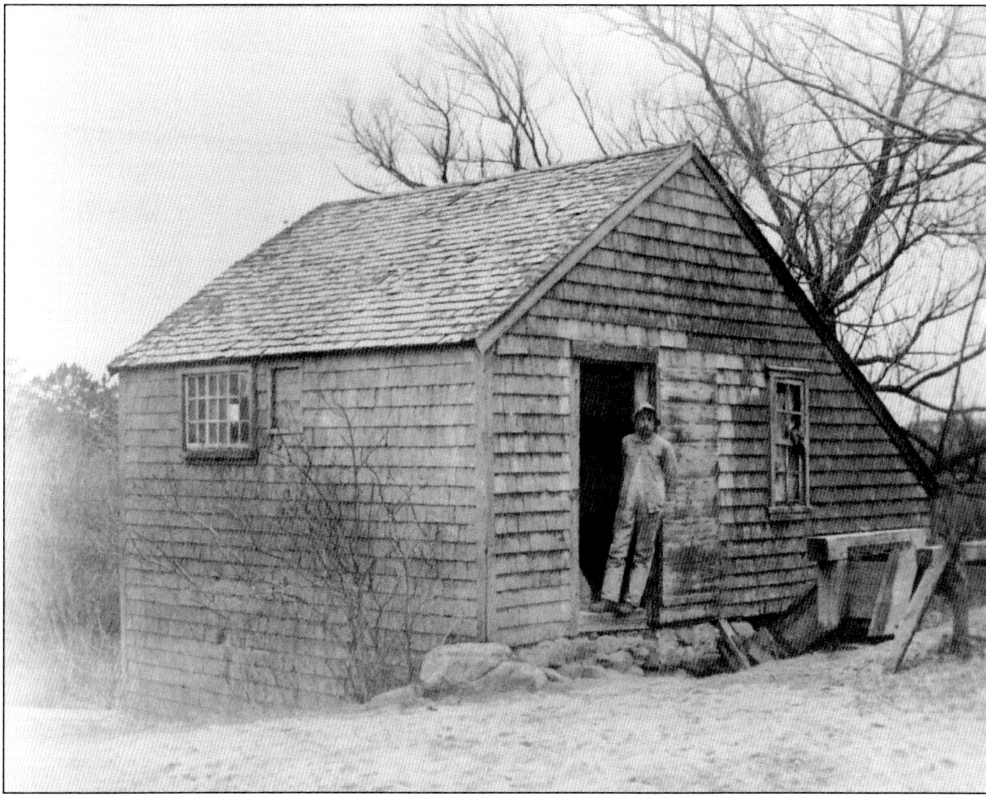

The Mill, Marstons Mills. Marstons Mills derives its name from the Marston family, who owned a fulling mill on the Marstons Mills River, once known as Goodspeed's River. In addition to the fulling mill, there were several other mills on the river, at least one of which was a gristmill. Records from 1704 show that the town granted John Stacy the right to build a dam, which he claimed was necessary for the operation of a gristmill.

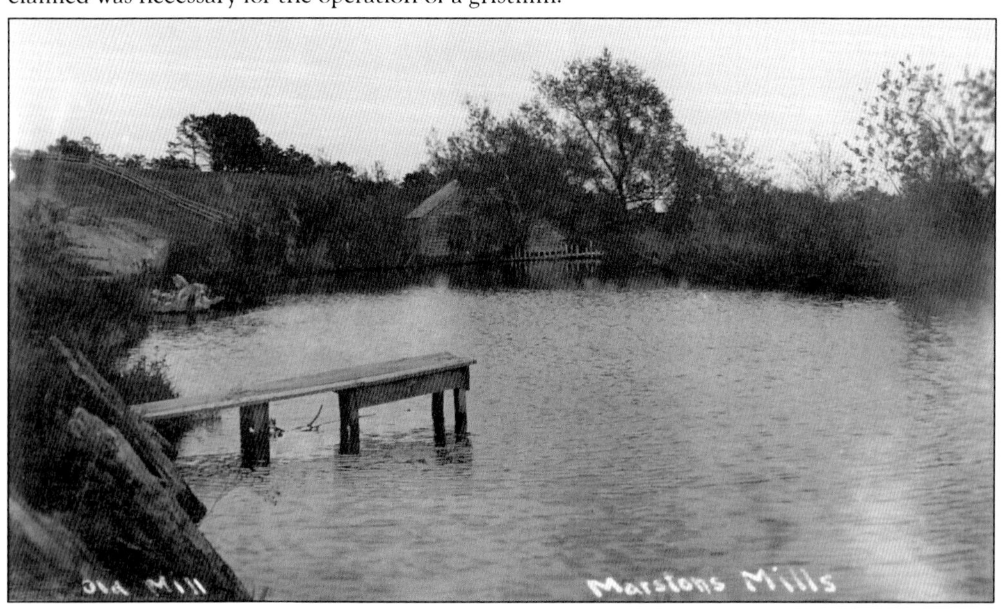

Bibliography

Allison, Robert J. *A Short History of Cape Cod*. Beverly, MA: Commonwealth Editions, 2010.

Bearse, Alvah. *Physic Point: Memoirs of Hyannis 1914–1929*. Hyannis, MA: The Patriot Press, 1976.

Barnstable Tercentenary Committee. Donald Trayser, ed. *Report of Proceedings of the Tercentenary Anniversary of the Town of Barnstable Massachusetts*. 1940.

Deyo, Samuel. *History of Barnstable County*. New York: H.W. Blake & Co., 1890.

Donald Trayser, ed. *Barnstable: Three Centuries of a Cape Cod Town*. Hyannis, MA: F.B. & F.P. Goss, 1939.

Green, Eugene and William Sachse. *Names of the Land*. Chester, CT: The Globe Pequot Press, 1983.

McKenney, O. Herbert et al. *The Seven Villages of Barnstable*. Binghampton, NY: Vail Ballou Press Inc., 1976.

Otis, Amos. *Genealogical Notes of Barnstable Families*. Barnstable, MA: The Patriot Press, 1888.

Vuilleumier, Marion R. *Churches on Cape Cod*. Taunton, MA: WM. S. Sullwold Publishing, 1974.

Consistent with our mission to preserve history on a local level, this book was printed in South Carolina on American-made paper and manufactured entirely in the United States. Products carrying the accredited Forest Stewardship Council (FSC) label are printed on 100 percent FSC-certified paper.

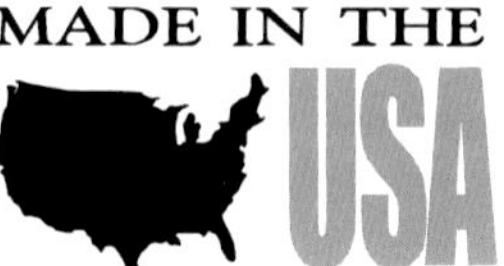